THE MIDDLE EASTERN ECONOMY

THE MIDDLE EASTERN ECONOMY

Studies in Economics and Economic History

Edited by

ELIE KEDOURIE

FRANK CASS & CO. LTD.

First published 1977 in Great Britain by
FRANK CASS AND COMPANY LIMITED
Gainsborough House, Gainsborough Road,
London E11 1RS, England

and in the United States of America by
FRANK CASS AND COMPANY LIMITED
c/o International Scholarly Book Services Inc
Box 555, Forest Grove, Oregon 97116

ISBN 0 7146 3074 8

This group of studies first appeared in a
Special Issue on The Middle Eastern Economy of
Middle Eastern Studies, Vol. 12, no. 3,
published by Frank Cass and Company Limited.

Printed in Great Britain by Unwin Brothers Limited.

Contents

Nineteenth-Century Egyptian Population

Justin A. McCarthy

1800[1]

In 1800 the population of Egypt was at its lowest point in history, perhaps half its ancient number. Josephus had felt the population in his time to be 7·8 million, Diodurus 7 million, and others had scattered their estimates even higher.[2] By early medieval times the numbers may even have grown. The Arab conquerors, for example, reportedly found 12–14 millions when they entered Egypt.[3]

After the Muslim conquest, the Egyptian population was in steady decline. Wars, plagues, and successions of indifferent rulers had destroyed the civic calm needed for population growth until, by the time of the French Expedition, Egypt had fewer than four million inhabitants. The downward trend was about to change, however, and the time of the Napoleonic conquest, 1800, can serve as a forward anchor for a study of that change.

The savants who accompanied Napoleon to Egypt were the first to put Egyptian population into a 'modern' enumeration. Their work, the *Description de L'Egypte*, has long been considered the primary source for the population of its period. With the exception of Volney's[4] account, it is the only detailed population record of the time, and surely the only one giving enough data to be verifiable. The author of the main sections of the *Description* dealing with population, Jomard, makes an attempt to ascertain the population of Cairo, the other large cities, and the country as a whole, scientifically. He fails, mainly because of his limited opportunity for accurate observations and his insistence on comparing Egypt to European models.

Jomard, his work limited by both available time and the difficulties of travel, was able to work extensively in only two areas—the city of Cairo and the province of Minya. He began examining Cairo's population by comparing the city to Paris, whose population was already known. In Cairo, observing and surveying the city walls, he decided that the city had a perimeter of around 24,000 metres,[5] an area of 793 hectares or 2,320 arpens, which was not one-fourth of the area of Paris. The roads were more narrow, however, and the houses close together. Most of the quarters were filled with gardens and tombs, but still contained much less open space than Paris.[6] All Paris and Cairo, he felt, could not be compared, and he chose only those areas which he felt were similar:

> En partant de la donnée qui est fournie par les quartiers du Louvre, de la Halle, de la Banque, des Arcis, de Saint-Avoie, du Mont-de-Pieté, et qui forment le 4e et 7e arrondissements de Paris, il trouve 102,692 individus pour une surface de 130 hectares. (C'est-a-dire 790 individus par hectare.) La population moyenne pour Paris entier est de 419 habitans par deux hectares.[7]

This number was obviously too great, since Jomard could see that houses in the Parisian quarters named had twice as many floors as those in Cairo, so he divided the population per hectare in half, multiplied by the area of Cairo, and came to a figure of 253,210 for Cairo's population.[8]

Jomard justified his figure by various other considerations. He stated that the French expedition figures gave a death rate for Cairo of 8,834 per year and that an unidentified enumeration one year before the French expedition showed a death rate of 9,125 per year,[9] proving that his figures did not sin by being too low. Indeed, he declared, they were accurate, because the population grew at a rate of one-sixtieth or one-fiftieth a year (no source or justification given). Thus, he reached an estimate of 9,000 births a year. The birth rate multiplier (i.e. Population/Births = Multiplier) for Paris was 29·3. Multiplying this by Cairo's 9,000 births, he arrived at a population of 263,700, verifying his first figure, but never noticing the circular reasoning process which gave him his birth rate in the first place. As the final proof:

> Enfin, on comptait alors au Kaire 26,000 maisons, qui, à 10 individus par chacune, supposent une population de 26,000 habitants.[10]
> (Le nombre des maisons habitées dans le Kaire est evalué a vingt-six mille, renferment, l'une dans l'autre, un peu plus de neuf individus, selon les uns, et même dix, selon les autres: ce n'est pas trop, attendu que, dans bien des maisons, les serviteurs reposent, réunis en grand nombre ensemble, dans une seule et même chambre. Il existe d'ailleurs, entre les massifs des maisons, de grandes cours ou enceintes pleines de cahuttes de 4 pieds de haut, où logent une foule de pauvres gens entassés pêle-mêle avec leurs bestiaux . . .)[11]

In essence, Jomard based all his conjectures on two assumptions: first, that Cairo could be compared with Paris; second, that there were ten persons per house. Both were false.

Little basis existed for a comparison of Cairo and Paris. If data on the size of buildings, number of people living in a room, etc., were unknown, no logical similarities could be drawn. Simple comparisons by eyesight have long been proven to be insufficient. Jomard estimated that there were one-half as many storeys in Cairo as in Paris, but Volney, writing only 15 years earlier, thought that the ratio was at most two floors in Cairo to five in Paris.[12] The construction situation could not have changed that rapidly. There is no reason to believe and, in fact, good reason not to believe that birth and death rates of Egypt and France could have been so similar. Furthermore, official lists of Egyptian births and deaths were notoriously inexact, as is demonstrated by the French expedition's own necrological tables,[13] which show almost three men dying for every two women; a conclusion which is highly unlikely, hence totally unreliable.[14]

Calculating population by house, while still unreliable, seems much more exact than any of Jomard's other methods. It is, in fact, the main method used by modern historical demographers (Russell and Barkan, for example) in similar situations. Although Jomard probably never actually counted the houses in Cairo, his estimate can still probably be considered relatively correct. While the French officers he relied on could not be expected to have entered houses and counted the number of inhabitants, they could, if only for military purposes, be expected to have an approximate knowledge of how many buildings were in the city areas under their command. Jomard's mistake lay in his figure of ten individuals to a house.

Modern analysis has indicated a rural figure of approximately 3·5 to 4·0 persons per family in medieval Europe, with a slightly higher rate for Syria, North Africa and Egypt.[15] Barkan uses a figure of five per hearth for the late medieval and early modern Balkans and Anatolia.[16] Since Egypt is operating under the same subsistence-level type of economy as the above and the figures for North Africa, Syria, Medieval Egypt, and Anatolia take into account the particular characteristics (e.g. occasional polygamy) of those areas, it is by no means ridiculous to accept similar figures for Egypt in 1800. General life-style in Egypt had changed little from medieval times. Since Cairo was a city of one and two storey houses,[17] the figure of eight per house seems to be realistic. To accept this figure simply on the basis of comparisons with other areas and times, however, would be to risk the same type of error Jomard fell into over Cairo and Paris. Further confirmation of the 'eight per urban house' multiplier is, however, needed. Contemporary confirmation exists in the fact that eight is the figure used by Mohammed Ali in estimating Cairo's population.[18]

At a ratio of eight inhabitants per house, Cairo's population in 1800 was 210,960.

Jomard's estimate of national population erred in the opposite direction from that of Cairo. It was far too low.

In attempting to find the total population of Egypt, Jomard found that he could not even obtain the real number of villages from the rolls of the Coptic scribes. Sometimes the scribes gave one name to many villages, sometimes many names to one; areas which paid no taxes (*waqf* lands, bedouin-controlled areas, etc.) were uncounted; many villages were simply never put on the registers; and many villages had been abandoned. Jomard, in the absence of data, arbitrarily decided 3,600 was an accurate figure.

Instead of doing any national 'average population per village' work, Jomard examined the province of Minya. He went through the province, questioning 'des cheykhs et des personnes instruites', taking their statements on population, correcting them as much as he felt necessary. He arrived at the figures in Table 1.

The province was computed to be 67·1 square leagues. Subtracting the populations of the two cities 'Minyeh' and 'Meylaouy', there were 1385 inhabitants per square league and 584 per village. Jomard stated that Minya was a 'good median' province, even though it was little inhabited, exposed to Arab attacks, and had ruined canals. He felt some provinces were better, some worse. Because of this, he assumed he could multiply the figures for population per square league by the number of square

TABLE 1

Minia	
Nombres des Lieux Habités	161
2 Villes (15–20,000 pop.)	11,750
39 Bourgades (1–3,000)	53,230
63 Villages (300–1,000)	30,820
57 Nazlets et Hameux (2–3,000)	38,850
Total	104,650
et sans les villes	92,900

Source: Jomard, *Description de L'Egypte*, IX, p. 119.

leagues in Egypt, reaching a population of 2,076,000, without counting the cities. The 'National Total' of villages (3600) multiplied by the Minya average per village (584) came very conveniently close (2,102,400), thus 'proving' the issue.

For the cities:

TABLE 2

A l'égard de celles-ci, nous avons des données dont l'approximation est suffisante. Le long sejour des ingenieurs ou des officiers de l'armee francaise dans chacune d'elles, a permis de savoir à quoi s'en tenir

Rosette	12–15,000
Alexandrie	15,000
Damiette	20,000
Syout	12,000
Mehallet-el-Kebyr	17,500
Qena	5,000
Girgeh	7,000
Beny-Soueyf	5,000
Medynet el-Fayoum	5,000
Atfyh	4,000
Gyzeh	3,000
Qelyoub	4,500
Belbeys	3,000
Mansourah	7,500
Menouf et Tant	15,500
Minyeh et Meylaouy	11,750
Total	149,250

Source: Jomard, *Description L'Egypte*, IX, p. 122 f.

To this total was added Cairo's 263,700 and the rural estimate for a grand total of 2,488,950, not including nomads.[19] (Chabrol calculated a nomad population of 130,000.[20])

Exceptions to Jomard's thesis arise from both within and outside his theories. The theories themselves at least have an internal consistency lacking in the evaluation of Cairo: (1) Take a representative province; (2) Find its population per square league; (3) apply the figure to the entire country; (4) add the population of the cities. If one assumes Jomard truly had a 'representative median' province, that he had the correct figures for that province, and that the density of all areas was almost the same, then his method would have been correct. Unfortunately, none of these assumptions was true.

First, there was no way to know whether or not Minya was truly representative. Based on such lack of confirmatory data, it is difficult to understand Jomard's assurance. Second, even if Minya were representative of Egypt as a whole, his figures for the province could not be correct. Looking at Minya in the years after 1800:

TABLE 3

Minya—Total Egyptian Population[21]

Year	Percentage
1947	6·7
1907	5·8
1897	5·6
1882	5·4
1846	6·3

Sources: Egyptian Censuses.

The 1846 percentage is probably close to the percentage in 1800, since Minya's population share seems to have gone down before it rose again. Assuming a 6·5 per cent share of Egypt's total population for 1800, and applying this to Jomard's population of 104,650, one gets a national figure of approximately 1,610,000, a ridiculous figure which shows that Jomard's Minya population estimate is very low. (Even if an impossible figure of 5 per cent of the national total is assumed for Minya, Egypt would still have only 2,100,000 inhabitants in 1800.)

Consideration by external factors, that is, comparing the 1800 figures to later, more positively accurate ones, also shows the weakness of the French statistics. If Jomard's national figures are correct, Cairo experienced a growth rate of 4·272 per thousand per year between 1800 and 1846.[22] The population as a whole would have had to increase three times faster than that of the capital city, a fact unprecedented in world history, and definitely false.

The percentage of Cairo's population in 1800 could never have been 10·6 per cent. In all other times in Egypt's nineteenth-century history the percentage of Cairo has grown with the country's growth, not lessened, as it would have had to have done between 1800 and 1846. (European cities of the time grew at a greater rate than the total population. Unless special natural or economic factors intervene, such growth could be considered natural.[23]) Nothing could explain such a drop except erroneous data. Since the Cairo data could not be in error to the extent needed (Cairo's population would have to be halved), the national figures must have been wrong.

TABLE 4

Jomard's Estimate Compared to Later Populations

Year	National Population	Cairo Population	Cairo Percentage
1800	2,488,950	263,700	10·6[24]
1846	4,476,439	256,679	5·5
1882	(6,817,265)[25]	374,838	5·4
1897	9,734,405	570,062	5·9
1907	11,287,359	678,433	6·0

Sources: Egyptian Censuses and the *Description de L'Egypte*.

Moreover, as will be shown below, the period from 1800 to 1846 was one of great plagues—both bubonic plague and cholera—and Mohammed Ali's wars. An impossible birth rate would have been needed to offset these factors and still allow a growth of two million between 1800 and 1846. The needed growth rate would have been as high as that between 1846 and 1882 or 1882 and 1897, both periods of comparative peace and lower mortality. Such a growth rate, in such critical times, surely cannot be expected. In times of disease, famine, war, and great taxation it would be indeed odd if the growth rate were greater than in times of peace and prosperity.

Jomard's national figure must be incorrect, both because of the method used to obtain it and the impossibility of the growth rate it demands. A more realistic approach would be to take the data from Cairo and multiply it by Cairo's expected place in the Egyptian population. Allowing for some war-caused increase in Cairo's 1800 population, we can infer that Cairo occupied about the same percentage of the 1800 Egyptian total as in 1846, namely 5·5 per cent. A normal progression in city size might indicate that Cairo's 1800 percentage might be less than that of 1846, but never more. With Cairo's population at 5·5 per cent, the population of Egypt would have been 3,835,633 in 1800. This study has adopted that number, using what is best in Jomard's study—Cairo house data—and discarding the rest.[26]

PESTILENCE[27]

Most Egyptian deaths can be included as part of normal population rate, causing a death rate which, over the nineteenth century, gradually decreased. This paper does not primarily consider such deaths, nor endemic diseases such as tuberculosis and dysentery, independently or specifically, but within the normal context of rate per year. They can be considered as a relatively constant function, slowly improving as the century went on. This is not true of the sporadic pestilences, diseases which took a great toll one year, were gone the next, and thus had a great effect on population rate. The presence or absence of these 'peaks of mortality' was most likely the most significant cause of change in population growth rate.[28] In studying nineteenth-century Egyptian population, two types of pestilence have to be considered—cholera and plague.

Like other statistics for Egypt, those of cholera are far more reliable as their dates approach the twentieth century. Statistics for deaths due to cholera are fairly good from 1883 on, but they are only truly reliable for the 1947 epidemic, thus any consideration of cholera in the nineteenth century must be based on very tentative data. Statistics on epidemics can be reworked, but they ultimately rest on contemporary data, which are by nature inexact.

Official cholera mortality records suffer from the cultural and political difficulties common to all Egyptian figures of the time.[29] Cholera also presents a special problem, in that its symptoms are so like those of other diseases; 'diarrhoea coupled with a high mortality rate does occur in other diseases and is not at all rare'.[30] The symptoms are even close to those of acute arsenic poisoning.[31]

The situation in Egypt was especially susceptible to mistake over cholera's death rate. Health conditions gave rise to all sorts of dysenteric diseases, one very hard to separate from the others. Death records in Cairo and Alexandria for 1859–60 show that the greatest cause of post-childhood death was 'fièvre gastro-enterique',[32] which seems to have meant (in the official statistics) any non-typhoidal intestinal disease.[33]

Dr. Shakespeare, sent by the United States government to investigate the 1883 Egyptian cholera epidemic, examined the registers of cholera deaths:

> It should be borne in mind: (1) The registers were not kept correctly with regard either to entries of deaths or names of diseases. There were causes of death put down which even the native doctor did not comprehend. (2) The case claimed by the authorities to be the first case of cholera was registered acute gastro-enteritis. (3) For at least two months previous to June 20 (the date of the 'first case') there had been an unusual number of cases marked down acute gastro-enteritis.[34]

In such a system, exact enumeration of victims of cholera would be impossible. The official data were, by necessity, corrected to arrive at the figures given in Table 5.

Cholera seems to have begun, in the modern period at least, in India, where it appeared with great loss of life in the late eighteenth century. From India it spread across the world. The first pandemic, which began in 1817, spared Egypt, but the second pandemic brought cholera to Cairo in July of 1831, probably carried there from Mecca, where it had killed nearly one-half of the pilgrims. The first Egyptian epidemic invaded the entire Delta and the Nile 'up to Thebes.' Cholera appeared again three times at mid-century, each time from Mecca—a minor attack in 1848

TABLE 5

Cholera Epidemics in Egypt

Year	Deaths
1831	180,000
1850	39,300
1855	116,020
1865	122,044
1883	58,511
1896	16,000
1902	34,590

Sources; Pollitzer's *Cholera* and Hussein.[35]

and two major epidemics in 1850 and 1855.[36] In 1865 the disease appeared in Alexandria, took a great toll in lives, and remained a minor trouble until it appeared again in 1883.

1831

> It [cholera] was carried in the Spring of 1831 by bands of pilgrims . . . by way of Suez to Egypt. It appeared in Cairo in July, and spread along the Nile upwards as far as Thebes and as far down as Alexandria, so that it overran the whole delta.[37]

Although it appears that this first cholera attack was Egypt's worst, no viable 1831 death statistics are available. The best sources seem to lie in diplomatic correspondence. (As will be shown later, such sources are untrustworthy for rural areas but fairly accurate for cities.) These state that 'official reports' claimed 9,000 dead of cholera in Cairo and 1,500 at Alexandria, 'at this time the populations of the two cities were 300,000 and 90,000 respectively',[38] figures more or less close to reality.[39] The figure of 9,000 seems to have been, if anything, small. Another source claimed 'it raged with such intensity at Cairo that 10,400 Mohamedans, besides Jews and Christians, were carried off . . .'.[40] The first figure was chosen for use here, however, because the correction factor to be applied was designed for and based on 'official' statistics. Taking Cairo's 9,000 dead and multiplying by 20 (a factor explained below—'1865') we arrive at the total of 180,000 deaths. Considering both the state of the cholera pandemic and that of Egypt in 1831, this figure seems not at all absurd. 18,402 died of the same pandemic in Paris in 1832,[41] and health standards in Egypt were very low.

Cholera existed in Egypt through 1837,[42] but seemingly not in significant virulence to have its death rate recorded. While cholera remained in Europe for a time, as well, and reached Persia from India in 1845–46, Egypt received a new pandemic only in 1850.

1850 AND 1855

Much of the information for the 1850 and 1855 epidemics comes from Europeans, especially French and Italian residents in Cairo and Alexandria. These were usually medical doctors, publishing their work in the Institut Egyptien publications. These did what they could with official records of the Egyptian government, usually recognising that, while the law demanded that all deaths be registered, many actually were not.[43] Data for the 1850 and 1855 epidemics were taken from these sources. The table below will demonstrate, however, that the data needed correction:

TABLE 6

Etats Comparatifs du Choléra-morbus qui a Regné au Caire en 1850 et en 1855

Nations	Nombre 1850	Nombre 1855
Européens	25	45
Grecs	6	20
Arméniens	5	12
Syriens		5
Cophtes	62	154
Israélites	15	15
Indigènes	1594	3074
Turcs	28	139
Mograbins	11	44
Barbarins	51	90
Noirs	168	465
Totaux	1963	4063

Source: M. J. Colucci Bey, 'Quelques Notes Sur La Choléra'.[44]

It seems very unlikely that the deaths of Greeks, Armenians, Copts, 'Mograbins', 'Barbarins', and 'Noirs' would triple, where that of the 'Indigènes' would less than double. The basic cause of cholera is fecal contamination, especially of water supplies, and the native Muslim of 1855 was surely as dependent, if not more so, on such water supplies as Copts, Greeks, or Armenians. The Jewish death rate is obviously also very much suspect. (The 'Syriens' who appear in 1855 may be in another group in 1850.) It was necessary, therefore, to change the data. This was done by tripling the 1850 number of native Muslim and Jewish deaths to obtain 4,782 and 45, respectively. The 1850 and 1855 figures were then multiplied by the factor of 20 to gain a cholera death rate of 39,300 for 1850 and 116,020 for 1855.

1865

In 1865 many more pilgrims than usual were gathered at Mecca when cholera struck. Probably not less than one-third died.[45]

> On the 19th of May a ship bringing 1,500 pilgrims from Jeddah arrived at Suez. Many of the pilgrims had died of cholera during the voyage, . . . The pilgrims were at once forwarded from Suez to Alexandria by rail, and on the 22nd of May the first case of cholera was noticed in a body of these people on their way to the port. Numerous pilgrims from Mecca followed by this route, and many of them embarked at Alexandria in vessels provided to carry them to their homes.
>
> Cases of cholera occurred in Alexandria early in June, and the disease spread rapidly over Egypt, destroying 60,000 of its inhabitants during the following three months. The panic was great, and the people fled from Egypt to Constantinople, and the various places along the Mediterranean coast.[46]

The figure of 60,000 was taken from government claims of 61,022 dead.[47] The statistics for Cairo, where deaths could be much more closely watched by the government, are probably not too incorrect, but as for the national figures: 'mortality figures for epidemics are considered to be grossly understated, and therefore these figures can scarcely be trusted'.[48] The reasons for this are obvious—natural reluctance of fellahs to register anything with the government, lack of effective communication, the natural confusion caused by an epidemic. Perhaps less obvious is the fact that village barbers were the keepers of the death records and that their profession, especially 'doctoring' the sick and preparing corpses, gave them a high mortality rate in any epidemic.[49] Often there was simply no-one to keep the records. Unreliable data resulted.

In his 1884 study, Rabino states, 'it must be borne in mind that the general impression (of the 1865 data) in Egypt is that the figures should be doubled'.[50] For 1883, that seems to be what Hussein has done. The same has been done here for 1865. As Rabino suggested, the figure has been doubled, an action made more acceptable by comparing Cairo's death rate to that of the entire nation. The official rate of cholera-death for Cairo (6,104) is 10 per cent of the total cholera death rate given for the country. This is doubly odd, since Cairo's population was only about one-twentieth of the total, and since the epidemic spread through the entire country. Doubling the national death total leaves a figure more in line with both Cairo's percentage of the Egyptian population and the national character of the epidemic.

The position that the official figures are too low is supported by the fact that, in Damietta, for example, in 1865 the registered death rate more than tripled—from 1,092 in 1864 to 3,747 in 1865 (and back to 987 in 1866). Undoubtedly the excess deaths were a product of cholera, although by no means always listed thus. 1,913 deaths were to be reported officially from Damietta as cholera deaths in the 1883 epidemic, and the population of the city changed little from 1865 to 1883.[51] Considering an improvement in health standards in 1883, the figure of more than 2,000 deaths in 1865 seems fairly correct.

The Damietta figure would lead us to suspect a much higher figure than the official one, even though Damietta lies in a high chlolera death area. If anything, such a high rate would tend to indicate that the 'multiple of 20' factor might be too low, but the tendency of chloera to strike much harder in the Delta and the generally unhealthy state of Damietta in 1865 tend to negate this somewhat.[52]

The figure of 122,022, as well as the other figures based on the 'Cairo times 20' rate, gains credibility when compared to the almost 60,000 death rate in 1883, when sanitary cordons, etc., were set up in Egypt, whereas in 1865 there were none. Neither was the 1883 pandemic as damaging world-wide as the 1865, yet 60,000 died in Egypt. In the 1947 epidemic 20,462 died, in spite of elaborate modern precautions:

> The Cairo–Port Said–Suez triangle was promptly isolated by the authorities, and travel in this area was prohibited, except for persons possessing certificates of immunization against cholera. An intensive immunization campaign was undertaken and approximately one-third of the six million inhabitants of the infected districts were innoculated with cholera vaccine. A fly-eradication program was also carried out in Cairo, the houses being sprayed with DDT, both from the air and the ground.[53]

If, despite all this, 20,000 could die, it is surely no exaggeration that 122,000 could have died in 1865, without DDT or cholera vaccine.[54] (The factor of 20 times the Cairo death rate is thus very credible, though admittedly still a matter of probability. It is used here for the previously calculated cholera death rates.)

1883

Between 1865 and 1883 cholera appeared to a small degree in Egypt, but was generally kept in check by the quarantine measures of the Intendance Sanitaire, the group empowered by the Egyptian government and foreign embassies to halt epidemics. Their quarantine surely kept cholera from Egypt in 1881. The proper procedures were not upheld in 1883, however, due to the British invasion, and the disease entered either with British Indian soldiers or pilgrims from Mecca:

> During this year a brigade of Indian troops landed in Egypt from Bombay, and took part in the occupation of that country by our forces, and the Egyptian quarantine procedures had to be relaxed

> in consequence of our military operations. At the end of June, 1883, cholera appeared at Damietta and afterwards at Rosetta, Port Said, and Mansourah. During July it spread from these locations; at Cairo it was very fatal, and also in Alexandria. It is estimated that from the 22nd of June to the first of September, 1883, cholera destroyed 50,000 people in Egypt. There can be little doubt that the Egyptian cholera of 1883 originated in the 1882 epidemic of India and Arabia.[55]

By the end of the 1883, epidemic cholera had surely killed more than 50,000. Shakespeare quotes many doctors present at the time who state the disease killed 'around 50,000', '56,000', etc., even though the government's official figures state approximately 28,600.[56] Factors previously mentioned, added to the fact that in 1902, under much better health and civil conditions, 34,595 died of cholera,[57] ensure that the government figures show the usual discrepancies and that Pollitzer's acceptance of Hussein's figure of 58,511 dead is as near to correct as possible.

1896 AND 1902

Pollitzer's figures for 1896 and 1902 are equally acceptable: 16,000 in 1896, 34,590 in 1902.[58] Both of these figures have been considered in the population totals.

Plague in Egypt was a far greater killer than cholera. It cannot, however, be considered in the same way. Unlike those due to cholera, plague deaths cannot usually be listed year by year. Cholera came, peaked, and was gone; plague was almost constant.

Plague was so constant in early nineteenth-century Egypt that it can generally be considered as a usual source of death, just like tuberculosis or dysentery. Between 1800 and 1844 there were plague epidemics in Egypt in 21 of the 44 years. Thus, plague can somewhat legitimately be placed in the general death rate. While this is by no means a satisfying method of dealing with the disease, lack of information on mortality makes it essential. If the records for cholera were meagre, those for plague are almost non-existent.

The exception to all this is the plague epidemic of 1834–35. Sources of the time agree that the epidemic was far worse than the others, worse even than the 'Great Plague' of 1783–84. Of that plague, Volney contended that 1,500 dead had been placed by the gates of Cairo in one day.[59] Even if that number were a gross exaggeration, the plague of 1835, worse than that of 1783, must have indeed been severe.

Contemporary estimates of 1835 plague deaths vary greatly. The same sources (e.g. Campbell[60]) list different results—either 31,000 or 35,000 dead, for example. The high figure above goes further to indicate a death rate of 150,000 for all Egypt, of which 75,000 were in Cairo, 18,000 in Alexandria.[61] For many reasons these figures are to be seriously questioned. First, analysis of plague later in Egypt's history has revealed certain patterns in the development of the disease:

TABLE 7

The Plague Season in Egypt

Region	Onset	Peak	End
Upper	March	April	May
Middle	April	May	June
Delta and Suez	April	June	July
Mediterranean Ports	May	July	October

Source: Pollitzer, *Plague*.[62]

The 150,000 report ends its estimate at 30 June, 1835. If the modern data in any way apply to 1835 Egypt, as they surely should, since the 'plague season' is caused by changes in temperature and humidity and these are roughly the same now as they were then, then the chroniclers missed much of the plague in their estimates. More important, any estimate of the plague which places one-half of the dead in Cairo cannot possibly be correct. It is possible that contemporary sources accepted such figures because fairly recent plagues in Europe had followed the one-city pattern. The plague of the last century in Marseilles, for example, had been restricted to that city by governmental action and climatic factors. This restriction, however, could not have applied to Egypt. If it had, one would be asked to believe that the plague fairly jumped from Cairo to Alexandria, missing the most populous areas of Egypt.

That the jump did not take place is demonstrated by modern, contemporary, and even medieval examples. The plague of the late Middle Ages is too well known to merit extensive discussion. It is enough to notice that its pattern surely did not spare the countryside.[63] It may be objected that medieval European examples do not apply to Egyptian climate and geography. Modern examples of Egyptian plague serve to answer such objections.

After an absence of 50 years, plague reappeared in Egypt in 1899. It came to the Mediterranean ports and from there spread inland, first to the chief towns and cities of each province, then to the villages. Egypt at the turn of the century was a far less fertile field for plague than at the time of Mohammed Ali's wars, and death rates were far lower. The pattern, however, still applies. If the much-lessened twentieth-century plague (19,386 died of plague between 1899 and 1930[64]) spread to all parts of the country, the earlier, more deadly pestilence should have spread there as well.

Contemporary sources support this thesis. Pictures of abandoned villages abound. In fact, the same sources which give incredibly low death figures for villages often mention the stark picture in the provinces. Count Medem, for one, travelling the Nile both before and after the effect of the 1835 plague and 1837 famine, saw whole villages empty, others vastly depopulated, and blamed the loss on plague, famine, and

Mohammed Ali's policies.[65] Bascombe, whose study of the movements of epidemic disease was the most complete of the time (written in 1849), compiled from contemporary sources a picture of Egyptian plague which affected the entire country terribly, up the Nile as well as in the capital. European consuls saw evidence of great death. Campbell, the British consul, even contended that one-fourth of the Copts perished in Cairo, yet he saw no contradiction in accepting both this statement and a very low estimate of total deaths.[66]

Clot Bey reported that only 50,000 died in all Egypt,[67] even though the official government figure for Cairo alone was 40,000 dead.[68] No reason is given for his estimate. In fact, he later states, in his *Mémoires*, that the first rural health teams went out in 1837. The first miniscule amount of good information came only then.[69] No government statistics for the rural Egyptian death rate seem to have been available. Death and birth records were only kept in the provinces after the 1846 census, and then not kept well. Where could Clot, or the rest of the European observers, have obtained their information? Probably, as was to be the case for almost all later population estimates, out of their imaginations.[70]

Given the nature of the disease,[71] it is extremely difficult to believe that the 1835 plague could have killed more than half of its victims in Cairo and Alexandria. In the plagues which occurred in the twentieth century, approximately 55 per cent of the plague deaths were in Upper Egypt,[72] since conditions made the plague more likely to spread there.

> Owing to the system used for irrigating the fields in the Southern areas of Upper Egypt, during the months of March, April, and May, when plague is most prevalent in Southern Egypt, as well as in the subsequent months, great numbers of inhabitants are obliged to remain idle in badly ventilated houses. There is thus a greater risk of the propagation of bubonic and pneumonic plague than in other parts of Egypt.[73]

Upper Egypt surely cannot have been adequately counted in an estimate that puts 62 per cent of the plague deaths in Cairo and Alexandria. Furthermore, the best rat host of the 'plague flea'[74] has a greater incidence in Upper than in Lower Egypt.[75] In a country whose transportation system is mainly made up of small boats and caravans, plague fleas cannot help but travel as widely as their human and rodent hosts. Therefore, from all evidence, the 1835 plague must have travelled to all parts of Egypt and caused far more than 150,000 deaths.

Since plague does affect different areas with varying virulence, it is probably impossible to give an estimate of the 1835 death rate with any degree of precision. We can only be sure that the contemporary figures are far, far too low. Therefore, death estimates of this study were designed to err on the low side, rather than the high. This was based on the assumptions that: (1) Though modern data seem to deny it, plague may possibly have had a greater death rate in Cairo and Alexandria than in the rest of Egypt, although never as great as contemporary Europeans asserted; (2) Plague touched at least most areas of Egypt; (3) Some plague deaths have already been included in the normal mortality (see above) of the time. Thus, erring on the low side for the 1835 plague would be the better choice.

For Cairo's 1835 plague deaths, Rabino's figure of 40,000 has been taken[76] (instead of estimates, like Lane's, of up to 80,000). If Cairo is considered to have had one-twentieth of the plague deaths, the national figure would be 800,000. Allowing for the above assumptions, a figure of 500,000 deaths has finally been set here, a figure whose very 'roundness' should indicate its uncertainty. The actual death rate could have been considerably higher, but not lower.

1800–46

The period between 1800 and 1846, most of which fell during the reign of Mohammed Ali Pasha, reversed the long downward trend in Egyptian population. Most sources agree that the population rose during the Pasha's rule, but there is little agreement on the amount of increase. In order to investigate the population of the time, it is necessary to consider contemporary events and the various estimates of population numbers.

Judging by the rates of the latter half of the century, the rate of unfettered population growth in Mohammed Ali's Egypt could have been as high as 15 or 17 per thousand per year. One of the main reasons for the actual, lower rate, i.e. pestilence, has already been discussed. Another factor was war.

The history of the Arabian, Morean, Syrian, and Sudanese wars need not be examined here. What is significant to this study is their effect on the male Egyptian population. Mohammed Ali's army, according to French sources, at the time of its greatest strength was composed of 207,653 men (naval forces included), of whom 130,302 were regular infantry or cavalry.[77] The strain of such a force on the population was tremendous.

One can argue that, while many died, the number who died in the wars was not nearly enough greatly to diminish the population. To the number of those killed in battle, however, must be added all those who died of war-time diseases. If the army of Mohammed Ali's days were not a terrible place, men would not have poked out eyes and maimed themselves to avoid it, nor would Mohamed Ali have been forced to use the measures he did in order to maintain an army.[78] More important is the effect of conscription and war on births. An Egypt of very low sanitary conditions needed a great birth rate to balance a great death rate. (In a country of almost universal marriage and constant childbirth a man could easily account for a child every three or four years and, where there is polygamy, obviously more.) Mohamed Ali's wars went on for twenty-five years. Conscripted soldiers contributed greatly to the death rate in those times, but were not at home to provide children. Debilitating wars took exactly those young men needed to maintain the birth rate.[79]

TABLE 8

The Population of Egypt 1800–45

Year	Population	Disease	Disease Deaths	Rate/ Year
1800	3,853,633			·006587
1801	3,879,020			
1802	3,904,574			
1803	3,930,297			
1804	3,956,189			
1805	3,982,252			
1806	4,008,487			
1807	4,034,894			
1808	4,061,475			
1809	4,088,232			
1810	4,115,165			
1811	4,142,275			
1812	4,169,564			
1813	4,197,032			
1814	4,224,682			
1815	4,252,513			
1816	4,280,528			
1817	4,308,728			
1818	4,337,113			
1819	4,365,685			
1820	4,394,446			
1821	4,423,396			
1822	4,452,537			
1823	4,481,869			
1824	4,511,395			
1825	4,541,116			
1826	4,571,032			
1827	4,601,145			
1828	4,631,457			
1829	4,661,969			
1830	4,692,681			
1831	4,543,596	Cholera	180,000	
1832	4,573,528			
1833	4,603,658			
1834	4,633,987			
1835	4,164,515	Plague	500,000	
1836	4,191,950			
1837	4,219,566			
1838	4,247,364			
1839	4,275,345			
1840	4,303,510			
1841	4,331,861			
1842	4,360,399			
1843	4,389,125			
1844	4,418,040			
1845	4,447,145			

The high rate of 'normal' diseases also served to limit population growth. While it is true that the ministrations of Clot Bey, Mohammed Ali's chief medical adviser, and others had destroyed many antiquated health practices in Cairo and Alexandria, there is little evidence that the new standards spread much beyond these cities during the Pasha's reign. Clot Bey recognised this, but his first move towards health teams for the provinces came only in 1837.[80]

The health teams sent out by Clot, while surely on no great scale, were the start of a long upward climb in Egyptian health standards. The fact that Clot found that such simple measures of hygiene as the teams could take had never been taken before indicates the abysmal health standards which had existed up to that time.[81]

What does seem to have improved under Mohammed Ali, and the single most important factor for population growth at the time, was civil order, internal peace. While the rate of population increase during the time of the Pasha was small compared to later periods, it should rightfully be compared to the time of the Mamluks. Almost from the time of the Muslim conquest Egypt had been losing population. Only with Mohammed Ali was the long decline halted. In spite of his wars, the population rose. Since there was little health improvement, and great military activity, the growth must have been brought about by better civil standards.[82] Unlike the Mamluks, the Pasha's army did not treat its own territories as conquered provinces.[83] It kept order. In such an atmosphere, despite plagues and conscription, peasants were obviously able to live and have children.

The actual population of Egypt in Mohammed Ali's time has long been a subject of confusion. In 1846[84] the Pasha took a census which, after nomads were included, arrived at a population of 4,476,440. His figures were, however, in complete disagreement with the opinions of the Europeans in Egypt. These observers estimated the population to be much smaller. Unfortunately, it was their figures which gained the widest acceptance.[85] For instance, in *The Agricultural Policy of Mohammad Ali in Egypt*, Helen Rivlin gives a summary of the European data, prefering them to that of Mohammed Ali:

> The final conclusion that can be drawn from the evidence is that the population figures were lower than those provided to foreigners by Mohammed Ali and that the foreign observers were fully aware of these inaccuracies and therefore relied on their own sources of information. Mohammed Ali may have genuinely believed that he had at his command a far larger population than actually existed. On the other hand, he may very well have exaggerated the size of the Egyptian population in his effort to justify his military and economic policies.[86]

To justify this position, Rivlin presents the following statistics, drawn from European consular officials in Egypt:

TABLE 9

Population of Egypt in 1840
European Estimates

Source	Population Estimate
Hamont	1,500,000
de Boislecomte	3,000,000
Bowring	2,500,000
Campbell	2,235,500 of whom 800,000 were peasants (!)
Barnett[87]	2,158,580 of whom 1,708,580 were 'agrarian' (1844)

Source: Rivlin, *The Agricultural Policy of Mohammad Ali in Egypt*[88]

Examination of these figures reveals them all as impossible. The first point against them is their obvious internal inconsistency. The data these 'experts' gave range over a difference, a deviation of 10 per cent from Hamont to Boislecomt. Which, if any, is to be trusted? Surely not Campbell, who held that only 800,000 of over 2,000,000 Egyptians were peasants.[89]

Comparative examination yields more evidence of error. If we select the figures given by Bowring (2,500,000) and Barnett (2,158,580) as indicative, and project them to the population of 1882, we arrive at:[90]

TABLE 10

Projected Rates of Change—to 1882

	Yearly Rate of Change Per Thousand
Bowring	26·597
Barnett	33·423

This compares to actual rates for 1882 to 1897 and 1897 to 1907 of:

TABLE 11

Actual Rates of Change—1882 to 1907

	Yearly Rate of Change Per Thousand
1882–97	15·142
1897–1907	15·246

If the Bowring or Barnett figures are correct, we are forced to believe that the Egyptian population of 1840 to 1882 increased at a rate double that of 1882 to 1907, inspite of huge cholera deaths in the former period and improvements in sanitation and agriculture in the latter. A rate of change of 30 indicates a growth of 3 per cent a year, above that of the most prolific countries today.[91] Considering both Egyptian history and the biological limits on birth,[92] such data indicate twice as many births as deaths. For a country of Egypt's nineteenth-century sanitary conditions, this is completely impossible. The European data must therefore be wrong, and very wrong, at that.[93]

The data of Mohammed Ali's 1846 census, however, fit times and events very well. The rate of change between his 1846 population and that of 1882 is 17·143 per thousand per year, slightly above the rates of 1882 to 1897 and 1897 to 1907. His figures could not, of course, have been as accurate as a modern census, not even the 1882 census could claim that. It was better than any other figures, though. When put into a picture of the revised 1800 data and the wars and plagues that came between 1800 and 1846, it presents a complete, rational image of population growth. As further proof, the provincial population data for 1846 put each province in approximately the same percentage of the total population as in the 1882, 1897, and 1907 censuses. All things considered, the virtue of Mohammed Ali's census is that its figures are probable. Those of the others are not.[94]

1846–82

So much of this study is based on comparisons using non-contemporary data that one question must inevitably arise, that is, why not make more use of the estimates of those who lived in nineteenth-century Egypt? It is true that a more complete study of the topic would, by necessity, involve extensive work in cadastral records, reports on conditions in provinces, etc. The contemporary sources that are usually quoted, however, and the ones which usually appear in a study of this nature are, first, the writings of European observers in Egypt and, second, the official records of births and deaths.

The mistake in trusting the consular sources of Mohammed Ali's period has already been shown. For this period, though, more extensive European analyses are available than those of Bowring or Barnett. Between 1846 and 1882 the Egyptian population was examined by men far more competent in population analysis than the consuls of Mohammed Ali's time. Many of them were doctors working in Egypt, officials of either the Intendance Sanitaire or the Census Bureau. They were by far the most qualified and concerned analysts of the time, yet they still did not arrive at acceptable population figures. Because of their standing, this study has chosen their work to demonstrate why, for this period, contemporary data are unusable.

The European savants were very confident of 'modern' methods. Among

TABLE 12

The Population of Egypt 1846–81

Year	Population	Disease	Disease Deaths	Rate/ Year
1846	4,476,439			·017143
1847	4,553,180			
1848	4,631,237			
1849	4,710,632			
1850	4,752,088	Cholera	39,300	
1851	4,833,555			
1852	4,916,418			
1853	5,000,702			
1854	5,086,431			
1855	5,057,610	Cholera	116,020	
1856	5,144,314			
1857	5,232,505			
1858	5,322,208			
1859	5,413,448			
1860	5,506,253			
1861	5,600,649			
1862	5,696,663			
1863	5,794,323			
1864	5,893,657			
1865	5,872,651	Cholera	122,044	
1866	5,973,328			
1867	6,075,731			
1868	6,179,889			
1869	6,285,833			
1870	6,393,594			
1871	6,503,201			
1872	6,614,688			
1873	6,728,086			
1874	6,843,428			
1875	6,960,748			
1876	7,080,079			
1877	7,201,455			
1878	7,324,912			
1879	7,450,486			
1880	7,578,213			
1881	7,708,129			

these was the registration of births and deaths. After the 1846 census, the Egyptian government made such registration mandatory. Some results of this enumeration, taken from Boinet Bey, later head of the Census Bureau, are contained in tables 13 and 14.

Interestingly, this table demonstrates that the areas where one would expect death rolls to be best kept are those with the highest death rates. Cairo and Suez head the list, with Alexandria closely behind. Farther from the government centres the people are much 'healthier'; officially, only one man dies for each 111 inhabitants in Beni-Suef, one

TABLE 13

Egypt—Birth and Deaths
January 1872 to December 1881

Administrative Divisions	Inhabitants/ One Birth	Inhabitants/ One Death
Cairo	19	21
Alexandria	23	26
Damietta	22	34
Rosetta	26	38
Port Said	24	28
Suez	16	18
Arish	22	35
Kosseir	25	34
Beheira	32	62
Sharqiya	34	48
Daqahliya	24	38
Gharbiya	27	41
Qalubiya	26	40
Minufiya	28	42
Asyut	43	77
Beni-Suef	40	111
Faiyum	34	66
Giza	29	45
Minya	44	107
Girga	38	94
Qena	42	75
Esna	31	54
Oases	33	47
Egypt	30	47

Source: A. Boinet Bey, p. 293.[95]

for 107 in Minya. In the rural areas of Upper Egypt, only one person for each 113 dies; in the cities of Lower Egypt, one per 23. Cities were indeed dangerous, but could they have been so much more fatal, especially in a period which contained no great epidemics?

The same is true of births. How could so many fewer children be born the farther one goes from Cairo? The returns are obviously deficient.[96]

Dr. Schnepp, writing in the 1862 *Mémoires* of the Institut Egyptien, is not confident of death registrations. He still feels, however, that they are fairly well registered, certainly better than births. His figures show his confidence to be unfounded. He quotes official figures which show that, for 1859–60, 14,985 persons died in Cairo and 10,701 were born, a very unlikely situation.[97] In Schnepp's general statistics, however, errors show in both births and deaths.

TABLE 14

Egypt—Births and Deaths by Regions
January 1872 to December 1881

Regions	Births	Inhabitants/ One Birth	Deaths	Inhabitants/ One Death
Lower Egypt				
Rural	99,932	28	63,384	44
Urban	37,087	20	32,771	23
Isthmus				
Rural	142	26	153	24
Urban	1,086	19	924	23
East				
Urban	125	22	81	34
Upper Egypt				
Rural	60,310	39	29,021	113
Urban	5,811	23	4,651	29
Oases				
Rural	797	32	554	47
Egypt				
Rural	161,181	32	93,112	56
Urban	44,109	21	38,427	24
Total	205,290	30	131,439	47

Source: A. Boinet Bey, p. 296.

TABLE 15

Schnepp's Estimates of Births and Deaths

	Births	Deaths	Increase
1857	128,128	107,936	20,192
1858	161,702	99,392	62,310
1859	159,345	100,929	58,416

Scource: Schnepp, pp. 534 and 539.

The rate of increase does not even closely approach that needed for the real growth rate,[98] which demands an increase of more than 65,000 for each of the three years. The figures of increase actually only come as close to the needed number as they do because both births and deaths are under-registered, the errors balancing each other. The figures could perhaps be doubled to approximate accuracy. For the cities, Schnepp is more correct:

TABLE 16

Schnepp's Estimates of Births According to Localities (indigenous population)

Localities	1858	1859	Inhabitants/ One Birth	Population
Cairo	11,200	10,701	24·85	265,000
Alexandria	6,725	6,634	25·62	170,000
Damietta	1,158	1,153	32·17	37,000
Rosetta	757	717	25·55	18,000
Suez	205	207	24·15	5,000

Source: Schnepp, pp. 533 and 535.

Schnepp's figures demonstrate a general truth of Egyptian contemporary population estimates—that death, birth and population statistics for large cities are generally fairly accurate. Rural and nationwide countings are nearly always suspect.[99] Schnepp, representing a trait common among his fellows, recognised that his data rested upon informants whose harems, fears of corvée, and knowledge of the tax-collector made them poor sources, yet still used these data, unchanged.

Finally, the general conclusion of contemporary and modern scholars has been that, while the official birth rates and numbers were wrong, death rates were fairly accurate, because of the need to obtain a death certificate before legal burial. The error in this reasoning can be seen in the previously cited tables of Boinet. The comparative study of F. Amici—Chef du Bureau Central de Statistique de L'Egypte—shows well the error of using such evidence for population estimation.[100]

Amici took the recorded birth and death rates, which, he contended, approached the truth closely enough to be used for his study,[101] and arrived at a figure of national increase:

TABLE 17

4,685,988	births (since 1846)
3,631,605	deaths (since 1846)
1,054,383	natural increase

He added this to the total from Mohammed Ali's 1846 census and arrived at a population for 31 December, 1878:

TABLE 18

4,463,244	(1846 population)
+1,054,383	(natural increase)
5,517,626	(1878 population)

Going further, Amici compared his mortality and nativity statistics with those of Europe, with interesting results:

TABLE 19

Births and Deaths in 1875 (Amici)

Country	Births/100 Inhabitants	Deaths/100 Inhabitants
Egypt	3·45	2·25
Great Britain	3·55	2·28
Bavaria	4·16	3·14
German Empire	4·04	2·74
Holland	3·63	2·54
Italy	3·79	3·07

Source: Amici, pp. 11 f. Table abridged.

According to his tables, Egypt had a lower birth rate than England, Austria, Bavaria, Germany, Finland, and most other European countries (only a few of those he lists are printed above), often a considerably lower birth rate. Egypt's mortality was also very low, lower than England, Italy, Holland, Germany, etc. Both assertions are so unlikely that they need no further rebuttal.

As the European observers of Mohammed Ali's time had an unfounded confidence in their powers of observation, so these latter-day evaluators felt confidence in their registration regulations. Some of them understood that births might be under-recorded, but they were sure that the 'death certificate law' would insure relatively accurate mortality tables. They were not in a position to conduct either empirical or mathematical analyses of their data, so many of their mistakes can be understood. Nevertheless, their data are useless for all but small, comparative purposes.[103]

1882–1907

The 1882 census was Egypt's first undertaken along 'Western' lines.[104] Europeans, headed by Boinet Bey of the Institut Egyptien, were chosen to supervise its enumeration. The census, however, was a failure. Its data were uniformly low, probably for all the usual reasons. While more than 40 years had passed since Mohammed Ali's conscription, not so long a period had passed since the corvée for the Suez Canal. Peasants still probably found it difficult to distinguish between the census taker and the tax collector. The tradition of never telling the truth to the government still applied. In such circumstances, it was remarkable that the 1882 census came as close as it did to accuracy.

The final total, beduins included, of the 1882 census was 6,817,262,[105] an estimate which showed a definite increase from the time of Mohammed

Ali, but an estimate that was not nearly high enough. If the 1897 population is compared to that of 1882, the population would have had to have increased at a rate of 24 per thousand per year (2·391 per cent) between those years. This is impossible, for two reasons:

1. Such a rate of increase was far beyond the biological potential of nineteenth-century Egypt.[106] Egypt's modern rate, in time of both 'population explosion' and modern medicine, is only 25 per thousand per year. Surely the Egypt of the 1890s could not have equalled it. Such a rate would be considerably higher than present-day India's (19/1000/year), almost equal to Turkey's (28/1000/year)—both countries at their highest growth rates in history.[107]

2. The Egyptian rate of growth between 1897 and 1907 was only 15 per thousand per year. The difference between this and the 1882–97 rate might not be unusual if the later period were economically and politically worse than the former, but the opposite is true. The period from 1882 to 1897 was the more unstable. It was the period of British occupation and solidification of power, a time of greater upheaval than 1897 to 1907, when the political system was more solidified.[108]

TABLE 20

The Population of Egypt 1882–1907

Year	Population	Disease	Disease Deaths	Rate/ Year
1882	7,840,271			·015142
1883	7,900,483	Cholera	58,511	
1884	8,020,119			
1885	8,141,566			
1886	8,264,853			
1887	8,390,006			
1888	8,517,055			
1889	8,646,027			
1890	8,776,852			
1891	8,909,860			
1892	9,044,781			
1893	9,181,745			
1894	9,320,782			
1895	9,461,925			
1896	9,589,206	Cholera	16,000	
1897	9,734,405			·015246
1898	9,882,823			
1899	10,033,504			
1900	10,186,482			
1901	10,341,793			
1902	10,464,882	Cholera	34,590	
1903	10,624,438			
1904	10,786,426			
1905	10,950,884			
1906	11,117,850			
1907	11,287,359			

The census figures, then, were very low. Perhaps a census taken in the time of Arabi and the British invasion[109] was doomed to be inexact. It is worth noting that this low enumeration of population followed a long-established trend. Boinet Bey was the same man who accepted the incredible birth and death rates mentioned above.[110]

In order to correct the 1882 results, it was necessary to deal with the data purely mathematically. A much more detailed investigation of conditions in individual provinces would yield facts which would surely affect the estimates drawn here. Bearing in mind that the estimates would be somewhat inexact by nature, this study proceeded with one assumption—that the general rate of increase between 1882 and 1897 would be very close to that of 1897 to 1907.

Since additions were to be made to the 1882 census figures, the danger was that the population would be overestimated. The political situation would tend to indicate, however, that the new figures are well within reason. The situation of the time would, if anything, have made the 1882 to 1897 rate lower than that of 1897 to 1907; overestimation cannot arise out of making them equal. Moreover, the new rates leave a more probable rate of progression than the old:

TABLE 21

Comparative Rates of Change

Period	Original Rate	Corrected Rate
1846–82	·013227	·017143
1882–97	·024830	·015142
1897–1907	·015246	·015246

While simply applying the 1897 to 1907 rate to 1882 to 1897 would have produced a fairly accurate answer, a more precise one was achieved by considering rates of growth in individual provinces and markazes:

Table 22 contains an analysis of each province's rate of growth per thousand per year for both periods. The rates are compared: If the 1882 to 1897 rate is more than five per thousand above the 1897 to 1907 rate, 'Analysis' registers 'Low'. If the first rate is more than five per thousand below the second, 'Analysis' reads 'High'. If both rates are within plus or minus five per thousand of each other, 'Analysis' is 'Good'. (That is, the *1882 population* is what is 'High', 'Low', or 'Good'.) Even with such a great deviation allowed, enough to cover any normal migration, only two provinces registered as 'Good'. None was 'High', and some 'High' provinces would be necessary if the 'Low' analyses were caused by internal migration. Both the 'Good' provinces were still low in population, but within the allowed deviation.

For the provinces which registered 'Low', new 1882 populations were

TABLE 22

Populations and Rates, 1907, 1897, 1882
With Correction Factor for 1882

Province	1907 Population	1897 Population	1897–07 Rate/Year	1882 Population	1882–97 Rate/Year	Analysis	1882 Corrected Population
Cairo	654,476	570,062	·013904	374,838	·028344	Low	463,414
Alexandria	370,009	319,776	·014697	231,396	·021800	Low	256,921
Beheira	792,242	636,825	·022077	415,234	·028920	Low	458,950
Daqahliya	912,428	780,480	·015742	586,033	·019285	Good	
Gharbiya	1,484,814	1,297,656	·013564	936,276	·021998	Low	1,060,210
Minufiya	971,016	864,206	·011721	646,013	·019588	Low	725,614
Qalubiya	434,575	371,602	·015777	271,391	·021171	Low	293,834
Sharqiya	886,346	748,972	·016983	464,655	·032338	Low	581,781
Beni-Suef	372,412	312,115	·017819	219,573	·023722	Low	239,472
Fayoum	441,583	371,006	·017567	228,709	·032776	Low	285,716
Giza	460,080	401,234	·013779	283,083	·023526	Low	326,774
Minya	663,144	550,971	·018703	314,818	·038017	Low	417,267
Asyut	907,435	782,720	·014894	562,137	·022313	Low	627,041
Girga	797,940	688,011	·014933	521,413	·018656	Good	
Qena*	685,653	626,869	·009003	386,249	·032810	Low	548,011
Aswan Mark.	75,532	67,440	·011396	13,962	·110703	Low	56,898
Edfu Mark.	101,694	86,218	·016445	57,444	·027440	Low	67,505
Esna Mark.	95,196	84,588	·011884	51,475	·033667	Low	70,851

*Corrected.

calculated, using the 1897 to 1907 rate. The new figures were then added as part of the new 1882 population.

In considering provinces for the above estimation, various factors were considered:

1. Small changes had been made in some provincial areas, especially in oases, etc. These were taken into account by using weight figures—those furnished by the *Statistical Yearbook* of 1909.[111] Kosseir was uniformly considered in Qena, Ramleh in Alexandria.

2. Changes in boundaries had occurred in Upper Egypt, land being lost to the Sudan. The Egyptian government's weighted statistics were again used and the markazes of Aswan and Edfu were taken separately, since considering the whole province of Aswan/Esna, from which the Sudanese subtractions had been taken, together would have given slanted figures.

3. The markaz of Esna, which was switched from Esna Province to Qena, was considered individually. Corresponding adjustments were made in Qena's total.[112]

4. Some areas which naturally experienced great growth were excluded from this consideration. Al-Arish, Suez, Port Said, and Ismailia all registered 'Low', but this resulted from natural, Suez Canal-inspired growth in the latter period. This omission, again, worked to insure that the estimate would not be over-large.

The difference between the new and old populations, added to the original 1882 total, gave a new population of 7,840,271.

The 1897 and 1907 census totals, while not perfect, were accurate enough so that no tampering would greatly improve them. The totals of both have been included here unchanged.[113]

TABLE 23

1897	9,734,405
1907	11,287,359

The purpose of this study has been to provide a starting-point for an accurate study of Egyptian population. The preceding analyses should serve that end. In conclusion, therefore, it is only necessary to mention a few major considerations:

First, in investigating the various sources on Egyptian population, European consular sources, hitherto acceptable, should be used with great care, since they are without exception incorrect.

Second, Mohammed Ali's 1846 census, previously ill-considered because it was at such variance with European statements, is the best population estimator for its time.

Finally, when considered through the viewpoint of population, the reign of Mohammed Ali and his family must be considered a distinct improvement on previous times. From 1800 to 1907 the population constantly rose, after falling for centuries. It rose in spite of plague epidemics, cholera, conscription, and corvée. More than anything else, this is a tribute to civil order. Improvements in health standards help explain an increased growth rate in later years, but it was civil order, from Mohammed Ali onward, long before modern medicine had any effect, that insured there always was a population increase. One can only conclude that, despite all the difficulties and errors in government, the rulers of nineteenth-century Egypt provided a climate amenable to population growth, something their predecessors notably failed to achieve.

APPENDIX

I. *Cairo*

Cairo, like almost all other capitals of the nineteenth century, grew faster than the country as a whole.[114] While no analysis of Cairo's population will be given here, an estimate, considering disease losses, is given below. It has not been greatly reworked and the population for 1882 is most probably low.[115]

The Population of Cairo 1800–1907

Year	Population	Disease	Disease Deaths	Rate/ Year
1800	210,960			·008050
1801	212,658			
1802	214,370			
1803	216,095			
1804	217,835			
1805	219,589			
1806	221,356			
1807	223,138			
1808	224,935			
1809	226,746			
1810	228,571			
1811	230,411			
1812	232,266			
1813	234,136			
1814	236,020			
1815	237,921			
1816	239,836			
1817	241,767			
1818	243,713			
1819	245,675			
1820	247,653			
1821	249,646			
1822	251,656			
1823	253,682			
1824	255,724			
1825	257,783			
1826	259,858			
1827	261,950			
1828	264,059			

The Population of Cairo 1800–1907 (cont.)

Year	Population	Disease	Disease Deaths	Rate/ Year
1829	266,184			
1830	268,327			
1831	261,487	Cholera	9,000	
1832	263,592			
1833	265,714			
1834	267,853			
1835	235,010	Plague	35,000	
1836	236,902			
1837	238,809			
1838	240,731			
1839	242,669			
1840	244,623			
1841	246,592			
1842	248,577			
1843	250,578			
1844	252,595			
1845	254,629			
1846	256,679			·011908
1847	259,735			
1848	262,828			
1849	265,958			
1850	267,160	Cholera	1,965	
1851	270,342			
1852	273,561			
1853	276,819			
1854	280,116			
1855	277,710	Cholera	5,741	
1856	281,018			
1857	284,364			
1858	287,750			
1859	291,177			
1860	294,645			
1861	298,153			
1862	301,704			
1863	305,297			
1864	308,933			
1865	306,508	Cholera	6,104	
1866	310,158			
1867	313,851			
1868	317,589			
1869	321,371			
1870	325,198			
1871	329,071			
1872	332,989			
1873	336,955			
1874	340,967			
1875	345,028			
1876	349,137			
1877	353,294			
1878	357,502			
1879	361,759			
1880	366,067			

The Population of Cairo 1800–1907 (cont.)

Year	Population	Disease	Disease Deaths	Rate/ Year
1881	370,426			
1882	374,838			·028988
1883	382,704	Cholera	3,000	
1884	393,798			
1885	405,213			
1886	416,960			
1887	429,047			
1888	441,485			
1889	454,283			
1890	467,452			
1891	481,003			
1892	494,946			
1893	509,294			
1894	524,058			
1895	539,250			
1896	554,002	Cholera	880	
1897	570,062			·017851
1898	580,238			
1899	590,596			
1900	601,138			
1901	611,869			
1902	620,992	Cholera	1,800	
1903	632,077			
1904	643,360			
1905	654,845			
1906	666,535			
1907	678,433			

II. *Modern Population*

This study attempts to demonstrate that some population estimates are faulty, some good, by comparing the estimates statistically with accepted data. Because of this, it is necessary to give some consideration to modern population rates.

The main factor used in examining population figures is 'rate'. This is the percentage gain or loss in population in a given year. Russell, in *Late Ancient and Medieval Population*, has demonstrated that the natural rate of increase (i.e. without migration) can never be more than 6·2 per cent.[116] Since, however, this figure assumes that in one year no-one will die and everyone who can will have children, it is never even closely reached. With medicine allowing developing countries tremendously high birth and low death rates, the modern area of greatest increase, Latin America, has not even reached 30 per thousand.

Population Rates 1965–70 (/1000/year)

Area	Birth Rate	Death Rate	Natural Increase
Africa	46	20	25
Asia	38	15	23
L. America	39	10	29
U.A.R.	44·1	16·5	27·6

Source: *United Nations Demographic Yearbook*, 1970.

For Egypt, a high rate of increase is a very modern phenomenon. Before World War II Egypt was still registering relatively low growth:

Egypt—Rates of Natural Increase[117] (*/1000/year*)

Year	Birth Rate	Death Rate	Natural Increase
1922	43·2	25·2	18·0
1927	44·6	25·2	18·8
1932	41·1	27·6	14·5
1937	43·4	27·1	16·3

Source: *United Nations Demographic Yearbook, 1948.*

In fact, not until the end of the Second World War did the rate of increase significantly rise:

Year	Birth Rate	Death Rate	Natural Increase[118]
1948	42·7	20·4	22·3
1949	41·8	20·6	21·2
1950	44·4	19·1	25·3
1951	44·8	19·3	25·5

Source: *Annuaire Stat. de L'Egypte, 1953.*

The rate of natural increase between 1966 and 1970 had risen to 27·6, one of the highest in the world, but this is a purely modern phenomenon. In the period studied in this work, 18 per thousand per year is the highest to be expected.

These figures must be kept in mind for comparisons. Birth rates may not have changed drastically from the nineteenth century, but death rates have. With the differences between the health standards of the two, the nineteenth-century rate of increase must necessarily have been lower than the modern figure. Any population estimate that demands a growth rate of perhaps 20 per thousand for the nineteenth century cannot be correct. Yet estimates that demand rates well above this have repeatedly been made. Comparisons to the above make it possible to judge their accuracy.

III. *The Population of Egypt 1800–1907*

Year	Population	Year	Population
1800	3,853,633	1845	4,447,145
1801	3,879,020	1846	4,476,439
1802	3,904,574	1847	4,553,180
1803	3,930,297	1848	4,631,237
1804	3,956,189	1849	4,710,632
1805	3,982,252	1850	4,752,088
1806	4,008,487	1851	4,833,555
1807	4,034,894	1852	4,916,418
1808	4,061,475	1853	5,000,702
1809	4,088,232	1854	5,086,413
1810	4,115,165	1855	5,057,610
1811	4,142,275	1856	5,144,314
1812	4,169,564	1857	5,232,505
1813	4,197,032	1858	5,322,208
1814	4,224,682	1859	5,413,448
1815	4,252,513	1860	5,506,253
1816	4,280,528	1861	5,600,649
1817	4,308,728	1862	5,696,663
1818	4,337,113	1863	5,794,323
1819	4,365,685	1864	5,893,657
1820	4,394,446	1865	5,872,651
1821	4,423,396	1866	5,973,328
1822	4,452,537	1867	6,075,731
1823	4,481,869	1868	6,179,889
1824	4,511,395	1869	6,285,833
1825	4,541,116	1870	6,393,594
1826	4,57,1032	1871	6,503,201
1827	4,601,145	1872	6,614,688
1828	4,631,457	1873	6,728,086
1829	4,661,969	1874	6,843,428
1830	4,692,681	1875	6,960,748
1831	4,543,596	1876	7,080,079
1832	4,573,528	1877	7,201,455
1833	4,603,658	1878	7,324,912
1834	4,633,987	1879	7,450,486
1835	4,164,515	1880	7,578,213
1836	4,191,950	1881	7,708,129
1837	4,219,566	1882	7,840,271
1838	4,247,364	1883	7,900,483
1839	4,275,345	1884	8,020,119
1840	4,303,510	1885	8,141,566
1841	4,331,861	1886	8,264,853
1842	4,360,399	1887	8,390,006
1843	4,389,125	1888	8,517,055
1844	4,418,040	1889	8,646,027

The Population of Egypt 1800–1907 (continued)

Year	Population	Year	Population
1890	8,776,952	1899	10,033,504
1891	8,909,860	1900	10,186,482
1892	9,044,781	1901	10,341,793
1893	9,181,745	1902	10,464,882
1894	9,320,782	1903	10,624,438
1895	9,461,925	1904	10,786,426
1896	9,589,206	1905	10,950,884
1897	9,734,405	1906	11,117,850
1898	9,882,823	1907	11,287,359

NOTES

1. Method: Unless otherwise stated, all rates and populations were computed by the author. Scarcity of data dictated the use of simple techniques and forced the assumption of constant rates of increase between any two census years (i.e. 1800, 1846, 1882, 1897, 1907). Consistent with the paper's assumptions, subtractions for population loss due to disease were taken as part of a general equation which insured a constant rate after subtractions. This was achieved through the use of a computerised iterative process which assured a rate which was precise to ·0000001.

The assumption that yearly inter-censal rates were alike is obviously a 'working hypothesis'. For example, the rate of growth at the beginning and end of Mohammed Ali's reign was surely not the same as during the middle period. Yet, without considerably more demographic information, such an assumption of constant rate is necessary.

2. See Craig, J. I., 'The Census of Egypt', *L'Egypte Contemporaine* (hereafter *EC*), VIII (1917); Azmi, H., 'The Growth of Population in Egypt', *EC*, XXVIII (1937); Darwish, M. M., 'Analysis of Some Estimates of the Population of Egypt before the XIXth Century', *EC*, XX (1929).

3. Craig, p. 212; Azmi, p. 268; Jomard, M., 'Memoire sur la population comparee de l'Egypte', *Description de L' Egypte* (hereafter *Descr.*), vol. IX, pp. 168–180.

Jomard quotes some incredible statistics, including an estimate of 40 million for only the Delta, which he agrees is ridiculous. He himself (*Descr.*, IX, p. 162) feels the ancient population to have been between 5½ and 6 million.

4. Volney, M. C-F., *Voyage en Syrie et en Egypte pendant les Anneés 1783, 1784, 1785.* Tome Premier, Paris, 1789.

5. 13,500 metres by the compass, adjusted to 24,000 on account of the winding of the walls.

6. Jomard, *Descr.*, IX, p. 122.

7. *Ibid.*, p. 123.

8. *Ibid.*, pp. 122 f.

9. *French Necrological Tables* (867 days)

3,897 men
5,261 women
11,827 infants
———
20,985 total

D'après un renseignement anterieur à l'expédition française, il mourait au Kaire environ 25 personnes par jour: 4 hommes, 6 femmes, 15 enfans, ce qui fait, pour toute l'année, 9125 . . . (*Descr.*, IX, p. 125).

10. Jomard, *Descr.*, IX, p. 127.

11. Jomard, 'Description de la ville et de la citadelle du Kaire', *Descr.*, XVIII, pt. 2, p. 367.

12. Volney, p. 215.

13. See note 9.

14. See the criticims of Jomard in Darwish.

15. Russell, J. C., *Late Ancient and Medieval Population*, Transactions of the American Philosophical Society, New Series, vol. 48, pt. 3, Philadelphia, 1958, pp. 45–59.

16. Barkan, Ö. L., 'Essai sur les données statistiques des registres de rencensement dans l'Empire Ottoman aux XVe et XVIe siecle', *JESHO*, Aug.–Oct., 1957–58, pp. 9–36.

17. Volney, p. 215.

18. Rabino, J., 'Some Statistics of Egypt', *Journal of the Royal Statistical Society*, Sept. 1884, p. 417. Four were counted for each village house, eight for houses in the cities.

19. Jomard, *Descr.*, IX, pp. 114, 115, and 122.

20. Chabrol, 'Essai sur les moeurs des habitans modernes de l'Egypte', *Descr.*, XVIII, pt. 1, p. 8. Chabrol arrives at population figures which are somewhat different from those of Jomard. They are, however, very close and it was felt better to analyse Jomard's figures, since Chabrol gives almost no justification for his opinions.

21. The 1882 figure given here is the official one, taken from the 1882 census. As will be seen later, it is in need of correction.

When statistics, especially those found in tables, are not identified as to source, it can be assumed that they are drawn from the Egyptian censuses.

22. These growth rates are drawn without consideration of loss from demographically significant disease. That is, operations such as those used to arrive at the final tables have not been performed (see note 1), though the figures are accurate enough for the purpose here.

23. *Percentage of National Population*

Vienna	*Berlin*
2% in 1830	1% in 1819
3% in 1890	3% in 1890
Paris	*Athens*
2% in 1801	3% in 1852
7% in 1896	5% in 1889

Source: Weber, Adna F., *The Growth of Cities in the Nineteenth Century*, Ithaca, N.Y. Cornell University Press, 1963 (originally published in 1899).

24. With the revised figure for Cairo, the percentage is 8·5 per cent.

25. The figure here is, again, the official one. This may account for 1882 being out of the normal progression.

26. Data are not sufficient to compare food consumption, cultivated land, or like bases of population estimation for this period. Only tax records, if one could make more sense out of them than could Jomard, and possibly more complete records from the French expedition on village size, etc., could help.

While some 1800 land estimates do exist, it was not possible to make use of them, since there was no way to check their accuracy. Jacotin's estimate in the *Description de l'Egypte* ('Superficie-totaux—5,542,250 feddan') was, for example, less than the area of *cultivated* land in 1930, even though Jacotin supposedly included ruins, villages, the Nile, desert, etc., in his estimate. Number of inhabitants to various areas is, in any case, almost impossible to ascertain. Jomard's attempt led him to his erroneous conclusions. (1930 data: Platt, Raye R. and Hefny, Mohammed Baly, *Egypt, a Compendium*, American Geographical Society, N.Y., 1958. See also: Girard, M. P. S., 'Memoire sur l'industrie et le commerce de l'Egypte', *Descr.*, XVII.)

27. Besides the sources listed below, see Hirst, L. Fabian, *The Conquest of Plague*, Cambridge, 1905, and Pollitzer, R. and Meyer, Karl F., 'The Ecology of Plague', in May, Jacques M. (ed.), *Studies in Disease Ecology*, M.D. Publications, N.Y., 1965.

28. 'Most students of the history of population seem to agree that a significant reduction in mortality was the primary cause of the demographic upswing; and, though the statistical evidence is inconclusive, we see no evidence why this proposition should be challenged. Indeed, it can be shown that when mortality was high a decline in the death rate is inherently a more powerful causative factor of population growth than a rise in the birth rate.

'We should argue, however, that it was the peaks rather than the plateau of mortality that were lowered. In other words, it was not so much a reduction in mortality in "normal" years that produced the secular downward trend of the death rate, but an unmistakeable abatement of the "great crises". The disappearance of plague, above all, but also a very sensible mitigation of subsistence crises seem to have been chiefly responsible for the increase in life expectancy.'

(Helleiner, K. F., 'The Vital Revolution Reconsidered', in Glass and Eversley (eds.), *Population in History*, Chicago, Aldine Publishing Company, 1965.)

29. See sections *1800–1846* and *1846–1882*.

30. Ackerknecht, Erwin, K., *History and Geography of the Most Important Diseases*, N.Y., Hafner Publishing Co., 1965, p. 23.

31. *Ibid.*, p. 25.

32. Schnepp, B., 'Considerations sur le mouvement de la population en Egypte', L'Institut Egyptien, *Mémoires*, I, Cairo, 1862, pp. 531 f.

33. See Sandwith, *The Medical Diseases of Egypt*, London, 1905.

34. W. I. Simpson, M.D., quoted in Shakespeare, E.O., *Report on Cholera in Europe and India*, The Miscellaneous Documents of the Senate of the United States, 1886–7, vol. 5, p. 28.

35. Which, in turn, draws on various sources for the disease. These will be identified as they are used.

36. Cholera in 1848 was not of enough demographic significance to be considered here.

37. Hirsch, *Handbook of Geographical and Historical Pathology*, vol. 1 ('Acute Infectious Diseases'), p. 398.

38. Barker, August 18 and 23 and September 2; Barker to Gordon, 29 September, 1831 (F.O), 78/202 quoted in Dodwell, H., *The Maker of Modern Egypt*, Cambridge, 1931, pp. 233 f.

39. Cairo in 1831—261,487, after subtraction for plague deaths. See *Cairo* section.

40. Bascome, E., *A History of Epidemic Pestilence*, London, 1851, p. 159.

41. Information on cholera in France is contained in Chevalier, L., *La Choléra*, La Roche, Impr. Centrale de L'Ouest, 1958.

42. Pollitzer, R., *Cholera*, Geneva, World Health Organisation, 1959, p. 25.

43. Schnepp, p. 539.

44. In L'Institut Egyptien *Mémoires*, I, Cairo, 1862, p. 606.

45. Pollitzer, *Cholera*, p. 96.

46. MacNamara, N. C., *Asiatic Cholera*, London, 1892, p. 21; see also Hirsch, p. 413.

47. Rabino, p. 419.

48. *Ibid.*, p. 420.

49. Shakespeare, pp. 21 f.

50. Rabino, p. 420.

51. Changes in trade caused Damietta to stagnate in the latter half of the nineteenth century, its population relatively stable. The city's death rate demonstrates this, normally registering around 1,100 deaths a year between 1860 and 1882. (Shakespeare, pp. 24 and 25.)

52. The believable data, that from the 1947 epidemic, show that cholera tended to hit hardest in the Delta, where population was packed closely together and, more important, where water sources were easily contaminated and usually shared by many. (May, Jacques M., *The Ecology of Human Disease*, N.Y., M.D. Publications, 1958; Shakespeare, p. 24.)

53. Simmons, James, *Global Epidemiology*, Philadelphia, J.B. Lippincott Co., 1951, p. 15.

54. Swaroop, S., 'World Distribution of Cholera Endemicity', *Epidemiological and Vital Statistics Report*, V, no. 11, pp. 569–616.
55. MacNamara, p. 28.
56. Shakespeare, p. 42; Rabino, p. 420.
57. Swaroop, pp. 570 f.
58. Figures drawn from Pollitzer and Swaroop and cross-checked.
59. Volney, p. 175.
60. Campbell, 18 May, 1835, in F.O. 78/260, 25 June, 1835, in F.O. 78/257, 30 June, 1835, in F.O. 142/7 (in Cattaui, R., *Le Regne de Mohamed Aly d'apres les Archives Russes en Egypte*, Tome II, pt. 1, 350), mentioned in Rivlin, Helen, *The Agricultural Policy of Mohammad Ali in Egypt*, Cambridge, Harvard University Press, 1961; Dodwell, p. 235.
61. *Ibid.*
62. Pollitzer, R., *Plague*, W.H.O., Geneva, 1954, p. 33.
63. See Russell.
64. Pollitzer, *Plague*, pp. 31 and 32.
65. Medem to Nesselrode, A. R. Carton 1838, no. 24, in Cattaui, p. 254.
66. Campbell, 18 June, 1835, in F.O. 78/257.
67. Clot Bey, A. B., *De La Peste Observée en Egypte*, Paris, 1840, p. 63.
68. Rabino, p. 419. Estimates covered such a wide range that it is not useful to mention more of them here. See Sandwith, pp. 159 f for examples.
69. Clot Bey, A. B., *Memoires de A. B. Clot Bey*, Cairo, Impr. de L'Institut d'Archeologie Orientale, 1949, p. 312.
70. See below, sections *1800–46* and *1846–82*.
71. Information drawn from Pollitzer, *Plague*, May, *Studies in Disease Ecology* (the Meyer article especially).
72. Pollitzer, *Plague*, p. 32.
73. Wakil, quoted in Pollitzer, *Plague*, p. 513. Wakil's complete treatment in Wakil, Abd a- Wahid, al-, *The Third Pandemic of Plague in Egypt*..., Cairo, Egyptian University, 1932.
74. Rattus Rattus and Xenospilla Cheopis, respectively.
75. Wakil, in Pollitzer, *Plague*, pp. 33 and 34.
76. Rabino, p. 419.
77.

130,302	infantry and cavalry
41,471	irregulars
31,804	in the two fleets
4,076	at the Alexandria Arsenal
207,653	total

Source: Cochelet to Thiers, 12 April, 1840, Correspondance Politique, Egypte, X, fos. 30–6, in Driault, E. (ed.), *L'Egypte et L'Europe, La Crise de 1839–1841*, vol. II, pp. 241–249.

With the enforced peace and troop reduction that ended Mohammed Ali's wars, the regular army dropped to 54,700 and the irregulars went back to agriculture. (Rohan-Chabot to Guizot, 16 August, 1841, Correspondance Politique, Egypte, IV, fos. 166–70, in Driault, vol. V, p. 230.)

78. See Rivlin, pp. 274 f. for Mohammed Ali's oft-quoted letters and statements on conscription policies.
79. The author is aware that Egyptian army camps sometimes contained wives (witness the need for civilian transport during the Syrian evacuation.) There were never enough, however, to affect the above statements.
80. Clot, *Memoires*, p. 312.

81. *Ibid.*, pp. 311 and 312.

82. The question of irrigation and agricultural improvement is too complex and the sources too divided to be discussed here. It seems that some population growth could have come as a result of better agricultural conditions, conditions of gradual improvement already reflected in this paper's computed statistics. However, problems such as computing the number of cultivated feddan or, indeed, stating exactly what a 'feddan' is at any given time, are beyond the scope of this study. For some of the differing views on matters agricultural see: Issawi, Charles, 'The Economic Development of Egypt, 1888– 1960', in *The Economic History of the Middle East*, University of Chicago Press, 1966; also Rivlin. For an investigation of the difficulties in land and cadastral investigations, see Lyons, Capt. H. G., *The Cadastral Survey of Egypt*, Cairo, Egyptian Ministry of Finance, 1908, pp. 9–40.

83. Dodwell, p. 228.

84. Mohammed Ali had taken another enumeration in 1821, but it was solely for tax purposes, a fact which guaranteed great inaccuracy.

85. For example, after quoting a long list of European consuls' figures, Issawi states that Mohammed Ali's 1846 figure is 'not very reliable' (p. 362) and he settles on an 1835 figure of 3–3·5 million (p. 373), far too low.

86. Rivlin, p. 280.

87. Supposedly taken from 'official' figures by one of Barnett's employees.

88. Rivlin, pp. 278 and 279. See also the estimates in MacGregor, John, *Commercial Tariffs and Regulations of the Several States of Europe and America*, part X ('Africa States'), London, 1843; and Waghorn, Thomas, *Egypt as It Is in 1838*, London, 1838.

89. There is perhaps a semantic difficulty here. It is difficult to see how anyone could believe this to be true.

90. The population for 1882 has been corrected, see below.

91. See section on *Modern Population*, below.

92. A two-to-one rate is a phenomenon of post-World War II Egypt.

93. For further comparisons see the section *Modern Population*, below.

94. The rate used between 1800 and 1846 has been computed as if it were the same for all these years. In reality, some change probably occurred as the economic and social conditions changed with the end of both the wars and the plague. Since these were close to the 1846 census point and thus difficult to compute, no alteration was attempted.

95. Boinet Bey, A., 'L'Accroissement de la Population en Egypte,' Institut Egyptien *Mémoires*, 2nd Series, no. 7, 1887.

96. Boinet accepts the figures without real question, satisfied that the low birth and death rates cancel each other out.

97. Schnepp, pp. 539 and 540.

98. Compare to the rate of growth and the 1859 and 1860 figures in the population table at the front of the section.

99. This holds true well through 1882.

100. In Amici', F., *Essai de Statistique Generale de L'Egypte*, *Années 1873*, *1874*, *1875*, *1876*, *1877*, Cairo, 1879.

101. Amici, p. 6.

102. If the 1882 population were uncorrected, this figure would still be wrong by almost a million.

103. Once again, extensive work in the area of agricultural lands, while beyond the scope of this work, would be valuable. In addition to the material mentioned in note 82, see Owen, E. R. J., 'Cotton Production and the Development of the Cotton Economy in 19th Century Egypt', in Issawi, *The Economic History of the Middle East*.

104. The 1882 estimation of De Regny ('Statistique d' Egypte') and Rossi Bey's 1875 figure are even less reliable than the 1882 census and so are not considered here. Their figures:

1872	5,203,405
1875	5,251,757

(See Rabino, pp. 418 and 419.)

105. Since some areas (e.g. Siwa Oasis) were not in the original report, slightly

different figures for this census will sometimes appear. The ones quoted here are the highest available.

106. See the section *Modern Population* below.

107. See the section *Modern Population* below.

108. The unrest of the period was obviously to have an unhappy effect on census-taking. The wartime 1917 census had similar problems and it too, arrived at somewhat faulty statistics. For this reason no comparisons have been drawn with its data.

109. The date of the census was 3 May, 1882.

110. See the previous section for Boinet's estimates.

111. 'The difference . . . is due to adjustments made by the Census Department on account of the change in the Sudan frontier since 1897 and the inclusion, in 1907, of the oasis of Siwa, omitted in the 1897 total. The adjustments were necessary in order to enable a comparison to be made between the figures of the two censuses.' (*1909 Statistical Yearbook of Egypt*, p. 22.)

112. The totals given for Qena in the table are not always exact, since they include the Esna Markza.

113. In computing national rates, the area of Egypt has been considered as constant. Some small error must be expected because of this.

114. See Clerget, Marcel, *Le Caire*, Tome 1, Cairo, 1934.

115. See Cairo's adjusted population for 1882 in the table of provinces in 1882, below.

116. Russell calculates that approximately one-third of women in a given population are of marriageable age and that 10% of all marriages are sterile. He quotes studies which show a woman can (statistically) have one child every 29 months, if no restraints exist. That is, there is a 41% chance of a woman being able to bear a child in any one year. Taking the one-third who are married, dividing out the men, he arrives at a 16·7% rate of child-bearing women. 41% of these can have a child in a year, or 6·9%, considering the 10% sterility rate, 6·2%.

117. The years were picked at five-year intervals from 1922 to avoid the effects of World Wars I and II.

118. It should be kept in mind that these are rates of natural increase and not absolute increase as used in the bulk of this paper. For absolute rate, migration will occasionally cause some small lowering of the natural rate.

Unless otherwise indicated, all census data come from official Egyptian Government reports on the topic. It was not considered necessary to list these sources.

The Egyptian Revolution of 1919: New Directions in The Egyptian Economy

Robert L. Tignor

As most political histories of Egypt indicate, the revolution of 1919 constituted an important turning point, if not a watershed, in Egyptian political development. The urban violence, rural discontent, and campaigns of assassination stymied British efforts to make Egypt into a full-fledged and indeed central Middle Eastern colonial state whence Britain would exercise political suzerainty and moral suasion over other Middle Eastern and Islamic states. Instead, in the treaty and constitutional formulations of the early 1920s, British imperialists were forced to settle for a much lesser degree of political control over the Egyptian polity—a control which guaranteed Britain dominance over certain key areas of Egypt's internal and external relations but which allowed Egypt some autonomy. The 1919 revolution also marked a peak period in the growth of Egyptian nationalism and saw the emergence of Egypt's most important political party. The Wafd was to remain at the centre of political life until the military *coup d'état* of 1952.

Less well appreciated were the new economic organisations and ideas accompanying and indeed growing out of the revolution of 1919. In 1920, landed magnates did what some Egyptians had been anticipating for four decades. They created a national bank—Bank Miṣr—the goal of which was to enable Egyptians to have more influence in their own economy and to diversify economic activities. The Bank sought to attract capital which would have lain idle or would have gone into banks run by foreigners. It hoped to use this capital to create new industries. Largely pioneered by a newly confident and resurgent foreign community residing in Egypt, an Egyptian Federation of Industries was established as a pressure group working to promote economic, social, and political conditions conducive to Egyptian industrial development. In the cotton crisis of 1921–22, Egyptian landed magnates established another important pressure organ, the Egyptian General Agricultural Sydicate, the purpose of which was to wrest from foreign merchants some measure of control over the financing and marketing of Egypt's most important export crop, cotton. Although these new institutions were just coming into existence during the conflict-torn years of the Egyptian revolution, and did not become powerful until the 1930s, they eventually constituted three of the most influential organs in pre-Nasser Egypt. Their founding reveals a great deal about an emerging Egyptian middle class, its economic attitudes and goals, and its relationship with Egypt's traditional source of wealth, the land. A study of the new economic philosophies and organisations crystallised during the political turmoil of 1919 to 1922 tells us much about the content and social structure of the revolution, and delineates new directions which were to propel the Egyptian political economy in the next three and a half decades.

Just as the political revolution of 1919 must be viewed against the backdrop of the First World War, so the accompanying economic changes reflected wartime economic developments. The war exposed major weaknesses in Egypt's pre-war economy. It demonstrated the vulnerability of an economy which depended so fundamentally upon the export of a single crop—cotton—and on substantial European financing for the marketing of this product. There were two peak moments of tension and discontent during the war: the first at the onset of the war in 1914–15 and the second during the last year. When the war broke out, in August 1914, the Egyptian government found itself faced with an immediate economic crisis. Nearly a quarter of Egypt's cotton exports had gone to countries which were now enemies of Great Britain or would be in a position to supply Britain's enemies.[1] Since the British prohibited cotton exports to these countries, the demand for Egyptian cotton declined abruptly. The price paid in the markets also fell. Moreover, the British found themselves unable to provide Egypt with gold, which was used to purchase the crop in the countryside. British officials in Egypt drew a picture of landholders seething with discontent, unable to find merchants willing to pay reasonable prices and yet still facing their regular tax payments.[2] Although the British closed the Alexandria bourse and declared a moratorium on debt payments, these measures were only palliatives. Finally, the government in London agreed to more radical measures, largely because they feared Egyptian rebellion. The British Treasury undertook to guarantee a loan of £E5,000,000, to be used to purchase cotton from smallholders and to enable Egyptian banks to make advances to large landholders.[3]

The value of the cotton crop exported declined from £E34,000,000 in 1913–14 to £E20,000,000 in 1914–15, prompting bitter complaints from Egyptian landlords against British policies.[4] Yūsuf Naḥās, who was to be the moving force in the Egyptian General Agricultural Syndicate after World War I, was one of the most outspoken critics. In an open letter to the British Financial Adviser, Edward Cecil, he accused the British of safeguarding their own financial interests and securing the financial stability of the Egyptian government at the expense of Egyptian cultivators. He felt that the British, instead of underwriting loans to banks and purchasing small amounts of cotton from the small landowners, should have guaranteed a minimum price for all cultivators. Expounding a criticism which was to recur frequently, he argued that, by providing the banks with funds, the state only strengthened the hands of the mercantile element to the detriment of farmers.[5]

Although this cotton crisis disillusioned many cultivators about the government, even greater antagonisms were generated in the last years of the war. Cotton prices had declined in 1914–15, but, with some reduction in the area cultivated, they quickly recovered and rose to record highs. The 1916–17 harvest sold for £E42,500,000 or £E22,000,000 more than the previous year.[6] Yet, in 1917–18, the British advisers in Egypt found themselves faced again with a need to regulate cotton marketing. Transport problems caused cotton to accumulate in the interior of the country, and reduced prices.[7] The British were also concerned about cotton supplies reaching enemy countries and, accordingly, the British Treasury agreed to purchase the entire cotton crop in 1918. A Cotton Control Commission was set up, largely dominated by British officials, with Ronald Lindsay as President and M. Hornsby as Vice-President. The Commission agreed to purchase the crop at a fixed price, which was held to be a fair one on the grounds that it was above the pre-World War I prices and assured cultivators a reasonable profit.[8]

These arrangements, like those at the outset of the war, created a storm of protests. Egyptian farmers felt that the prices had been fixed at artificially low levels and that, in estimating a farmer's costs, the state had not taken into account the enormous inflation in 1918. Yūsuf Naḥās published an article in *al-Muqaṭṭam* on 26 October, 1918, charging that prices had been established before substantial increases in wages, transport costs and other expenses had occurred.[9] The Egyptian Chamber of Commerce in Cairo filed a formal complaint with the President of the Egyptian Council of Ministers, claiming that the costs of production had gone up some two or three times and that the government's prices were too low.[10]

Although the government's economic policies left a legacy of bitterness and suspicion which economic nationalists exploited after the war, in fact the economic changes fostered by the war had a variable impact on different segments of Egyptian society. In their propaganda, the British emphasised the financial gains achieved during the war. Arguing that British troops had protected Egypt from military hardships, British apologists claimed that Egypt emerged from the war a much more prosperous country than it had entered the war. They had much evidence in their favour. In a memorandum by L. G. Roussin on 27 August, 1917, for example, the British Financial Adviser estimated that in the first year of the war the value of Egyptian exports had declined significantly, but that these financial losses were compensated by the expenditures of British troops garrisoned in Egypt. By the third year of the world conflict, rising cotton prices and vastly increased British military expenditures in the country caused the favourable financial balance in trade to total £E35,000,000.[11] The wealth of large landed magnates was clearly on the rise, as an article by a European economist, S. Avigdor, demonstrated. Using reports by Egypt's leading banks, Avigdor showed that the customary arrears on loans owed to the Agricultural Bank of Egypt, which were £E1,394,546 in the first year of the war, had been reduced to £E151,326 in 1918–19 and to £E83,724 in the next year. In addition, the landed debt of Egyptians had been reduced an extraordinary £E12,000,000 from £E40,328,914 to £E27,964,196, while private deposits in banks increased from £E6,498,828 to £E35,479,673.[12] This was dramatic evidence that substantially increased wealth was circulating in the Egyptian economy and that Egypt was dealing successfully with one of its traditionally intractable economic problems—landed indebtedness.

But, of course, much of this wealth was superficial and had been generated by the rapid inflation of the latter war years. In inflationary circumstances, the large landholders were favoured since their debts became less burdensome. Additionally, since they tended to be the major exporters of cotton, which was enjoying high prices, they realised the gains from this crop. Much less fortunate were the urban and agricultural proletariat and small landowners, who felt the pressure of rising prices and did not enjoy the compensation of large profits from cotton exports. This lower segment of Egyptian society suffered a number of economic hardships which were as influential in producing the urban and rural discontent of 1919 as some of the better known political causes of the revolt, such as surging nationalist sentiments and hostility against *mudirs* and British officials for carrier corps recruitment.

The most serious economic problem Egypt faced in the latter war years was rampaging inflation. This inflation was related to many governmental economic policies, for the state had increased the amount of currency in circulation at a time when, because of reductions in imports, the quantity of goods available for purchase was severely limited. Prices for all commodities were on the ascent, causing the state to set up a Supply Control Board in March, 1918, with the duty of fixing maximum prices on cereals, meats, and other necessary items and seeing that the cities and the British troops were properly supplied.[13] The Supply Control Board was as unsuccessful as its predecessors in coping with rising prices. Merchants and cultivators held back produce which they felt to be priced too low, thus forcing the state to set higher price ceilings. Lacking an efficient administrative organisation, the Board was unable to enforce its rulings, and goods were sold in market places at prices well above those fixed by the state. The result was that the poorer classes, especially those in the cities, were unable to afford many necessities and were forced to go without.

Spiralling inflation, however, afforded golden opportunities for powerful business firms controlling the manufacture and distribution of necessities to reap unanticipated profits. The huge gains of these companies, coming, as they did, at the expense of the rank and file of the population, caused Egyptian nationalist critics to scrutinise and attack the behaviour of these firms, all of which were dominated by foreign capital and foreign administrators. The Egyptian press shaped Egyptian thinking about the exploitative nature of foreign business companies in Egypt and the need for governmental regulation. Egyptians began to call for the creation of Egyptian-financed and -run firms which would have a more sympathetic attitude toward the plight of the people. Two firms aroused the most intense criticism and are deserving of attention: the Salt and Soda Company, and the Egyptian Sugar Company.

Both of these companies were run and financed by European capital. Both were industrial firms with a monopoly over the supply and manufacturing of essential products. Although they had struggled to realise profits before the war, they prospered when the war cut off competitive imports from the Egyptian market. The Egyptian Salt and Soda Company was the object of bitter attacks from the Egyptian Chamber of Commerce in Cairo and from an Egyptian-based but European-dominated newspaper, *Bulletin Commercial.* The Egyptian Chamber of Commerce in Cairo was composed of a small group of Egyptians interested in commercial and industrial matters. From its inception, it issued a journal. Although the articles written in the Chamber of Commerce's journal attacking the Salt and Soda Company and the Sugar Company were unsigned, their careful critique of the companies' balance sheets, their attack on the exploitative nature of foreign capital in Egypt, and their implied call for the emergence of Egyptian firms, bear the imprint of the ideas of Ṭal'at Ḥarb, who a few years later was to realise the changes espoused in these articles through the creation of Bank Miṣr. The Salt and Soda Company had a monopoly over the extraction and sale of soda which in the last year of the war was selling at £E60 per ton, compared with £E9 to £E12 before the war. While admitting that the costs of production had risen, the critics argued that they had not risen so steeply as to justify the company's price. The author of the articles in the journal of the Chamber of Commerce claimed that the company had ceased to manufacture oil since it could make profits of 700 per cent from soda. Dividends were said to be five times what they had been before the war.[14] The *Bulletin Commercial* accused the company of operating 'without any other motive than to enrich itself to the detriment of the population'.[15] Since soda was used in the manufacture of soap, the two attacking journals pointed out that the company's drive for high profits was affecting the hygienic standards of the masses. Indeed, the anonymous author of the articles in the journal of the Egyptian Chamber of Commerce wrote that the municipality of Alexandria had established a hygienic campaign for the population and had organised a number of public baths. This effort had been defeated as a result of the high price of soap.

Even harsher criticisms were launched at the Egyptian Sugar Company. Again, the Egyptian Chamber of Commerce led the campaign, and the unsigned articles bear the mark of Ṭal'at Ḥarb. The cultivation, refining, and distribution of sugar had long antecedents in nineteenth-century Egypt. A number of processing factories had been created under Ismāil; just before the turn of the twentieth century these diverse activities were brought under the control of a single firm, the Egyptian Sugar Company. Although in theory not a monopoly, this company was, in practice, the only technologically modern industry in Egypt, hence its only internal competition came from local artisans. None the less, before World War I it had to face external competition, since Egypt imported refined sugar, and before the war it struggled to remain in existence. The war, with its attendant restriction on sugar imports, proved a great boon.[16] But the company's profits, coupled with rising sugar prices, aroused complaints. There were many criticisms of sugar shortages, and charges that sugar was sold above the official price. The distribution system of the company was attacked. It was argued that only a small number of merchants possessed the right to sell sugar, and that these individuals were interested in making speculative profits rather than ensuring the wide circulation of this vital product.[17] A close critique of the company's balance sheets appeared in the journal of the Egyptian Chamber of Commerce in Cairo. Citing figures from the company's annual reports, this article showed that, while the costs of production were steadily reduced, both the sales price and profits had risen dramatically. Besides paying handsome dividends, the Sugar Company was able to set aside large sums of money for amortisation projects.[18]

The Egyptian revolution of 1919 was rooted in deep and obvious political grievances. Educated Egyptians resented the creation of a British protectorate at the outbreak of the war and then the introduction of martial law. The masses suffered when peasant livestock and then peasants themselves were recruited to participate in the military campaigns in Palestine. The educated élite, alive to world events, was captivated by Woodrow Wilson's call for national self-determination, and wanted this principle applied to Egypt after the war.[19] But the economic impact of the war was equally important in firing revolutionary enthusiasms and arousing Egyptian concern about the country's economic well-being. The war revealed Egypt's dependence on overseas financial and commercial markets and prompted Egyptian nationalists to argue that complete independence (*al-istiqlāl al-tāmm*) needed to be buttressed by economic independence. Inflation produced massive discontent among the lower classes. At the same time, it reduced the weight of indebtedness on Egypt's landed class and, through the sharply rising cotton prices, it permitted wealth to accumulate in the hands of this group. A nascent bourgeoisie was about to emerge as a force in the Egyptian political economy. Prior to World War I, a number of large-scale or modern commercial and industrial ventures were in the hands of foreigners residing in Egypt. The economic consequences of the war strengthened this group, but it also enhanced the wealth of Egyptian landed magnates, some of whom began to diversify their economic interests from agriculture and land into commerce and industry. The new institutions and ideas which we shall be discussing marked the emergence of what can loosely be called an Egyptian bourgeoisie. These words must be used with caution. It can be argued that this group was neither very Egyptian nor very bourgeois. Many of the economic leaders of inter-war Egypt were foreigners resident in the country who often liked to call themselves Egyptians because of their long residence in the country and their dedication to it. But they also stressed their apartness from rank-and-file Egyptians, and they were sometimes viewed with distrust by pure Egyptians. Moreover, this bourgeois class, especially those who were unquestionably Egyptians, retained their large landed estates and blended their developing interest in industry and commerce with their fundamental and deep-seated attachment to the land.

Just as the war and the attendant British military and political programmes were seen as an affront to Egyptian national pride, so the war revealed in stark terms the foreign control of the Egyptian economy and the disabilities created by this dependence. Nationalist economic critiques were directed at the foreign firms in the Egyptian economy, which were shown to dominate nearly all of the export-import institutions in Egypt. To be sure, most of the land of Egypt was Egyptian-owned, although foreigners, especially foreign land companies, did possess substantial tracts. But much of this Egyptian-owned land was mortgaged to European-dominated land banks, the most powerful of which was the *Crédit Foncier Egyptien.* Indeed, all of the banks in Egypt were foreign-controlled. In 1898 a National Bank was established, but this organ was run by leaders of the British community in Egypt and even had a separate London executive committee. The other banks were either branches of major European firms or banks opened with their headquarters in Egypt but funded and administered from overseas. The main Egyptian export was cotton, and the preparation and movement of this crop from Egypt to Europe was controlled at all levels by foreign interests. Banks played a major role in purchasing the crop for overseas shipment. The ginning firms in Egypt and the export-import houses were also run by Europeans, while a select group of brokers and merchants, called the Alexandria General Produce Association, monopolised the grading and overseas sales of Egyptian exports. Although there had been remarkable growth in the number of joint stock companies operating in Egypt during the British occupation, nearly all of these firms were run by Europeans. In his close study of the Egyptian economy, A. E. Crouchley estimated that, of the slightly more than £E100,000,000 of paid-up capital in joint stock companies operating in Egypt in 1914, £E92,000,000 was controlled by foreign interests.[20] Thus, as Egyptian nationalist aspirations began to be expressed after World War I, it was inevitable that nationalists should call attention to the overweening economic power of the foreigners and should demand a more genuinely national economy.

Perhaps the clearest statement of Egypt's frightening dependence on European capitalism was drawn up by Yūsuf Naḥās, who wrote a note for the Wafd attacking Britain's wartime economic policies, and pointing out the folly of relying on the outside world for economic well-being. In this critique, he wrote that 'the war made clear . . . the great losses which occur in a country lacking those organisations which solve difficult problems created by unexpected events, like agricultural and co-operative unions, lending institutions, genuine national banks, and administrative organisations composed of specialists in economic, financial, and commercial matters'. He went on to add: 'The war also made clear the great deception which can be carried out against a country which is ruled on the basis of non-responsibility for affairs, whether these men be ministers or English advisers'.[21]

The war years had initiated a cascade of press and journal articles identifying the weaknesses in the obviously troubled Egyptian economy, and offering prescriptions. This tendency continued at an accelerated rate during the years of institutional formation after the war. Although many of these ideas were articulated in connection with the new organisations coming into being, and are best discussed in their appropriate institutional context, some warrant special treatment here. The starting point of much of the economic thought of these years was an attack on the prevailing colonial economy inherited from the days of Lord Cromer, the British Consul-General in Egypt from 1883 until 1907. In so far as the economy of this era had any coherent rationale, it was based on the idea that the world should be divided economically into regional specialisations, with each region producing those articles for which it had a natural advantage and exchanging them through a system of free trade. In this scheme of things, Egypt was depicted as a pre-eminently agricultural country, and its agricultural exports, most notably cotton, were supposed to enable it to purchase European-manufactured products and to enjoy the same prosperity as its European neighbours. When a group of British entrepreneurs residing in Egypt came forward with the idea of establishing a textile factory there, Cromer opposed their project. After the factory had been established, he placed an excise duty of 8 per cent on textiles and other manufactures, equivalent to the Egyptian customs duties, hence denying these industrialists any tariff protection, since Cromer felt that this protection would violate the principles of regional specialisation and spawn uneconomic activities.[22] The First World War, however, showed many concerned Egyptians the folly of this arrangement. It demonstrated that commercial intercourse was interrupted by acute political and military crises, and a dependent country was denied vital products. Moreover, as innumerable commentators noted, the British system of regional specialisation and free trade was exceedingly self-serving. European states were accorded the right to be the industrial centre, while the colonies and states in the rest of the world were the suppliers of raw materials.

In inter-war Egypt, the most powerful driving force calling for new economic arrangements was the resident foreign community. Cromer and other British officials delighted in talking about the cosmopolitan nature of Egyptian society. Straddling Asia, Europe, and Africa, Egypt was seen as a melting-pot of Levantines, Turks, and Europeans. Often, when resisting nationalist demands for increased autonomy, the British cited the cosmopolitan nature of Egypt. During and just after the war, British officials drew up constitutional proposals in which an upper house or Senate representing foreigners would have a veto over certain types of Egyptian legislation. No doubt foreigners exaggerated their own importance, but the foreign communities in 1919 were large and influential. According to the census of 1917, there were residing in Egypt 24,354 persons of British nationality, 21,270 of French nationality, 40,198 of Italian nationality, and 56,731 of Greek nationality. The Jewish community, which was to play such a large role in the inter-war Egyptian economy, totalled nearly 60,000.[23] Foreigners were not exclusively in commerce and industry, nor were they all wealthy. Large numbers of Greeks and Italians were artisans or members of the urban work-force. But there was a small segment of this community which had great power in commerce, access to European capital, and plans for diversifying the Egyptian economy.

The ideas of this community gained their most forceful articulation in three weekly economy journals: *Bulletin Commercial*, founded before World War I and later called *Economiste Egyptien; Revue d'Egypte Financière et Economique*, founded in 1927, and *L'Informateur*, opened in 1929. These three newspapers were run by Europeans resident in Egypt, and espoused the economic point of view of members of this community. These journals published the annual reports of the business firms operating in Egypt and wrote editorials, calling for a more balanced national economy, in which industry and commerce would play as prominent a role as agriculture. In contrast to the purely Egyptian bourgeois element, these newspapers were more favourably disposed toward an economy open to foreign capital and foreign technicians. The *Bulletin Commercial* wrote in 1919, at a time when nationalist agitation was at its peak, that 'modern Egypt has been created and prospered especially through the active and intelligent collaboration of the European element introduced into the country'.[24] This attitude toward the role of the foreign element in the Egyptian economy always troubled relations between the Egyptian middle class and the foreign bourgeoisie, and made their alliance a tenuous one. All three journals wanted to see the country freed 'from the slavery of the monoculture' and were keen advocates of a new tariff system behind which Egyptian industrialisation could take place.[25] Like many others concerned about Egypt's economic growth, they were apprehensive of Egypt's expanding population, and felt that only through agricultural diversification and, most important of all, a vast industrial expansion would Egypt be able to find gainful employment for these increased numbers. The journals called upon the Egyptian government to regulate Egyptian marketing arrangements, which were largely in the hands of a few wealthy European merchants, and thereby to ensure more decisive Egyptian control over the economy. In short, these papers championed the erection of a national economy which, while not independent of foreign capital and technical assistance, would produce whatever it could and would keep profits from agricultural, commercial, and industrial enterprises within the country.

Many purely Egyptian journals and thinkers echoed these themes. A favourite argument of the intensely nationalistic newspaper, *al-Akhbār*, was the need for Egypt to create the economic infrastructure for the political independence which it hoped that Zaghlūl and the Wafd would soon win.[26]

The most impressive of the Egyptian governmental figures articulating new economic approaches was unquestionably Ismā'īl Ṣidqī. Even the usually cynical British conceded his intellectual talents and regarded him as the most astute economic thinker among Egyptian politicans. Lord Lloyd, in condescension typical of this proconsular figure, remarked that 'he is the only Egyptian I know whose conversation is a real intellectual excitement'.[27] Ṣidqī burst onto the economic horizon with his critique of the 1920 budget, published by most of the daily Arabic newspapers.[28] Egyptian criticisms of British policy had tended to be confined to political issues, but Ṣidqī proved himself bold enough to level an attack on the economic arrangements drawn up by the British Financial Adviser. Expounding themes which were to recur in subsequent criticisms of Egyptian budgets, including his own, he argued that this budget had been drawn up by one man, without any parliamentary review, and that it was full of waste and extravagance. He was especially critical of the large proportion of revenue earmarked for governmental salaries; he was worried lest the bureaucracy cease to be an instrument of modernisation and become merely an agency for doling out pay-cheques to educated Egyptians. Ṣidqī demanded that some of these funds be reallocated to programmes of economic development, which would create genuine and sustaining gainful employment for the Egyptian population. Shortly after the publication of this critique, Ṣidqī was named Finance Minister in the 'Adlī government, in 1921. He established a new governmental organisation, the Economic Council, which was composed of leading foreign and Egyptian economic thinkers in the country. The Council was supposed to give advice on the major economic programmes being discussed by the government. Its members included such influential personalities as Ṭal'at Ḥarb, Henri Naus, Midḥat Yakin, 'Alī Manzalauī, Hornsby, and I. G. Lévi. Although the Council never exercised much authority, it did reveal Ṣidqī's economic strategy of uniting the foreigners resident in Egypt—the cosmopolitans—with the emerging Egyptian bourgeoisie and making this group an engine of economic transformation.[29] At the time that he created this organ, Ṣidqī also put forward his vision of an altered Egyptian economy. He called for the extension of arable land, the development of the irrigation system, and the exploitation of mineral wealth. These were traditional themes with which Lord Cromer would have had no quarrel, but Ṣidqī added to them a call for industrial and commercial development. By the mid 1920s, Ṣidqī was beginning to elaborate what he meant when he spoke of industrialisation. He felt that Egypt was ripe for the foundation of what we would call today import substitution and secondary industries. He wanted entrepreneurs to establish textile, food processing, and construction industries, and he believed that the Egyptian government should support these endeavours. In an effort to entice European capital, he portrayed the Egyptian labour force as disciplined and cheap, and he regularly opposed any labour legislation which would raise labour costs. Ṣidqī saw industrial development as the only solution to Egypt's burgeoning population, and as a necessary economic direction if Egypt was to prevent social discontent and even revolution. He and others skillfully used the spectre of revolution to press wealthy landlords to transfer investments from land to industry.[30] In 1926 he published a powerful appeal for the abolition of the capitulations, those rights and privileges enjoyed by foreigners residing in Egypt.[31] He claimed that these arrangements gave foreigners an unfair economic advantage over Egyptians and impeded the powers of the government to tax forms of wealth other than the land. While still favouring a close alliance between foreign and Egyptian capitalism, he appealed to the foreign communities to renounce these privileges and to work even more closely with their Egyptian colleagues. Ṣidqī's call forced this issue into public, even international, prominence, but the capitulations were not abolished until 1937, after the conclusion of an Anglo-Egyptian treaty of co-operation in 1936.

The most important new economic institution created after World War I was Bank Miṣr, the brainchild of Ṭal'at Ḥarb. Ṭal'at Ḥarb was the ideal founder of an institution which proved to be such an interesting and curious mixture of the old and the new. To be sure, there were other outstanding figures whom one might have expected to take a leading role in the founding of a national bank. Two names spring immediately to mind: Aḥmad 'Abbūd and Amīn Yaḥya. Aḥmad 'Abbūd was perhaps the most energetic and successful inter-war Egyptian entrepreneur. From a family of modest means he had studied engineering at Glasgow, financed by the Turkish government through the mediation of that extreme Egyptian Muslim nationalist, 'Abdul 'Azīz Shawīsh. A condition of his fellowship was that 'Abbūd enter Turkish service upon graduation, and between 1913 and 1920 he worked as an engineer and contractor in Iraq and Syria. Although he returned to Egypt in 1920 with a certain amount of capital, he was not yet a financial force.[32] A much more likely founder was Amīn Yaḥya. Born in 1866 to a wealthy Alexandrine family and educated in foreign schools, Amīn Yaḥya was interested in establishing new industrial and commercial ventures, as he did in the 1920s when he created a whole array of linked commercial and industrial firms. But as an Alexandrine, and reflecting the mentality of this mixed European and Egyptian community, he was at a disadvantage. Egyptian nationalists were calling for genuinely and purely Egyptian political and financial structures, and were suspicious of foreign influences.[33] Indeed, Ṭal'at Ḥarb was the logical creator of a banking organ born of the nationalist and anti-foreign ferment of this period.

Ṭal'at Ḥarb's early career blended the traditional and modern in ways which were to prove fortunate after the war. A graduate of the Egyptian Law School, he worked as a translator in the *Daira Saniya* and rose to head one of its departments. After this administration was dissolved, he moved to one of Egypt's powerful, European-dominated land companies, the Kom Ombo Company, and also became an associate of the great Egyptian land bank, the *Crédit Foncier Egyptien*, where he seems to have come to the attention of its leading administrators—Suares, Rolo, and Cattaui. His skills in finance and estate management were noted, and he was selected to administer the vast estates of 'Umar Sulṭān.[34] Thus, in his early career he had established connections with leading Egyptian land magnates, like 'Umar Sulṭān, as well as powerful financiers, like Suares and Rolo. A further manifestation of his early relationship with the European-dominated aspects of the Egyptian economy was his membership in the *Union des Agriculteurs*, a pressure group which represented mainly European landed magnates and foreign land companies.

Ṭal'at Ḥarb's reformist and forward-looking tendencies were combined with a deep veneration of traditional Islam as a religious and social system of value in a changing world. In 1905 he wrote a history of Arab and Islamic civilisation.[35] Far more revealing of his religious and ethical values was his rejoinder to the well-known book published by Qāsim Amīn under the title, *Taḥrīr al-Mar'a* (The Liberation of Woman). This work called for the liberation of Muslim women and opposed their veiling. Its publication caused a great stir in Egypt, and one of those who attacked it was Ṭal'at Ḥarb whose essay, entitled *Tarbīyat al-Mar'a wa al-Ḥijāb* (Female Education and the Veil), was published in 1899. In this treatise Ṭal'at Ḥarb opposed Qāsim Amīn's view, and cited *Quranic* and *Hadīth* texts to demonstrate that, indeed, women were not equal to men and should remain veiled. His use of traditional religious argumentation to substantiate his ideas seems to stand in glaring contrast to the innovative and rationalistic thinking he employed in the economic sphere. The most revealing section of the book was the chapter on the veil, where Ṭal'at Ḥarb portrayed the unveiling of Muslim women as leading to a marked decline in Islamic morality and to the intrusion of evil Western influences. The veil symbolised for him essential differences between the East and the West, and should be retained if only to assist the East in maintaining its integrity in the face of the Western cultural onslaught. Moreover, he saw the unveiling of women as part of a movement for relaxing the virtuous Islamic legal and moral codes and leading inevitably to the free mixing of the sexes, drinking, drunkenness and prostitution.[36] Although his extensive use of religious texts to buttress his arguments seems out of place in a man who already had much contact with Western thought and institutions and who was to be the founder of Egypt's leading, modern banking institution, still the essay revealed a cultural pride and nationalist thrust which also infused the programmes of Bank Miṣr at its inception.

In the decade before the outbreak of the war, Ṭal'at Ḥarb began to focus his attention on national economic problems. As a co-founder of the *Umma* Party's newspaper, *al-Jarīda*, he made certain that the paper carried articles dealing with economics. He himself wrote articles, one of which contained a plea for creating the economic bases of political independence. While admitting that almost all Egyptians favoured *al-istiqlāl al-tāmm* (complete independence), he reminded readers that Egypt still depended on foreigners as doctors, engineers, merchants, and industrialists. He bemoaned the absence of factories producing clothing and other articles of consumption, and felt chagrin that the coffee shops and hotels of Ezbekiah so popular with Egyptians were owned by foreigners. In concluding this article, he exhorted Egyptians to establish their 'domestic independence' first, by becoming good hotel managers, cooks, and builders; from this economic base he expected Egyptians to enter the medical, engineering and banking professions.[37] He continued to display his expertise in economic matters when he published a book (*Qanāt al-Suways*) attacking the British plan to extend the Suez Canal concession for an additional forty years. He showed that, despite having invested huge amounts of labour and capital in the construction of the canal, Egypt had realised trifling gains. He also argued that the company made its huge profits at the expense of the Egyptian people and its government, and that the Egyptian Parliament should not extend the concession unless the company was willing to make far-reaching changes in the distribution of funds between shareholders and the Egyptian people and to allow Egyptians a voice in the company's administration.[38] This work reflected a dominant theme in Ṭal'at Ḥarb's writing, namely, a concern with the exploitative nature of foreign business organisations in Egypt and the loss of Egyptian capital through the repatriation of profits. This essay was followed shortly by another study on the Egyptian economy. *'Ilāj Miṣr al-Iqtiṣādī*, published either in 1911 or 1913, contained a critique of British rule based on a close perusal of the annual reports of Lord Cromer and his successor, Eldon Gorst.[39] While conceding that British suzerainty in Egypt had brought a unification of the currency system, a reduction in taxes, significant irrigation works, and an improvement of the legal system, Ṭal'at Ḥarb contended that the condition of the fellahin was not much better than it had been before the coming of the British.[40] Moreover, this work contained a plea for the creation of a national bank serving Egyptian needs and not merely those of its shareholders.[41]

At the Muslim conference of 1911, Egyptian nationalists had propounded a number of demands, one of which was the establishment of a genuine national bank. So enthusiastic were some of the conference members about this idea that Ṭal'at Ḥarb was delegated to make an examination of banking arrangements in Europe, as a preliminary to the founding of a bank in Egypt. Although enthusiasm soon waned, Ṭal'at Ḥarb's European tour proved fruitful. In 1916 he and his colleague, Yūsuf Aṣlān Qaṭṭāwī, submitted a report on German banking and economic development to a special committee established under the presidency of Ismā'īl Sidqī to draw up a report on industrial and commercial development in Egypt. The ideas enunciated in the report proved to be a preview of many of the plans he sought to implement at Bank Misr in the 1920s and 1930s. Ṭal'at Ḥarb and Yūsuf Aṣlān Qaṭṭāwī found German economic development extremely stimulating and pertinent to Egyptian conditions. The key to German economic success, they felt, was the capacity of German leaders to rally the nation around the single goal of German pre-eminence (*tafawwuq*). The authors paid much attention to the role of banks in Germany's economic progress. Believing that the salient feature of the German economy was that industrial development tended to outstrip capital formation, they argued that banks had played a critical role in mobilising much-needed capital. Additionally, Germany had shown the advantages that cartels possessed over numerous smaller industrial forms. They were able to act as instruments of central economic planning, and maximise the use of scarce resources.[42]

Ṭal'at Ḥarb's last major writing prior to the founding of the bank was the publication in 1919 of a series of newspaper articles attacking the Belgian-owned and -run tramway company operating in Cairo. These articles criticised the company for its inordinately high profits which were wrung from the Egyptian common people and flowed into the coffers of Belgian shareholders. Particularly outrageous to Ṭal'at Ḥarb was the amount of money turned over to holders of founders' shares. According to the original charter of the company, the ordinary shareholders were limited to a 5 per cent return on their investment; any additional profit accrued to the board of directors and the founders, who had not been required in fact to put up any money at the time the company was established.[43]

All of these writings demonstrated Ṭal'at Ḥarb's unmatched talent for simplifying and publicising economic issues and linking them with national concerns—a capacity he continued to employ with great success when he wrote his annual reports for the general shareholders meetings of Bank Miṣr. His economic writings stressed a number of themes. Running through his attack on the tramway company and other European-dominated firms, like the Suez Canal Company, was a strong populist orientation, for he thought that these and other European firms displayed little concern about the well-being of their Egyptian consumers. He accused the tramway company of realising 'easy spoils' (*qhanīma bārida*) from their Egyptian operations, and he portrayed the board of directors and the founders of the company as 'predators' on Egyptian wealth. In addition, he attacked the tramway company for its lack of concern for its workers and the low wages it paid despite its huge profits. Ṭal'at Ḥarb remained ambivalent about the contribution of foreign firms to Egyptian economic progress. While admitting that foreign banks provided access to capital which otherwise would have been lacking in Egypt, he also portrayed foreigners as rapacious, concerned only with maximising profits for their shareholders at the expense of the Egyptian population, and lacking in regard for Egyptian prosperity. Although his writings did reveal this suspicion of foreign economic dominance over the Egyptian economy, and although Bank Miṣr was founded on deeply-rooted nationalist principles, Ṭal'at Ḥarb personally and professionally enjoyed many contacts with leaders of the foreign economic community. He remained a member of the European-dominated *Union des Cultivateurs* and was one of the early participants in the predominantly European-run Egyptian Federation of Industries. Both of these organisations advocated developing the Egyptian economy through an alliance of foreign capital and technical skills with the nascent Egyptian middle class and the Egyptian working class. In short, Ṭal'at Ḥarb was an enigmatic and complex figure—a devout and traditionalist Muslim, who defended Muslim ethics by appealing to religious texts, yet an exponent of economic rationality; a keen nationalist, suspicious of foreign capital, yet a member of the *Crédit Foncier Egyptien* and other European-dominated organisations. In fact, it was this combination of the old and the new—of the traditional Egyptian with the modern Western—which was such an essential part of the 1919 revolution.

Bank Miṣr officially came into being on 8 March, 1920. It had long historical antecedents.[44] Egyptians had tended to call for a national bank during times of acute economic and political crises and to see it as an economic panacea. The first epoch in which propaganda for a national bank became prominent was during the 'Urābī revolt. The notion was put forward by a number of persons, including 'Umar Sulṭān, Ṭal'at Ḥarb's patron. Later, Ṭal'at Ḥarb and 'Umar Sulṭān proposed to establish a number of local banks in the provinces, starting in Minyā, the home area of 'Umar Sultān, and eventually building up to a central bank. These ideas lost their force during the first two decades of the British occupation, but the fiscal crisis of 1907, demonstrating as it did, the vulnerability of an economy dependent on foreign capital, again occasioned pleas for the establishment of a national bank which would enable Egyptians to defend themselves against this foreign economic control. This thinking culminated at the Muslim Congress of 1911, where a number of influential nationalists signed a petition calling for a national bank. The architect of this document was not Ṭal'at Ḥarb, as historians have since come to think, but the influential Yūsuf Naḥās.[45] The latter attacked the domination of foreign capital, which he held to be more degrading than the British military occupation. In these early calls for an Egyptian bank, what was envisaged was primarily an agricultural credit organisation which would make loans to landowners and assist Egyptians with the marketing of their chief export, cotton.

In considering the background to the foundation of Bank Miṣr, no discussion would be complete without mention of 'Umar Luṭfī.[46] His thoughts contained within them the seeds not only for Bank Miṣr, but also the Egyptian General Agricultural Syndicate. Like other concerned nationalists, he was alarmed at the weaknesses of the Egyptian economy as revealed by the financial crisis of 1906–07, and began to argue that Egyptians must develop institutional underpinnings if they were to win their political freedom. His overarching concern was the inability of Egyptians to mobilise large amounts of money, hence their dependence on foreign banking and lending institutions. Because foreign firms monopolised the capital available in Egypt, they were able to fix the prices for Egyptian exports and expropriate the lion's share of Egypt's foreign trade earnings. Thus, despite the fact that Egypt had a prosperous overseas trade, the country did not retain this wealth. This concern led him to take an interest in co-operative organisations. He made a trip to Italy to study agricultural co-operatives. The so-called father of the Egyptian co-operative movement, 'Umar Luṭfī, also championed the idea of 'a big national bank' (*bank waṭanī kabīr*), and he founded an Egyptian Financial Co-operative Company (Sharikat al-Ta'āwun al-Mālīya) in 1909.[47] Although this firm remained extremely small, and without influence in raising Egyptian cotton export prices, as 'Umar Luṭfī hoped it would have, it had on its board Ṭal'at Ḥarb and Fu'ād Sulṭān. They remained in the firm even after the founding of Bank Miṣr, and used this company to collect funds from small investors interested in buying a few Bank Miṣr shares.[48]

Heightened interest in the founding of an Egyptian bank began to be felt at the end of the war. The journal of the Cairo Chamber of Commerce became a forum for these ideas. It published numerous letters and queries discussing the purpose of such a bank, one of which was answered by Ṭal'at Ḥarb himself.[49] One letter argued that a bank was needed to guard against 'the pilfering of the national wealth', while another coupled a demand for a bank with proposals for industrialisation and tariff reform.[50] The more widely-read journals, like *al-Ahrām* and *al-Muqaṭṭam*, also participated in the publicity campaign. By this time Ṭal'at Ḥarb was the acknowledged leader of this effort and had put himself in touch with landed magnates. At first his pleas did not yield solid results. As he later indicated, one person whose help he solicited replied that one of his principles was not to participate in commercial endeavours. Another said that he invested only in well-established enterprises.[51] There was much concern over the Islamic injunction against usury, which many Muslims believed forbade the paying of interest on bank deposits. Probably most fundamental of all, the wealthy landed class still remained attached to the land and was loath to redirect its investments.

According to Ṭal'at Ḥarb, the turning-point came when he received a letter from Midḥat Yakin approving the idea and agreeing to work hand-in-hand with him.[52] *Muḥāfiẓ* of Alexandria and a descendant of a Macedonian noble who had married a sister of Muḥammad 'Alī, Midḥat Yakin was a man of considerable wealth. Educated in Egypt and France, where he had taken a law degree, he was portrayed in British reports as a person 'inclined to lead a life of ease and pleasure'. But he was rumoured to have made over £E200,000 during the cotton land boom in the spring of 1920. Moreover, he was a close associate of the king, and his cousin was 'Adlī Yakin, Prime Minister in the 1920s.[53] Hence, he gave the national bank project needed respectability and increased the circle of landed magnates willing to back Ṭal'at Ḥarb.

The conditions, at least in the early months of 1920, were favourable to the creation of this new financial institution. As we have seen, the inflation of the latter war years had wiped out much of Egypt's landed indebtedness and had increased Egyptian bank deposits. World cotton prices continued to rise in 1919 and the early part of 1920, but so did the price of land, causing people to consider new economic alternatives for their investments. In Ṭal'at Ḥarb's estimation; wealthy Egyptians possessed a great deal of idle money; he was hopeful of attracting some of these funds to his new bank.[54]

In reality, his success in obtaining backing for his bank was limited, in part, as we shall see, because there was a radical downswing in cotton prices in late 1920. The bank had no fewer than 124 founders, far more, for example, than the small number who created the National Bank of Egypt in 1898. But these 124 men subscribed only £E80,000 in capital. Most of the original subscribers represented wealthy landed families. There were eight pashas and 57 beys. None the less, the largest subscriber was 'Abd al-'Aẓīm al-Miṣrī, holding only 250 shares worth £E1,000.

'Alī Ismāīl contributed £E600 and six others £E500 apiece: Midḥat Yakin, Ṭal'at Ḥarb, Muḥammad al-Sharī'ī, 'Abd al-Rāziq al-Fār, Muhammad Mūsa al-Fiqā'ī and the sons of Badawī al-Shaytī.[55] It was not at all surprising that most of the founders were men from wealthy landed families, not only because land was still the chief source of Egyptian wealth, but also because many of these individuals believed that the bank would support their agrarian export endeavours. They hoped that the bank would provide loans at rates lower than those offered by the foreign banks in Egypt. Nor were these rather traditional views of what a national bank should be unfounded. Although it is not possible to make a detailed study of the early history of the bank here, it was not coincidental that the bank created a subsidiary cotton ginning company which opened its first factory in Upper Egypt at Maghāgha, the home of 'Abd al-'Aẓīm al-Miṣrī, the bank's largest original subscriber, and another factory at al-Maḥalla al-Kubra in a region where Midḥat Yakin had considerable landed interests.[56]

The sum of £E80,000 was an exceedingly small amount and must have been a bitter disappointment to Ṭal'at Ḥarb. Opponents of the bank wondered whether this money would suffice to pay the rent of a bank building as well as employees' salaries. But on 8 March, 1920 the charter of the bank was promulgated, and on 8 May, 1920 the bank held a formal ceremony to celebrate its inauguration. The new bank had a number of novel features which reflected its nationalist orientation. All shares had to be owned by Egyptians—a restriction justified on the ground that otherwise foreigners would buy up most of the shares and take control of the bank. The language of the bank was to be Arabic, despite the fact that almost all of Egypt's financial and commercial firms employed French. Ṭal'at Ḥarb was anxious to demonstrate that Arabic could be developed as a language of modern commerce, and he felt that an institution employing Arabic would open up employment opportunities other than government service for educated Egyptians.[57]

Although the bank was founded on a small scale, it commanded immediate attention in the press. One of its most vigorous champions was *al-Akhbār*, run by Amīn al-Rāfi'ī, who ran regular advertisements in the paper exhorting the people to purchase shares. His brother, the Watanist lawyer and writer, 'Abd al-Raḥman al-Rāfi'ī, wrote an article on the Polish national bank which he depicted as an economic bulwark of Polish political independence.[58] The European press in Egypt, however, was not so enthusiastic. The *Bulletin Commercial* tempered its support with a word of caution: 'A long education is necessary in order to adapt to the principles and prescriptions of modern finance—in a word European assimilation. In everything there must be an apprenticeship. One does not become a master at a stroke. . . . Without wishing to diminish whatsoever the merit of this new activity, we can say that limited strictly to the indigenous element in capital, administration, and direction its hour has not yet come.'[59]

The bank's early growth was slow. Despite its link with Egyptian nationalism, less than £E100,000 of additional capital had been raised by the end of 1920. Nevertheless, the capital did begin to increase. Since the original subscribers wielded enormous influence in the countryside, they were able to persuade others to invest money. 'Alī Islām, a landed magnate from Beni Suef, related that he rallied support in his district from the lesser gentry, and although many of these new subscribers gave money out of loyalty to the great magnates and looked upon their investments as donations, the capital of the bank rose from £E474,924 in 1924 to £E720,000 in 1925 and then to £E1,000,000 by 1927.[60]

Ṭal'at Ḥarb used Bank Miṣr as an instrument of industrial development, as he had predicted. In 1923 he began to employ a small amount of the bank's surplus profits to found national industries, and he extended this programme in subsequent years. The industries he sponsored were closely related to Egypt's cotton economy. The first company founded was a printing firm for which the bank itself had much use. This was followed by a ginning company. By 1926, the bank had become the largest purchaser of Egyptian cotton and had established a navigation company to transport cotton and other produce.[61] In 1927, Bank Miṣr moved into the textile industry by creating three new firms for the manufacture of cotton and linen.[62]

All of these industries operated on a small scale, since industrialisation did not begin to secure a firm foothold until after the tariff reform of 1930, and especially after the outbreak of World War II, when Egypt's trade with Europe was again interrupted. But the bank had made an important initial impact on Egyptian society. It symbolised for many a genuinely Egyptian financial institution which offered competition to European-run banks and industries. Although its industrial endeavours were embryonic and regarded with suspicion by some, the bank had managed to popularise the notion that Egypt should diversify its economy and balance its agricultural wealth with industrial growth. So closely linked with Egyptian national aspirations had the bank become that it was difficult for the state to deny it economic support or to refuse it government contracts or government concessions when bargaining in competition with foreign firms. In 1929, just prior to the tariff reform, the bank published a far-ranging study of Egyptian industrialisation and called upon the state to create an industrial bank as the primary vehicle of financial support for new Egyptian firms. The bank's shareholders and its board of directors continued to be Egyptian. The bank was suspicious of combining with foreign firms for fear of losing its purely Egyptian quality and being submerged in a foreign company. Recognising its technical limitations, however, Ṭal'at Ḥarb did engage certain foreign experts known for their sympathy to Egyptian nationalist aspirations. Richard Adler of the German Orient Bank helped to set up the bank's accounting system, while the well-known German cotton merchant, Hugo Lindemann, was brought into the Miṣr company for the export of cotton.[63] The Miṣr companies displayed an interest in prestigious national undertakings as well as pan-Arab and pan-Islamic projects. In 1930, Bank Miṣr founded the first Egyptian airline, which linked Egypt with other Arab states. It also created a shipping company and won the governmental concession for transporting pilgrims to the Arabian peninsula.

A second institution which reflected new directions in the Egyptian economy was the Egyptian Federation of Industries. Founded in 1922, this body represented the modernising industrial sector, rather than the still persisting artisan and local handicraft groups. The Federation's organising genius and intellectual stimulus was I. G. Lévi, a remarkable man in modern Egyptian history, whose talents have not gained the recognition they deserve. Born in Istanbul in 1878 and a graduate of the University of Naples in law, political science, and oriental languages, Lévi settled in Cairo in 1903. He worked first as an advocate, then as attaché to the Italian embassy in Cairo, and director-general of the Egyptian Bureau of Statistics, before helping to found the Federation of Industries. Although men like Henri Naus and, later, Ismā'īl Ṣidqī received the credit for this organisation, I. G. Lévi was its secretary-general. He was also the secretary-general of many other industrial associations which were the constituents of the Federation. He was a member of Ṣidqī's Economic Council and secretary of the intellectually influential Egyptian Society for Political Economy, Statistics, and Legislation, the publisher of the journal *L'Egypte Contemporaine*.[64]

Lévi was not simply an organiser, however. He had one of the most fertile economic minds of inter-war Egypt; his articles and editorials, many of which appeared in *L'Egypte Industrielle*, the organ of the Egyptian Federation of Industries, probably contain the most lucid statement of Egypt's inter-war strategy of economic development. As the First World War was drawing to a close, Lévi began to warn that the wartime prosperity would be lost if Egypt did not put its economic house in order. Writing in 1927 in *L'Egypte Contemporaine*, he argued that under Cromer and Kitchener the British had brought major economic gains to Egypt. They had established tight control over the finances, reformed a corrupt administration, and modernised agriculture and hydraulics. But this policy, he believed, needed to be 'revised and simplified in the light of the development of the country. It neglected internal and external commerce, industry, branches of agriculture besides cotton, technology, and economic institutions'.[65] He sought to create conditions favourable for industrialisation. To this end he worked diligently to influence the tariff reform programme carried out in 1930. He agitated in favour of allowing foreign capital and foreign technicians easy entry into the country, and since he believed that Egyptian industrial development could thrive only if labour costs were kept low, he tried to block the introduction of labour legislation based on what he considered to be inappropriate European models. But clearly his major contribution was his work at the Egyptian Federation of Industries.

The reason the Egyptian Federation of Industries came into being when it did was related to the First World War. During the European conflagration, trade with Europe was severely curtailed, and Egypt was unable to obtain many of its traditional imports. This provided an unanticipated opportunity for capitalists to found Egyptian industries or to expand the production of those already in being. As we have seen, the Salt and Soda Company and the Sugar Company enjoyed unrivalled prosperity. The textile company which Cromer had done so little to assist—*La Filature Nationale d'Alexandrie*—finally began to make some headway. At an exhibition held in 1916 and displaying only Egyptian manufactures, a vast array of products gave proof of Egypt's expanding industrial sector. On display were cigarettes, cement, sugar, alcohol, furniture, simple agricultural and industrial machinery, textiles, rugs, metal, leather and copper products, pottery, processed foods, and many other items.[66] Thus, the First World War implanted in Egypt a few financially powerful industries and some influential personalities concerned about the fate of Egyptian industrial development. The post-war years were harsh on these firms. Egypt resumed its trade with the outside world, and most industries found themselves unable to compete with cheaper European manufactures. Many firms were forced to close. The Sugar Company and *La Filature Nationale d'Alexandrie* were barely able to eke out profits. They looked to the state for assistance. It was under these conditions that leading industrial magnates decided to organise a pressure group to agitate in favour of their interests. Known first as the Association of Egyptian Industries, this organ quickly began to exercise influence in Egyptian politics. Two of its most prominent founders were Henri Naus of the Sugar Company and M. Sornaga, head of the Greek community, a ceramics manufacturer in Cairo, and an associate of *La Filature Nationale d'Alexandrie*.

This organisation espoused some of the newly emerging bourgeois economic ideas. It pointed to the alarming statistics on Egypt's rising population and argued that, unless industrial development was supported, rural discontent and urban unemployment would disrupt Egyptian society. The Federation agitated vigorously for tariff reform and had a substantial impact on the new tariff structure introduced in 1930. Although these new customs duties remained primarily revenue-earning, the Federation was able to persuade the government to protect certain nascent industries, like textiles, and to allow vital raw materials and machinery used in Egyptian industries to enter the country at low rates. Although the tariff reform was the focus of its interest in the 1920s, it also succeeded in pressuring the government into making other, smaller changes in its economic policies. The state altered its railway rates in order to assist Egyptian industries. It changed governmental purchasing arrangements and required the state to use Egyptian manufactures if they were not more costly than imported commodities. It abolished the eight per cent excise tax on many Egyptian-manufactured products which Cromer had defended on free-trade grounds.[67] The Federation helped to link industries engaged in the same undertakings. Associations of brick-makers, builders, cigarette and tobacco manufacturers, milk manufacturers, and river transport firms were established and then incorporated into the Egyptian Federation of Industries. Although the Federation was dominated by European industrialists resident in Egypt, and always championed economic development by means of these foreign cosmopolitans, it began to associate Egyptians more closely with its organisation in the 1930s. Ṭal'at Ḥarb and the Miṣr companies had been members from the early years. Aḥmad 'Abbūd began to exercise power and Ismā'īl Ṣidqī was appointed vice-president.

A third new economic institution founded after the war was the Egyptian General Agricultural Syndicate. It represented the interests of Egypt's large landed magnates and their desire to gain greater control over the marketing of cotton. A great deal of its activity was directed against the Alexandria General Produce Association, which dominated Egyptian cotton marketing. A brief glance at this organ is in order if we are to understand the founding of the Agricultural Syndicate. From 1821 to 1883 there were no formal rules dealing with the export of cotton. On 17 February, 1883, a group of Alexandrine merchants and brokers met and established the Alexandria General Produce Association.[68] Controlling Egypt's main export market at Mina al-Basal, this association drew up regulations for the marketing of produce—especially cotton, cotton seed, and cereals. Called by its critics 'a state within a state', the Produce Association purchased cotton and other export commodities, graded products, and delegated to itself the authority to settle all disputes, not only between its own members but between its members and outsiders.[69] These prerogatives were bitterly resented by Egyptian cultivators, who felt that the Produce Association used its far-reaching powers to deflate prices and to monopolise most of the profits from Egypt's exports. Cultivators were also upset that merchants and brokers alone were represented on the Produce Association. Its operations were managed by a select committee of 32, of whom 20 (Committee A) controlled the marketing of cotton, while a committee of 12 (Committee B) took charge of the marketing of cotton seed and cereals. To its numerous Egyptian critics, the representatives of the Produce Association argued that their body maintained a high reputation for Egyptian exports and thereby assured favourable prices.

Although the Egyptian General Agricultural Syndicate grew out of Egyptian cultivators' discontent over the Produce Association, it was galvanised into being during the cotton crisis of 1920–21. The steady increase in world cotton prices was shattered in late 1920. British and American production declined, and the price of cotton fell from $187 a qantar in February 1920 to $18 in February 1921.[70] The leading figure in organising Egyptian cultivators was Yūsuf Naḥās. A French protégé of Syrian parentage, he was born in Cairo and educated in France, where he studied agriculture and economics. He was one of the largest landowners in Egypt, and was French consular agent at Zaqaziq and friend of Zaghlūl.[71] One of his close associates in this enterprise was 'Alī Manzalawī, another large landowner who had bitter experiences with the vagaries of cotton marketing. A bankrupt in 1910, he had led a crusade against European merchants in Tanta district before World War I, arguing that cultivators should be paid a fair price.[72] Naḥās and Manzalawī organised meetings of princes, ministers, large landowners, and Egyptian and foreign merchants to discuss the best means to enable Egyptian cultivators and merchants to gain control over cotton marketing and stop the precipitate decline in cotton prices. A Syndicate for the Protection of the Interests of Cultivators was formed, later changing its name to the Egyptian General Agricultural Syndicate.[73] Although this body was holding meetings in 1921, it did not begin to act on a regular basis until the following year.[74] The Agricultural Syndicate became primarily a pressure group, composed of large landowners, many of whom were deeply involved in politics and commerce, and who were themselves speculators on the cotton market. At first, the Syndicate drew up an ambitious and far-reaching programme. It called upon its members to donate funds for an executive committee and to hold back the cotton crop for sale until the price had reached a certain level. The Syndicate, however, was unsuccessful in implementing this extensive programme, mainly because its members were not willing to hold back cotton for sale. Yet, as a pressure group, the Agricultural Syndicate exercised much influence over the government's cotton policy.

The Syndicate's programme was almost entirely focused on ways of raising the price of Egyptian cotton. Believing the Produce Association to be the major cause of low prices, and often labelling it 'the party of falling prices' [Ḥizb al-Nuzūl], the Syndicate demanded that the state regulate marketing so as to break the stranglehold of the Alexandria Produce Association. It also pressured the state to use its resources to buy cotton or to lend funds to cultivators as a means of sustaining higher prices. It favoured the limitation of cotton cultivation to a third of the land. One of its favourite targets was the system of cultivators' arranging to sell their cotton to a merchant with the price to be fixed later. This complex system of marketing, called selling 'on call', gave cultivators advances before the harvest season at a time when many desperately needed funds, but in the view of the Syndicate it enabled the Alexandria General Produce Association through its control of financing and marketing to depress the final sales prices to the disadvantage of the cultivators. The Syndicate agitated for the abolition of this system.[75]

The Syndicate enjoyed enormous success in persuading Egyptian ministries to implement its suggestions. No doubt this was because both bodies were heavily representative of large landed interests. Indeed many Egyptian ministers were members of the Syndicate. In 1927 the Syndicate pressured the Egyptian government to legislate against all cotton sales in which prices were to be fixed later. This law was later overturned by the Egyptian Mixed Courts, on the grounds that it was injurious to foreign interests.[76] Despite opposition from all British financial experts, the Syndicate persuaded the Egyptian government to intervene in the cotton market, either to purchase cotton or to make advances to cotton cultivators. The British regarded this endeavour as economically unproductive and costly. Believing that Egyptians did not sell enough cotton on the world market to influence prices, they felt that the state could not have any influence on world cotton prices.[77] Yūsuf Naḥās published a spate of articles in the Arabic press in the early 1920s, however, calling on the government to purchase portions of the crop and portraying men like Ṣidqī who opposed this policy as agents of the British and economic traitors to Egypt. In one article, he accused government leaders of preferring to see '£E4,000,000 go into the pocket of the foreigner as a gift without any government resistance on the grounds of not gambling with money'.[78] The British advisers pointed out that, even if minimally effective, government financial intervention would only benefit the already well-to-do large landowners and would be of no help to small cultivators. But the campaign for state assistance succeeded. Between 1921 and 1926 the state entered the cotton market as a buyer. In 1926 it spent nearly £E3,000,000 to purchase almost 500,000 qantars of cotton.[79] These purchases proved to be such a financial burden that the state devised new formulas before the depression of 1929. It advanced money to cultivators or guaranteed a minimum price. Neither of these arrangements proved entirely satisfactory, and the government embarked upon new cotton policies, following the publication of 'Abd al-Waḥāb's famous report on cotton in 1930. Even so, two British commercial agents Turner and Larkin estimated that by 1931 the Egyptian government had expended over £E19,000,000 in purchases or advances on cotton.[80] Perhaps the reform that gave the Syndicate its greatest satisfaction was the regulation of the Mina al-Basal market and the Alexandria General Produce Association. The state broke the monopolistic marketing powers of the Produce Association and created new committees on which cultivators and merchants from the interior of the country were represented. The entire marketing operation was also supervised by the state.[81]

These three new economic institutions were consequences of the Egyptian revolution of 1919. Like the political movement of Zaghlūl, they reflected a vigorous nationalist orientation. Moreover, the desire to establish such institutions, apparent in Egypt before the war, was intensified by the economic impact of this conflict. Claiming to be a purely Egyptian bank, with only Egyptian shareholders and an Egyptian board of directors, Bank Miṣr was committed to creating the economic underpinnings for Egypt's political independence. The Egyptian Federation of Industries, although dominated by the so-called cosmopolitans of Egypt, also sought to create a more diversified Egyptian economy with a strong industrial sector. The Egyptian General Agricultural Syndicate agitated against the dominance of a small group of European merchants over the marketing of cotton and wanted to gain a larger share of the profits from Egypt's main export. All of these patently nationalist demands were couched in powerful nationalist imagery. The proponents of these new bodies were not trying to create an autonomous and self-sufficient national economy. They all recognised Egyptian backwardness and the need to rely on a certain amount of foreign capital and technical assistance. But at the same time they sought to dismantle the old Cromerian arrangements, in which Egypt was seen only as an agricultural country, exporting cotton. They favoured industrial development, a modified tariff system affording protection to nascent industries, and an end to monoculture.

It would be tempting to assert that the founding of these new organisations marked the emergence of the Egyptian bourgeoisie, and to use this evidence to argue for the bourgeois nature of the Egyptian revolution of 1919. In reality, these societies were established on a very small scale in the early 1920s, so they can not be cited as evidence of the emergence of a strong, self-confident Egyptian middle class. Nor does the term bourgeoisie appear appropriate. While it could be applied to the cosmopolitans who led the activities of the Egyptian Federation of Industries, it presents more problems when applied to the Egyptian General Agricultural Syndicate and Bank Miṣr. Both of these organs were controlled by landed magnates who were just beginning to turn their attention from agriculture to commerce, finance and industry. Indeed, one reason Bank Miṣr had such an appeal to this group was that its programmes for the purchase of cotton and the creation of ginning, shipping and textile firms could be seen as a force supporting the agrarian economy. These new institutions manifested a new power and confidence on the part of nineteenth-century Egyptian families who had been fortunate enough to become large landholders as a result of the changes in land laws and the distribution of private estates carried out by Muḥammad ʻAlī and his successors. As is well known, the nineteenth-century economy witnessed the growth of vast inequalities in landholdings, so that by the outbreak of World War I, a tiny proportion of the total Egyptian population possessed a huge percentage of the land. Although the revolution of 1919 involved all segments of Egyptian society —peasantry and urban proletariat—the landed families made vast political, economic, and social gains. They dominated all the major inter-war parties and the new bicameral Egyptian legislature. Bank Miṣr and the Egyptian General Agricultural Syndicate represented the efforts of these families to invest their wealth in new undertakings and to compete with European capital in Egypt. The Egyptian Federation of Industry marked an effort to implant Egyptian industries in Egypt through an alliance of cosmopolitan Egyptians, native-born Egyptians, and foreign technical and capital skills.

NOTES

1. J. M. 'La Situation Économique en Égypte', *Bulletin de l'Union des Agriculteurs d'Egypte*, vol. 12, no. 108, July to October, 1914, pp. 218–23.

2. See especially no. 51341, Telegram, Cheetham to Grey, 7 September, 1914, Foreign Office (hereafter FO) Public Record Office (hereafter PRO) 371/1969. The entire file 45836 deals with this cotton-marketing crisis.

3. No. 63063, Telegram, Cheetham to Grey, 24 October, 1914, PRO FO 371/1969.

4. J. Schatz, 'Chronique Agricole de l'Année, 1914–15', *L'Egypte Contemporaine*, 1916, vol. 7, pp. 253–68.

5. 'Khiṭāb Maftūḥ' (Open Letter), *al-Jarīda*, 23 September, 1914, in Yūsuf Naḥās, *al-Quṭun fī Kḥamsīn 'Aman* (Cotton over Fifty Years) (Cairo, 1954), pp. 6–7; and

'Mudhakkira Thānīya min Taṣrīf Maḥṣūl al-Quṭun Muqaddamma ila al-Mālīya' (Second Note on the Marketing of Cotton sent to the Treasury), *al Jarīda*, 6 October, 1914, in Naḥās, *ibid.*, pp. 8–9.

6. Annual Report of the Crédit Foncier Egyptien, *Bulletin Commercial*, 24 February, 1918.

7. *Ibid.*, 21 April, 1918.

8. *Ibid.*, 17 March, 1918.

9. 'al-Quṭun wa Athmānuhu wa Taslīmuhu' (Cotton, its Prices and its Sale), *al-Muqaṭṭam*, 26 October, 1918, in Naḥās, *al-Quṭun*, pp. 22–4.

10. *al-Ghurfa al-Tijārīya al-Miṣriya* (The Egyptian Chamber of Commerce), vol. 3, no. 11, November 1918, pp. 428–9.

11. No. 199, Wingate to Balfour, 2 September, 1917, enclosing memorandum on Egypt's war investments by L. G. Roussin, 27 August, 1917, PRO FO 371/2932 f. 110832.

12. S. Avigdor, 'Modifications de Situation Economique des Classes Rurales Egyptiennes entre 1912/13 et 1919/20', *Bulletin de l'Union des Agriculteurs d'Égypte*, vol. 32, no. 250, February 1934, pp. 94–105.

13. No. 32, Wingate to Curzon, 20 January, 1919, PRO FO 371/3713 f. 20835; *Journal Officiel*, 14 October, 1918; and *al-Ghurfa al-Tijārīya al-Miṣriya*, vol. 3, no. 2, February 1918, pp. 46–47.

14. *al-Ghurfa al-Tijārīya al-Miṣriya*, vol. 3, no. 11, November 1918, pp. 434–41.

15. *Bulletin Commercial*, 14 July, 1918.

16. See Jean Mazuel, *Le Sucre en Egypte: Etude Geographique Historique et Economique* (Cairo, 1937).

17. *al-Ghurfa al-Tijārīya al-Miṣriya*, vol. 3, no. 8, August 1918, pp. 308–10. This issue contains a formal note of complaint from the Cairo Chamber of Commerce to the Supply Control Commission on 2 July, 1918, describing the crisis in sugar and oil. See also *al-Ghurfa al-Tijārīya al-Miṣriya*, vol. 3, no. 6, June 1918, pp. 239–40.

18. *Ibid.*, vol. 3, no. 4, April 1918, pp. 140–4.

19. See the work of P. G. Elgood, *Egypt and the Army* (Oxford, 1924).

20. A. E. Crouchley, *The Investment of Foreign Capital in Egyptian Companies and Public Debt* (Cairo, 1936), p. 73.

21. Yūsuf Naḥās, *Juhūd al-Niqāba al-Zirā'īya al-Miṣriya al-'Amma fī Thalāthīn 'Amin* (The Struggle of the General Egyptian Agricultural Syndicate over Thirty Years) (Cairo, 1952), p. 13.

22. E. R. J. Owen, 'Lord Cromer and the Development of Egyptian Industry, 1883–1907', *Middle Eastern Studies*, vol. 2, no. 4, July 1966, pp. 282–301.

23. Egypt, Ministry of Finance, Statistical Department, *Census of Egypt*, 1917, vol. 2, *passim*.

24. *Bulletin Commercial*, 28 September, 1919.

25. See, for example, *La Révue d'Egypte Financière et Economique*, vol. 1, no. 1, 10 March, 1927.

26. See, for example, *al-Akhbār*, 22 February, 1920.

27. No. 277, Lloyd to Chamberlain, 6 May, 1927, PRO FO 371/12388 f. 1353.

28. *al-Akhbār*, 30 March, 1920.

29. *Bulletin Commercial*, 10 September, 1922.

30. *al-Siyāsa al-Usbū'īya*, 13 March, 1926.

31. *Ibid.*, 27 March, 1926.

32. Personalities file, 1 January, 1931, PRO FO 371/15420.

33. On Amin Yaḥya one should consult Arnold Wright (ed.), *Twentieth Century Impressions of Egypt, its History, People, Commerce, Industries, and Resources* (London, 1909), p. 439; *L'Informateur*, 10 April, 1936, and 23 April, 1948; and *Majallat Ghurfa al-Qāhira* (The Journal of the Cairo Chamber), vol. 1, no. 4, April 1936, pp. 3–5.

34. There are many accounts of Ṭal'at Ḥarb's life. Especially useful is the work of Ḥāfiz Maḥmūd, Muṣṭafa Kāmil al-Falkī, and Maḥmūd Fatḥī'Amr, *Ṭal'at Ḥarb* (Cairo, 1936) and Tal'at Ḥarb's own short account in Ṭal'at Ḥarb, *Majmū'at Khutab* (Collected Speeches) (Cairo, 1927), vol. 3, pp. 79–84.

35. Ṭal'at Ḥarb, *Tā'rīkh al-'Arab wa al-Islām* (Cairo, 1905).
36. Ṭal'at Ḥarb, *Tarbīyat al-Mar'a* (The Education of Woman) (Cairo, 1899).
37. *al-Jarīda*, 1 October, 1907.
38. I have not been able to obtain a copy of this work. My interpretation is based on short descriptions of the work in *al-Jarīda*, 3 February, 1910, and after, and the study by Ḥāfiz Maḥmūd, *Ṭal'at Ḥarb*.
39. 'Abd al-'Azīm Muḥammad Ramaḍān, 'Nisf Qarn min Kifāḥ al-Burjuwāzīya al-Misrīya linsh'a Bank Miṣr' (A Half-Century in the Struggle of the Egyptian Bourgeoisie in the Creation of Bank Miṣr), *al-Kātib*, vol. 11, April 1971, pp. 170–184. Ramaḍān questions whether this work, with its powerful appeal for the establishment of an Egyptian bank, was published at the time of the Muslim Congress, and suggests that it was published in 1913 instead.
40. Ṭal'at Ḥarb, *'Ilāj Miṣr al-Iqtiṣādī*, pp. 38 ff.
41. *Ibid.*, pp. 3–30.
42. This prescient report is to be found in Ṭal'at Ḥarb, *Majmū'at Khuṭab*, (vol. 1, pp. 13–44) under the title 'Taqrir 'an al-Sinā'a wa al-Tijāra al-Almānīya' (Report on German Commerce and Industry).
43. *al-Akhbār*, 14 April, 1920; Ṭal'at Ḥarb, *Majmū'at Khuṭab*, vol. 3, pp. 63–67; and Ḥāfiz Maḥmūd, *Ṭal'at Ḥarb*, pp. 77 ff.
44. See the interesting article by Ramadān in *al-Kātib*, vol. 11, April 1971; the historical account in Ṭal'at Ḥarb, *'Ilāj Miṣr al-Iqtisāḍī*, pp. 3–30; and Ra'ūf 'Abbās Ḥāmid, *al-Nizām al-Ijtimā'i fī Miṣr fī Ẓill al-Milkiyāt al-Zira'īya al-Kabīra* (The Social Structure of Egypt under the Influence of Large Agricultural Estates) (Cairo, 1973), pp. 169–174.
45. This is the argument made by Ramaḍān in *al-Kātib*, vol. 11, April 1971.
46. 'Abd al-Raḥman al-Rāfi'ī, *Niqābāt al-Ta'āwun al-Zira'īya* (Agricultural Cooperatives) (Cairo, 1914), pp. 159–255.
47. *Ibid.*, p. 208.
48. *Yūbīl Bank Miṣr* (The Jubilee of Bank Misr) (Cairo, 1970), p. 54.
49. *al-Ghurfa al-Tijārīya al-Miṣriya*, vol. 4, no. 1, January 1919, pp. 16–18.
50. *Ibid.*, vol. 3, no. 12, December 1918, pp. 468–72, and vol. 4, no. 2, February 1919, pp. 44–5.
51. Ṭal'at Ḥarb, *Majmū'at Khuṭab*, vol. 3, pp. 246–9.
52. *al-Tayms al-Miṣrī*, 4 May, 1935.
53. No. 277, Lloyd to Chamberlain, 6 May, 1927, PRO FO 371/12388 f. 1353.
54. For a discussion of background conditions favouring the establishment of this bank, see Muḥammad Rushdī, *al-Taṭawwur al-Iqtiṣādī fī Miṣr* (Economic Development in Egypt) (Cairo, 1972), vol. 2, pp. 13 ff. and *Yūbīl Bank Miṣr*, pp. 37 ff.
55. A list of the original subscribers exists in *Yūbīl Bank Miṣr*, pp. 153–4.
56. Maḥmūd Mutawallī, *al-Usūl al-Tā'rikhīya lil-Ra'smālīya al-Miṣrīya wa Taṭawwuriha* (Historical Roots of Egyptian Capitalism and its Development) (Cairo, 1974), p. 179.
57. The nationalist orientations of the bank were elaborated upon in many speeches and press articles. Perhaps the most insightful is Ṭal'at Ḥarb's speech of 8 May, 1920, at the formal opening of the bank. Ṭal'at Ḥarb, *Majmū'at Khuṭab*, vol. 1, pp. 45–63.
58. *al-Akhbār*, 17 May, 1920.
59. *Bulletin Commercial*, 11 April, 1920.
60. Interview with 'Ali Islām and annual reports of Bank Miṣr.
61. *Yūbīl Bank Miṣr*, p. 123.
62. *Saḥīfathal-Tijāra*, vol. 4, no. 2, January 1928, pp. 21–22, and Bank Miṣr, *Taqrir*, 1927.
63. Bank Miṣr, *Taqrīr*, 1920 and 1929.
64. *Annuaire des Juifs d'Égypte et du Proche Orient* (Cairo, 1942), p. 254.
65. I. G. Lévi, 'L'Industrie et l'Avenir Economique de l'Egypte', *L'Egypte Contemporaine*, vol. 18, no. 100, April 1927, p. 361.
66. René Maunier, 'L'Exposition des Industries Egyptiennes', *ibid.*, vol. 7, 1916, pp. 433–43.

67. The activities of the Federation are best followed through its publication, *L'Egypte Industrielle*.

68. Fritz Alleman, 'Aims and Objects of the Alexandria General Produce Association', *Egyptian Cotton Congress*, 1927, pp. 127–30.

69. *Bulletin Commercial*, 27 October, 1918, and Yūsuf Naḥās, *Juhūd*, *passim*, but especially pp. 78–91.

70. Great Britain, Division of Overseas Trade, *Report on the Economic and Financial Situation in Egypt*, April 1922, by E. Homan Mulock, p. 9.

71. Telegram, no. 898, Allenby to Foreign Office, 2 June, 1919, PRO FO 371/3717 f. 24930.

72. E. H. Mulock to Department of Overseas Trade, 10 February, 1921, PRO FO 371/6281.

73. Yūsuf Naḥās, *Juhūd*, pp. 14–16.

74. Yūsuf Naḥās, *Quṭun*, pp. 54–7.

75. A collection of Yūsuf Naḥās's press articles dealing with these subjects may be found in the two books cited in the two previous footnotes.

76. No. 657, Henderson to Chamberlain, 5 November, 1927, PRO FO 371/12391.

77. No. 246, Allenby to Curzon, 26 March, 1921, PRO FO 371/6330.

78. Yūsuf Naḥās, *Quṭun*, p. 75.

79. Great Britain, Department of Overseas Trade, *Report on the Economic and Financial Situation in Egypt*, June 1926, E. H. Mulock, p. 11.

80. Great Britain, Department of Overseas Trade, *Report on the Economic and Financial Situation in Egypt*, July 1931, Turner and Larkin, p. 12.

81. Pilavachi (ed.), *Egyptian Cotton Yearbook*, *1931–32*, pp. 43–50 and *L'Egypte Contemporaine*, vol. 23, no. 135, April 1932.

Bank Misr and the Emergence of the Local Bourgeoisie in Egypt

Marius Deeb

Our conception of the local bourgeoisie differs from that held by many writers on Egypt by being confined to that social class or socio-economic group which sought the protection and the establishment of industrial and financial enterprises as such, and that independently from, and at the expense of, foreign commercial interests. The latter consisted of agents of foreign commercial firms who were opposed to the development of local industry in Egypt. Only Egyptian merchants, whose interests were strongly tied to local industry, are regarded here as members of this bourgeoisie.

The inter-war period is of paramount importance in understanding the emergence of the local bourgeoisie and clarifying some of the misconceptions concerning the role of this bourgeoisie. Contrary to what Abdel-Malek and Girgis claim, the two main groups of the local bourgeoisie, namely, the Bank Misr group and the Association of Industries, were basically at loggerheads with foreign commercial interests such as the British Chamber of Commerce of Egypt, during the 1920s. Both glossed over the important distinction between the role of the Bank Misr group and even that of the local bourgeoisie as a whole, and the foreign commercial interests. Abdel-Malek grouped, unjustifiably, what we have called the local bourgeoisie and the foreign commercial interests into one group or class, namely, the 'upper bourgeoisie'. Girgis used the term 'national bourgeoisie' exclusively with respect to the Wafd.[1] Furthermore, the Bank Misr group tried to act as the nucleus of a national and an independent bourgeoisie in spite of its reliance on large landowners. However, both Abdel-Malek and Girgis underestimated Bank Misr's contribution to the economic ideology of the nationalist movement in Egypt and in particular of the Wafd.

Thus the aim of this article is to trace the emergence of a local bourgeoisie in Egypt as a fully-fledged class by the end of the 1930s. We called it local and not Egyptian because it was predominantly composed of members of the local foreign minorities, although there was also an important Egyptian section, namely, the Bank Misr group. The latter began as the nucleus of a national bourgeoisie, that is, an Egyptian and independent bourgeoisie, whose ideology was embodied in the doctrine of 'economic independence'. The other section of the local bourgeoisie was the Federation of Industries, which was dominated by local foreigners. We shall examine each section separately during the 1920s and 1930s because they had basically different objectives. Nevertheless, we show the factors which led to their eventual coalescence and the consequent formation of a local bourgeoisie, which continued to exist until the early 1960's. Finally, we shall also examine this local bourgeoisie as it emerged by the late 1930s, in relation to other classes in Egypt, such as the landowning classes, the petty bourgeoisie and the working class.

The idea of establishing an Egyptian national bank goes back to the aftermath of the 1907 economic crisis and was discussed in the Egyptian Congress of April–May 1911, which in fact passed a resolution for the formation of a national bank.[2] It was this resolution, probably, which prompted Muhammad Tal'at Ḥarb to publish his book *'Ilaj Misr al-Iqtisadi Aw Mashru' Bank al-Misriyyin Aw Bank al-Umma*, in November 1911.[3] The conditions which prevailed during World War I made the Egyptians realise more than ever the need for such a bank. Foreign banks, Tal'at Ḥarb maintained in 1915, were unable to get the credit on which they depended from abroad, in times of crisis. Consequently, if there were national banks formed with Egyptian capital, they would not need credit from abroad during such crises, for they would be relying primarily on internal funds, which would be available in Egypt.[4] In a prophetic note, Ḥarb thought of the possibility of the project of a national bank materialising after the end of the First World War.[5]

The campaign for the establishment of Bank Misr started on 1 August, 1919, when Tal'at Ḥarb sent a circular to prospective shareholders.[6] On 3 April, 1920, the official decree concerning the establishment of Bank Misr was promulgated, and on 7 May, 1920 the bank was officially inaugurated. Muhammad Tal'at Ḥarb, its founder, conceived of Bank Misr as the necessary prerequisite for the achievement of economic independence, *al-istiqlal al-iqtisadi*. The latter meant that Egypt had to have an independent economic policy which would be supported by a purely Egyptian bank.[7] The National Bank (*al-Bank al-Ahli*) in Egypt was not national, as it was foreign both in capital and in management,[8] and consequently Bank Misr was to be formed to satisfy this need for a national bank. As Bank Misr was supposed to be Egyptian in character, it restricted the buying of its shares to Egyptians only—otherwise it would not have differed from any foreign bank operating in Egypt.[9] To achieve this goal of economic independence, Bank Misr was to 'encourage the various enterprises . . . and assist in the establishment of financial, commercial, industrial, agricultural, transport and insurance companies'. It was also to 'pursue a policy which would give Egypt a say in its economic affairs and defend her interests as other banks defend their countries' interests'.[10] Egyptians, according to Tal'at Ḥarb, did not lack the necessary funds for such projects. Money was available, but it was either hoarded, or deposited in foreign banks or invested in land. Ḥarb, therefore, urged Egyptians to invest in joint-stock companies, to have at least a share in the financial, commercial and industrial sectors of the economy, which were mostly in the hands of foreigners.[11]

Bank Misr was founded in the midst of the economic boom that immediately followed World War I, and it was only with the surplus money accumulated by the two classes which profited from the boom, namely, large landowners and big Egyptian merchants, that the project materialised. In fact, these two classes, and especially large landowners, constituted the bulk of the shareholders, as described by Tal'at Ḥarb, who drew up a list of the names of those who would accept to participate in the project.[12] Large landowners were probably most of the 126 Egyptians, who bought shares amounting to the total of £E80,000.[13]

This reliance on large landowners was reflected, to a certain extent, on the board of directors of the Bank. Out of the ten members of that board, six were either large landowners, like Ahmad Midhat Yaghan, Fu'ad Sultan, 'Abd al-'Azim al-Misri and 'Abbas Basyuni al-Khatib; or associated with land companies, like Yusuf Qattawi, one of the owners of the Société Foncière d'Egypte, and Tal'at Ḥarb, who was working for the latter, and during World War I was charged with organising the estates of large landowners whose confidence he was able to win.[14] Two members were big merchants: 'Abd al-Hamid al-Siyufi and Joseph Cicurel; and the other two, 'Ali Mahir and Iskandar Masiha, were high-ranking officials. During the 1920s there were three new members, 'Abd al-Fattah al-Lawzi, a merchant and owner of a silk factory in Damietta; Ahmad 'Abd al-Wahhab, a high-ranking government official; and Mustafa Mahir, a large landowner and president of the General Agricultural Syndicate. However, Bank Misr's board of directors was not a very representative body, in the sense that there was probably a greater proportion of large landowners as shareholders, who, being first and foremost landowners, did not participate more actively in Bank Misr.

It could be seen from the early annual reports, and throughout the 1920s, that Bank Misr dealt at great length with agricultural problems and in particular with the activities and demands of large landowners. The Report for 1921 covers the major activities of the General Agricultural Syndicate, for the latter's objectives were another brick in the construction of the 'economic edifice'.[25] The 1922 Report reiterated the Syndicate's demand for the formation of a strong joint-stock company whose objectives were to be the prevention of speculation, the decrease in the number of middlemen between cultivators and consumers, the supervision of the trade in the various crops, and which should act as the central organ for agricultural co-operatives.[16] It was on the latter's development on which Egypt would depend for the protection of crops and through which it would, eventually, find a remedy for its agricultural ills; and Bank Misr was willing to assist and give loans to, and even participate in organising agricultural co-operatives.[18] On the other hand, it condemened, as the Agricultural Syndicate did, the sale of cotton *on call*, because it worked against the interests of cultivators.[19]

Bank Misr's reliance upon large landowners was also manifested in the formation of its subsidiary enterprises. During the 1920s, nine new companies were formed or promoted by Bank Misr. The sum total of the initial capital of these companies amounted to £E460,000.[20] Some of the joint-stock companies formed between 1924 and 1927 were: Misr Paper Manufacturing Company (capital £E30,000) and Misr Trading and Cotton Ginning Company (Capital £E30,000), both of which were established in 1924 and had a majority of large landowners as shareholders;[21] Misr Silk Weaving Company (Capital £E10,000), which had three members of al-Lawzi family of merchants (the silk enterprise originally belonged to them), other than members of the board of directors of Bank Misr itself;[22] Misr Fisheries (Capital £E20,000) and Misr Flax Company (Capital £E10,000), which had only large landowners as founding members.[23] Misr Cotton Spinning and Weaving Company deserves special attention, as its initial capital of £E300,000 amounted to almost two-thirds the total initial capital of the Bank Misr subsidiaries in the 1920s. The predominance of large landowners among the founding members was obvious, as at least 87 per cent[24] of the capital was paid up by large landowners such as Muhammad Badrawi 'Ashur, al-Sayyid Badrawi 'Ashur, Muhammad Sha'rawi, Sayyid Khashaba, 'Ali Islam, 'Ali al-Manzalawi and Muhammad Ahmad al-Sharif.[25]

Thus, the Bank Misr group relied primarily on large landowners and therefore was able to finance those subsidiary companies during the 1920s. On the other hand, this reliance on large landowners was in itself a weakness, for when the great economic depression affected the land-owning classes, the Bank Misr group consequently suffered and had to become gradually less and less dependent on landowners as shareholders of its industrial and financial enterprises.

However, in the aftermath of World War I, the Bank Misr group also had strong ties with Egyptian merchants, going back to the first Egyptian chamber of commerce which was established in November 1913. Tal'at Ḥarb and other founding members of Bank Misr were prominent members of this Egyptian Chamber of Commerce. It was on the pages of the latter's journal that Tal'at Ḥarb urged Egyptians, in the summer of 1919, to buy the shares of Bank Misr. Moreover, the Egyptian Chamber of Commerce in Cairo paved the way for the formation of chambers of commerce in the main towns, as it already had branches in the provinces by the end of World War I. In 1919, the Daqahliya Chamber of Commerce was formed in Mansura, the Gharbiya Chamber in Tanta; in 1920 the Cairo Chamber was reorganised; in 1922 Alexandria, Mit Ghamr and Zifta chambers came into being. However, this movement among Egyptian merchants, which flourished in the midst of the wave of nationalist enthusiasm engendered by the 1919 popular uprising, subsided and consequently resulted in the inactivity or even the dissolution of most of these newly-formed chambers, with the notable exception of that of Alexandria.[26]

In June 1924, the Department of Commerce and Industry of the Ministry of Finance issued a circular to the Mudirs of the provinces to urge merchants to set up new chambers of commerce, and chambers were in fact, formed in most of the important towns of the various provinces.[27] In March 1926, a conference of Egyptian chambers of commerce was held, in Cairo, with a view to forming a Federation of the Egyptian chambers of commerce. It was an attempt to foster co-operation among these chambers, so that they would be able to act in unison for the attainment of their objectives, and to encourage the setting up and organisation of new chambers.[28] Tal'at Ḥarb played a conspicuous role in convening this Congress, because he conceived the organisation of Chambers of Commerce and their aims as an integral part of the doctrine of economic independence.

A peculiar feature of these Egyptian chambers of commerce was their weakness, the result of for instance, the small number of merchants who joined them. The basic causes of this phenomenon lay in the very structure of Egyptian commerce itself: the numerical preponderance of small merchants.[29] According to the 1927 commercial census, there were 100,788 establishments, but 53 per cent employed no staff, and 44 per cent employed one to four employees.[30] In 1937, the number of commercial establishments increased to 138,675, out of which 74 per cent employed no staff and 23 per cent employed one to four employees.[31] Another indication in support of this numerical preponderance of petty traders was given for the first time in the 1937 census, namely, the capital invested in commerce: out of the 118,548 commercial establishments with a declared capital, 91,821, i.e. 78 per cent, had a capital of £E1–49.[32]

It goes without saying that small merchants were bedevilled with middlemen, and that the crude and old-fashioned techniques used made them an easy prey for the latter. However, even big Egyptian merchants were not free from the activities of middlemen. Perhaps the most significant characteristic of Egyptian commerce was that the external trade (import-export) was almost entirely in the hands of non-Egyptians.[33] Hence, the activities of purely Egyptian merchants were primarily confined to internal trade. Even in this latter sector of commerce, competition from Greeks, Armenians and Italians residing in Egypt was quite strong.

It was because of this exclusion of Egyptian merchants from playing a significant role in the export-import trade that they pursued a policy of full support of local industry, and very strong ties with the latter were maintained throughout the inter-war period. The development of local industries widened the scope of their activities and enhanced their position *vis-ā-vis* import traders. One significant function of most of the Egyptian chambers of commerce was to hold industrial exhibitions (the Alexandria chamber held a permanent one) to display the various products of local industrialists and craftsmen. One of the major objectives of the Alexandria chamber of commerce, for instance, was to strengthen the ties between merchants and industrialists, to work for the advancement of both sectors and to protect the rights of the two groups.[34] It called for the establishment of various industries, and particularly the weaving industry, so that merchants would find a new market for the cotton bought from cultivators. This was eventually to lead to the liberation of the Egyptian economy from foreign domination.[35] Similarly, in the statute of the proposed Federation of the Chambers of Commerce, the improvement and encouragement of Egyptian industry was put forward as one of the main objectives,[36] and it was reiterated in 1927, after the cotton crisis of 1926, with an emphasis on the establishment of weaving industries to consume part of the cotton crop.[37]

Another important policy pursued by the Egyptian chambers of commerce during the 1920s was the demand for the diversification of agricultural crops. The growing of one major crop, i.e. cotton, had been the cause of the country's maladies. On the other hand, to diversify agricultural crops would have led to the creation of local markets for these products.[38] In 1927, the representatives of the Egyptian chambers of commerce met to examine and recommend remedies for the economic crisis which hit the economy with the fall of cotton prices. The measures recommended were the restriction of cotton acreage to one-fourth the cultivated area for three years, and, simultaneously, the encouragement of the growing of cereals and fruits by decreasing the cost of their production and by increasing railway freight rates and even customs duties on similar imported agricultural products.[39]

The aftermath of World War I also witnessed the formation of the Association des Industries en Egypte in June 1922. The members of this group were mainly local foreign industrialists of such varied nationalities as Belgian, Greek, Italian, French, British, etc. Their ideas were formulated by industrialists such as S. Sornaga, the owner of a building materials factory, and H. Naus, the president of the only sugar refinery in Egypt, and a former member of the Commerce and Industry Commission of 1916, both of whom played an important role in the founding of this Association des Industries.[40]

Three major factors led to the formation of the Association des Industries, or the Federation of Industries, as it came to be known after April 1930. The first factor was the breaking down of the artificial protection which local industry enjoyed during World War I. In other words, foreign competition became rampant and, consequently, the need was felt for the protection of local industry by the means of preferential treatment in matters such as Government adjudications, ordinary freight rates, import tax on raw materials, and semi-manufactured goods used by local industrialists. The second cause was, perhaps, the series of labour strikes which took place immediately after World War I, and which affected most of the major industries. For instance, during the period 1919–21, 81 strikes (67 general and 14 partial strikes) took place.[41] And, thirdly, there was the wave of popular enthusiasm, witnessed by the foundation of Bank Misr in 1920, for the establishment and promotion of industrial undertakings. The main objective of the Federation of Industries, as Article 2 of its Statute stated, was 'to bring together the important industrial establishments so that industrialists will be able to pursue their common interests and study the means for the advancement . . . and if necessary the protection of local industry.[42]

The Federation of Industries represented, from its very inception, big industry. At least seven out of eleven members of the first board of directors represented big enterprises in sugar, cement, salt, clothing, cotton, and mining industries.[43] Moreover, the Federation was predominantly foreign in character, as eight of the eleven members of the board of directors were non-Egyptian. In fact, when the Federation was founded there was only one Egyptian member on the board of directors, and two vacancies were left open for two other Egyptians who would accept to be appointed members of that board.[44]

The Federation of Industries had, in 1925, 90 members, of whom 22·2 per cent were Egyptian. This was less than the share of Egyptians on the board of directors, which was 28·5 per cent. The members had a total capital, in 1925, of more than 30 million, and employed approximately 150,000 workers.[45] By 1930, the membership of the Federation more than doubled, with a total of 226 members, of whom only 15·9 per cent were Egyptians, whilst the Egyptian proportion on the expanded board of directors of twenty-four members was 33·3 per cent.

The Federation of Industries had, during the 1920s, some basic demands such as protective tariffs for local industries against the inflow of imported manufactured goods. Consequently, it demanded a revision of the *ad valorem* system of duties by introducing specific duties on some of the imported articles, especially on those produced in Egypt. The new tariff system was, in fact, implemented in 1930. Some of the other demands which were put into effect were the preferential treatment of local products in Government adjudications, even if imported products were equal in quality and 10 per cent cheaper than those produced locally. This became applicable to certain products during the 1920s, but was adopted as a general principle by the Egyptian Government in July 1930.[46] Customs rebates on machinery, and preferential railway freight rates and even remission on exported products, were granted by the Egyptian Government to certain local industries and certain local products. Finally, the Federation of Industries was much concerned with labour legislation and trade unionism during the 1920s. It criticised as premature attempts made by some members of Parliament to pass labour laws. It also opposed the proposals suggested by the Rida Commission Report on Labour, which was completed in 1929. It was only with the coming into power of Isma'il Sidqi (who was Vice-President of the Federation of Industries) that the Government's labour policies came to be in harmony with those of the Federation.[47]

Although the Bank Misr group and the Federation of Industries were two separate and distinct groups in the twenties, they also had some interests in common, such as preferential treatment of local products in governmental adjudications, the lowering of freight rates for raw materials, etc. Also, as early as 1925, Bank Misr and its enterprises had joined the Federation of Industries, and Tal'at Ḥarb sat on its board of directors. Moreover, Bank Misr had been connected from its earliest stage with continental interests: it had some links with Banco di Roma[48] and its financial consultant was a former employee of Deutsche Orient Bank.[49] Furthermore, the origin of the capital invested in local industry was predominantly continental. Finally, both groups were struggling against foreign commercial interest as represented mainly by the British Chamber of Commerce in Egypt. The latter was accused of obstructing the realisation of the demands of local industrialists. Thus, the ground was furnished for the co-operation between the Bank Misr group and the Federation of Industries.

The second stage in the development of Bank Misr can be said to have started with its report of 1929 on the establishment of new industries and an Egyptian industrial bank for financing them. Bank Misr, from its foundation in 1920, represented the nucleus of a 'national bourgeoisie' which wanted to develop the industrial sector of the economy so that Egypt would not remain a purely agricultural country. 'Egypt with its agriculture only would remain incomplete in its economic formation'.[50] It would continue to depend upon others if its agricultural production was not accompanied by industrial production to increase its national wealth and substitute its own products, manufactured in Egypt, for those imported. Only industry could absorb the increasing number of educated Egyptians, rural immigrants to towns, let alone the increase in the population itself. Moreover, the growth of industry would necessarily lead to the development of commerce and thus open new fields for employment.[51]

The report of 1929 proposed the fields in which industry could be developed, and gave a tenative list of 28 joint-stock companies that could be formed to fill the gap in the industrial sector.[52] It demanded the laying down of a ten years' plan of industrialisation, and the formation of a permanent organisation representing industrialists, the Government, financiers, and others for the examination of industrial projects.[53] The Report took into consideration the difficulties of establishing industries, and was not too ambitious in its objectives. The new industries, according to the report, were to satisfy the real needs of the country and be mainly for domestic consumption; they were not to cost more than similar goods produced in other countries, and the number of factories of a particular industrial product were not to exceed the domestic needs.[54] Moreover, the report recommended the formation of joint-stock companies as the best form of enterprise suited to both future expansion and Egyptianisation.[55]

The demand for the establishment of an Egyptian Industrial Bank was partly an admission of the fact that Bank Misr was not and would not be able to shoulder alone the burden of industrialisation. Bank Misr had, in these circumstances, three options in its industrial policy: first, to induce Egyptians to invest more in industry and commerce—however, the experience of the 1920s did not make this alternative very promising;[56] second, to accept non-Egyptians as shareholders (although keeping the majority of the shares in the hands of Egyptians); third, to seek Government participation in an Egyptian industrial bank. The Report sought the third course as the only plausible alternative for the development of the industrial sector on a 'national' (*qawmi*) basis.[57] The participation of the Government in a national bank would, it was thought, encourage more of the reluctant Egyptians to invest their money in such ventures.[58]

The necessity and urgency of such a project could not, according to the Report, be over-emphasised, as Egypt had lagged behind other countries for several generations in industrial development.[59] Moreover, Egypt was on the eve of adopting a new system of tariffs which was to attract foreign capital and capitalists to establish financial, industrial and commercial enterprises.[60]

The 1929 Report of Bank Misr was important in the sense that its proposals and suggestions were a continuation of the policy of 'economic independence' pursued by Bank Misr. In other words, the ideals of 'economic independence' and the emergence of a viable and developed 'national bourgeoisie' were contingent on the implementation of its programme. However, for this the Government's support was necessary. It is true that Egyptian cabinets were pursuing a favourable policy with respect to local industry. This policy had evolved around three basic principles: first, protective tariffs; secondly, preference being given to local products over foreign ones, even if the cost of the former exceeded that of the latter by up to ten per cent; and thirdly, preferential railway freight rates were given to local industry. However, Bank Misr realised, as was clearly expressed in its 1929 report, that those measures were not sufficient to achieve its objectives. Consequently, it demanded that the Egyptian Government should actually participate in the establishment of an Egyptian industrial bank to foster industrial enterprises. Despite the Egyptian Government's continued support of local industry, it did not take any concrete step to meet these new demands.[61] Thus, the Government's failure to respond to these suggestions forced Bank Misr from the early 1930s on the new course of co-operation with foreign capital, as there was no other alternative to provide sufficient capital for the realisation of its economic programme.

Thus, co-operation between Bank Misr and foreign capital became the feature of its newly formed enterprises during the 1930s. Misr Air Works Company, formed in 1932, had an initial capital of £E20,000, with 40 per cent of the shares held by the British partners.[62] Misr Insurance Company was formed in 1934, in agreement with the British Bowring Company and Assicurazioni Generale di Triesta, and had the majority of shares held by Egyptians.[63] Misr Shipping Company was formed in 1934 with the help of Cox and Kings.[64] Misr Tourism Company was formed in 1934 and had a capital of £E7,000 comprising 1,400 shares, of which 770 were held by Egyptians.[65] This co-operation between the Bank Misr group and foreign capital reached its culmination in the late 1930s. The best illustration of this important development was the formation, in 1938, of the Beida Dyers and the Misr Spinning and Dying of Fine Cotton of Kafr al-Dawar companies, as a partnership between the Bank Misr industrialists and the Bradford Dyers Association.[66] The initial capital of these two companies was £E500,000, of which 50 per cent was held by Bank Misr and other Egyptians.[67]

Another aspect of co-operation between the Bank Misr industrialists and foreign capital was the former's participation in companies dominated by local foreigners. By the late 1930s, one notices that the main founders of Bank Misr, like Muhammad Tal'at Ḥarb, Ahmad Midhat Yaghan, and Fu'ad Sultan were sitting on the boards of 'foreign' companies such as the Alexandria Insurance Company,[68] Rosetta and Alexandria Rice Mills[69] and The Engineering Company of Egypt.[70]

Nevertheless, whenever possible, Bank Misr continued to pursue the policy of establishing purely Egyptian enterprises, as, for instance, Société des Tabacs et Cigarettes (Capital £E40,000), formed in 1937; Société Misr pour l'Industrie et le Commerce des Huiles (Capital £E30,000), and Société des Mines et Carrières (Capital £E40,000), formed in 1939.[77] However, one notices the small capital of these companies in comparison with some of the companies formed in conjunction with foreign capital, such as Misr Spinning and Weaving of Fine Cotton and Beida Dyers.

The qualitative change which began in the early 1930s with the participation of foreign capital in financing even the purely Egyptian enterprises, inevitably had its repercussions on Egyptian Chambers of Commerce. The former urging of Egyptians to participate in industrial and commercial undertakings,[72] and the denouncing of the control over external trade by foreigners,[73] were replaced by a new attitude towards the role of foreign capital, heralding a new phase in the development of industry and commerce, which was to characterise the 1930s. 'It was inevitable that this [foreign] capital would find a meeting point with the Egyptian renaissance to co-operate for their mutual interests, and that the Alexandria Egyptian Chamber of Commerce . . . would provide the atmosphere for the participation of the various interests under the banner of "one Egyptian general interest for all" . . .'[74]

As the purely Egyptian industrialists actively co-operated with the Federation of Industries, the Egyptian Chambers of Commerce followed suit. In fact, with the development of local industry in the 1930s, domestic Egyptian commerce expanded, and thus the ties between Egyptian merchants and local industrialists became stronger. The interdependence of their interests could be seen by the sitting of representatives of the Egyptian Chambers of Commerce on the board of directors of the Federation of Industries, from 1935 onwards.[75]

The Federation of Industries, on the other hand, during the 1930s represented primarily big industry and to a lesser extent medium-sized industry. This is clear from its total membership, which did not exceed by June 1939 more than 427 members. Another indication to this effect was the Federation's conscious effort to differentiate between its interests and those of small industry.[76] It was estimated in the late 1930s that the Federation's members had a capital of approximately £E120 million and employed 250,000 workers.[77] In the period from January 1936 to June 1939 the Federation had 130 new members, an increase of approximately 44 per cent.[78] More significantly more than half of these new members were Egyptian. It seems that the Federation of Industries made special efforts, from the mid-1930s, to attract Egyptian members. In contrast to earlier periods, as shown in the Table, the late 1930s can be regarded as the culmination of the overlapping of interests of purely Egyptian and local foreign elements, and the consequent emergence of a local bourgeoisie.

By January 1939, the Federation of Industries had eleven industrial chambers, seven of which were formed from 1935 onwards. The total membership of these industrial chambers was 243, of which 100, that is 41 per cent, were Egyptians.[79] Moreover, seven of the eleven industrial chambers were presided over by Egyptians.[80] In spite of this apparent Egyptianisation, the Federation of Industries remained predominantly foreign in character. Although 18 out of 41 members (approximately 44 per cent) of the Federation's board of directors in January 1940 were Egyptian,[81] only 117 out of 427 (i.e. 27·4 per cent) of the total membership of the Federation were Egyptian.[82]

Membership of the Federation of Industries

	1925–1930	1930–1936	1936–1939
Increase in total membership	226−90=136	297−226=71	427−297=130
Increase in Egyptian membership	36−20=16	50−36=14	117−50=67
Percentage of new Egyptian members to total new members	11·7	19·7	51·5

Moreover, an examination of the directors of joint-stock companies operating in Egypt would furnish more evidence to the view that the local bourgeoisie was overwhelmingly foreign. In 1931, Egyptian directors of joint-stock companies constituted less than 10 per cent of the total (50 out of 504).[83] In 1937, the proportion of Egyptian directors had increased to 16·4 per cent, that is, 72 out of 496 directors.[84] If we examine these 72 directors, we notice that most of them could not be classified as belonging to the local bourgeoisie as such, because they were appointed by the various joint-stock companies in a conscious effort to include Egyptians. Therefore, most of them were still at this stage high-ranking ex-civil servants or prominent politicians or professionals. The notable exceptions were some members of the Bank Misr group, and others like Ahmad ʻAbbud, Ahmad Farghali, Ismaʻil Sidqi and Muhammad Mahmud Khalil.

Thus, Bank Misr by the late 1930s ceased to be 'national' in character and consequently lost its original *raison d'être*. In other words, the aim of Bank Misr had been to form the nucleus of a 'national' and independent bourgeoisie in Egypt which could have industrialised to a certain extent, and thereby have modified the colonial character of the Egyptian economy. However, by the late 1930s, Bank Misr became an integral part of the

Federation of Industries, which was predominantly constituted of foreign elements. The Federation of Industries favoured in the late 1930s the co-operation between local industrialists and foreign capital. All matters which could obstruct foreign capital from entering into Egypt were to be removed, and co-operation between foreign capital and local industry was to be encouraged. The protagonists of this co-operation pointed to the benefits which could be obtained in terms of greater tax revenue and more opportunity for employment for Egyptian workers.[85] Foreigners who brought their capital into Egypt during the 1930s and invested it in industry made a great contribution, according to the Federation of Industries, to the nascent industry in Egypt.[86] As Sidqi argued in the 1940s, from an economic point of view, a foreign industrialist who worked for the benefit of the country and the national interest of Egypt ceased to be a foreigner.[87]

The change which took place in the role of Bank Misr reached its culmination in the Bank Misr crisis of 1939. It is not clear how this crisis started. The Bank was not able to meet its obligations as depositors began to withdraw their money in the early summer of 1939. Tal'at Ḥarb, however, insisted that the Bank needed no assistance from the Government, until it was realised, by late August 1939, that Bank Misr was undergoing a real crisis. The basic causes of this crisis were: the generous credits given to large landowners, coupled with the mortgage debts legislation in their favour, as well as the Bank's policy of participation in its industrial subsidiaries. Consequently, the Government stepped in to help the Bank, put pressure on Tal'at Ḥarb to resign, and appointed Hafiz 'Afifi to replace him.[88] This was of great significance, as 'Afifi believed that Bank Misr should be merely a credit bank and should cease to foster the establishment of new industrial enterprises.[89] This was in sharp contrast to its avowed objectives which had been formulated by its founder, Tal'at Ḥarb, in 1920. Moreover, 'Afifi was not a protagonist of a 'national' and independent bourgeoisie, as he served, almost uninterruptedly, on the board of the British National Bank of Egypt from 1934, and he welcomed, as did other members of the local bourgeoisie, foreign capitalists who invested in Egypt. He believed that would lead to the employment of more Egyptian workers whose wages would be much higher than the wages of those employed in agriculture.[90]

This new local bourgeoisie suffered from social and political timidity which was, perhaps, rooted in its predominantly foreign character. On the whole it was on the defensive, as no taxes were levied on financial, commercial, and industrial establishments until 1939, due to the existence of the system of Capitulations.[91] It was attacked in the parliamentary debates on Law No. 14 of 1939, concerning the taxation of profits, salaries and wages. Large landowners and even members of the urban middle class argued that it was high time for financiers, industrialists, and merchants to pay taxes, as the burden had hitherto been borne by the landowning classes.[92] The timidity of this class was also rooted, perhaps, in the fear of rising trade union consciousness among the workers. Combating labour legislation in general occupied the Federation of Industries throughout the inter-war period. The local bourgeoisie demanded gradualism in labour legislation, as industry was still in its formative years and, consequently, labour laws would weigh heavily on it. Moreover, the local bourgeoisie feared that some restrictions would be made on the employment of women and children, as they constituted cheaper labour during the 1930s.

The local bourgeoisie was more contented with non-Wafdist regimes or cabinets, because those were less amenable to workers' demands. The Wafd had always had a strong following among the working class, and trade union leaders were Wafdists, and consequently had a greater influence on Wafdist Cabinets than on non-Wafdist ones. The Federation of Industries was particularly satisfied with the Palace-Sidqi regime of 1930–33, as it complied with their wishes, whether on labour legislation or in undermining the trade union movement.

Because of its fundamental weakness as a predominantly foreign class, the local bourgeoisie shied away from directly attacking Cabinets or members of Parliament who advocated labour legislation and official recognition of trade unions. They merely demanded the application of those laws on industrial and agricultural workers, so as to get the support of the landowning classes who did not want agricultural labourers to associate themselves with trade unions and syndicates. These attempts to link the fate of industrial workers and agricultural labourers were made in order to prevent labour legislation as such, and to appeal to the landowning classes by causing them to have apprehensions concerning the harmful effect of such legislation on agricultural labourers. The local bourgeoisie did not need to raise the wages of industrial workers to attract labourers to town, because their wages were already much higher than those of agricultural workers. In fact, the increase in population and the economic depression of the 1930s made labour abundant in towns, and the Government had to take measures to curtail the immigration.[93]

Furthermore, as the local bourgeoisie represented big and medium-sized industries, its interests were in opposition to those of the Egyptian petty bourgeoisie. For instance, the Federation of Industries urged the Ministry of Commerce and Industry to confine its encouragement of small industries to those products which were not manufactured by big industry, especially with respect to weaving, as it would otherwise expose small industries to competition from big ones.[94] Moreover, it claimed that taxation could not be levied equally on big and small industry, as in the former's case it could be enforced effectively, while in the latter's case it would be difficult to do so. Thus, taxation would be favourable to small industry and would enable it to compete with big industry, because of the former's work conditions, let alone fraudulence and other forms of illegitimate competition.[95]

The local bourgeoisie's attitude towards the landowning classes was of paramount importance. Leading members of the local bourgeoisie demanded an amelioration of the condition of the fellah, for instance, the improvement in his housing conditions on *'izab* (landowners' estates), where the number of agricultural labourers exceeded one million, and the exemption of small and poor landowners from paying land taxes.[96] Undoubtedly, the low standard of living of the peasant class worked against the expansion of the domestic market by limiting the purchasing power of the fellah, a fact which was of great concern to the local bourgeoisie. Instead of assisting the peasant class, the Egyptian Government's only help was given to a very small number of land-owners, namely, the large landowners, who were the main beneficiaries of the mortgage debts legislation in Egypt.[97] Bank Misr criticised the mortgage debts legislation, demanding that the creditor and the debtor should be left alone to reach an agreement between themselves, and hoping that no more laws would be enacted to intervene in this relationship.[98]

EPILOGUE

The failure of the Bank Misr group to act as a 'national' and independent bourgeoisie by the late 1930s did not mean that the doctrine of 'economic independence' became obsolete. If it ceased to inspire the Bank Misr group or the Egyptian members of the local bourgeoisie, there still remained a group of Egyptians who continued to adhere to this doctrine, among them a prominent member of the Cairo Chamber of Commerce, 'Abd al-Majid al-Ramali. He expressed apprehension about the attempts that were made by foreign capitalists to establish industrial enterprises in Egypt. This inflow of capital, he believed, was to be stopped even by resorting to legislation, otherwise it would result in a neocolonial or new economic dependency.[9] In this attitude, al-Ramali was voicing the opinion of the Egyptian urban middle class or 'effendiya' and the Egyptian petty bourgeoisie. Many members of the urban middle class were unemployed by the late 1930s, as the industrial and commercial enterprises which were dominated by local foreigners tended to employ members of their own communities. Thus, the full co-operation between purely Egyptian and local foreign elements of the local bourgeoisie was not accompanied by a similar co-operation between the Egyptian urban middle class and the petty bourgeoisie and their local foreign counterparts. On the contrary, they remained at loggerheads, and perhaps the antagonism at those levels even increased.[100]

Although the Bank Misr group failed to achieve its goals of economic independence and the formation of a 'national bourgeoisie', these ideals continued to be pursued by this petty bourgeoisie and by the Egyptian 'effendiya', who launched a campaign against this predominantly foreign local bourgeoisie and demanded the use of the Arabic language in commercial affairs. This was an attempt to Egyptianise the bourgeoisie and create employment opportunities for Egyptians in the foreign-dominated industrial and commercial enterprises operating in Egypt.[101] It was regarded by those Egyptians as part and parcel of an 'economic nationalism' which was never realised either by the pioneering projects of Tal'at Ḥarb and the Bank Misr group or by the abolition of the capitulary system in 1937.

A major achievement in this struggle of the Egyptian 'effendiya' and petty bourgeoisie to 'Egyptianise' the local bourgeoisie was the joint-stock companies law of 1947, which stipulated that 51 per cent of the capital, 40 per cent of the board of directors, 75 per cent of the employees and 90 per cent of the workers of joint-stock companies should be Egyptian.[102] This law was critised by the local bourgeoisie on the grounds that it would discourage foreign capital investment in Egypt, badly needed by the country, and that it did not take into consideration the 'acquired rights' of local foreign elements who had faithfully participated in the economic development of Egypt.[103]

NOTES

1. Anouar Abdel-Malek, *Egypt: Military Society* (New York, 1968), pp. 10–12; Fawzi, Girgis, *Dirasat fi Tarikh Misr al-Siyasi Mundhu al-'Asr al-Mamluki;* (Cairo, 1958), pp. 139–41.
2. *Minutes of the Proceeding of the First Egyptian Congress* (Alexandria, 1911), pp. 295–6; Muhammad Tal'at Ḥarb, *Majmu'at Khutab*, vol. I (Cairo, 1927), p. 130.
3. Ibrahim 'Abdu and 'Ali 'Abd al-'Azim, *Tidhkar Muhammad Tal'at Ḥarb* (Cairo, 1945), p. 57.
4. *Majallat al-Ghurfa al-Tijariya al-Misriya*, vol. I, nos. 10, 11, 12. January–March 1915, p. 433.
5. *Ibid.*, p. 434.
6. *Ibid.*, vol. IV, no. 9, September 1919, pp. 274–6.
7. Muhammad Tal'at Ḥarb, *Majmu'at Khutab*, vol. I, p. 50.
8. *Ibid.*, p. 51.
9. *Ibid.*, p. 49.
10. *Ibid.*, p. 57.
11. *Ibid.*, pp. 46, 59–60.
12. *Ruz-al-Yusuf*, no. 593, 22 July, 1939, p. 27. He encountered difficulties in convincing some of them that investing in a bank is not a form of usury (*riba*), which was contrary to their beliefs. *Ibid.*, p. 28.
13. Ibrahim 'Abdu and 'Ali 'Abd al-'Azim, p. 51; *Ruz-al-Yusuf*, no. 593, 22 July, 1939, p. 29.
14. *Al-Musawwar*, no. 793, 22 December, 1939, p. 4.
15. Bank Misr, *A'mal al-Jam'iya al-'Umumiya al-I'tiyadiya*, held on 31 March, 1923 (Cairo, 1924), pp. 9–10.
16. Bank Misr, *A'mal al-Jam'iya al-'Umumiya al-I'tiyadiya*, held on 25 March, 1922 (Cairo, n.d.), pp. 16–17.
17. Bank Misr, *A'mal al-Jam'iya al-'Umumiya al-I'tiyadiya*, held on 14 March, 1926 (Cairo, n.d.), p. 9.
18. Bank Misr, *A'mal al-Jam'iya al-'Umumiya al-I'tiyadiya*, held on 20 March, 1927 (Cairo, n.d.), p. 10.
19. Bank Misr, *A'mal al-Jam'iya al-'Umumiya al-'Adiya*, held on 18 March, 1928 (Cairo, n.d.), pp. 13–14.
20. Bank Misr, *Insha' al-Sina'at al-Ahliya wa Tanzim al-Taslif al-Sina'i, Mashru' Bank Sina'i Misri* (Cairo, 1929), p. 6.
21. *Mulhaq al-Waqa'i' al-Misriya*, no. 34, April 10, 1924, p. 2; *Mulhaq al-Waqa'i' al-Misriya*, no. 96, 6 November, 1924, p.2.
22. *Sahifat al-Tijara wal-Sina'a*, vol. IV, no. 2, January 1928, pp. 25–6.
23. *Ibid.*, pp. 27–8, 30.

24. Excluding the portion of the capital paid by Bank Misr, its subsidiary companies and the members of its board of directors, which amounted to 56·6 per cent of the total capital. *Ibid.*, pp. 25–6.

25. The two Badrawi 'Ashurs held 25,000 shares, that is £E100,000. *Ibid.*

26. *Sahifat al-Tijara wal-Sina'a*, vol. I, no. 3, April 1925, p. 35.

27. *Ibid.*, p. 36.

28. *Al-Mu'tamar al-'Am lil-Ghuraf al-Tijariya al-Misriya bil-Qahira* (Cairo, n.d.) pp. 3–4.

29. *Al-Balagh al-Usbu'i*, no. 39, 19 August 1927, p. 23.

30. *Egypt*, *Industrial and Commercial Census*, *1927*, (Cairo, 1931) pp. 234–5, 276–7.

31. *Egypt*, *Industrial and Commercial Census*, *1937*, (Cairo, 1942) pp. 502–3, 558.

32. *Ibid.*, pp. LXI, 736–7.

33. *Taqrir al-Ghurfa al-Tijariya al-Misriya bil-Iskandariya*, for the year 1924–25 (Alexandria, n.d.), p. 13; *Al-Balagh al-Usbu'i*, no. 39, 19 August, 1927, p. 22; *Sahifat al-Tijara wal-Sina'a*, vol. V, no. 1, October 1928, pp. 82–4. In 1924, the Alexandria Chamber of Commerce had only ten members out of one hundred full members, i.e. 10 per cent engaged in some form of import-export trade, and three out of these ten were non-Egyptian. See *Taqrir al-Ghurfa al-Tijariya al-Misriya bil-Iskandariya*, for the year 1923–24 (Alexandria, n.d.).

34. *Taqrir al-Ghurfa al-Tijariya al-Misriya li-Madinat al-Iskandariya*, for the year 1922–3, (Alexandria, n.d.) p. 16.

35. *Taqrir al-Ghurfa al-Tijariya etc.* (Alexandria), for the year 1923–4, p. 8.

36. *Al-Mu'tamar al-'Am lil-Ghuraf al-Tijariya al-Misriya bil-Qahira*, pp. 3–4.

34. *Taqrir al-Ghurfa al-Tijariya al-Misriya li-Madinat al-Iskandariya*, for the year 1922–23 (Alexandria, n.d.) p. 16.

35. *Taqrir al-Ghurfa aliTijariya etc.* (Alexandria), for the year 1923–24, p. 8.

36. *Al-Mu'tamar al-'Am lil-Ghuraf al-Tijariya al-Misriya bil-Qahira*, pp. 3–4.

37. *Taqrir al-Ghurfa al-Tijariya lil-Qahira, 1926–1927* (Cairo, 1927), pp. 21–2.

38. *Taqrir al-Ghurfa al-Tijariya etc.* (Alexandria), for the year 1923–24, p. 20. The excessive concern of the General Agricultural Syndicate with cotton hindered co-operation between the Alexandria Chamber and the Syndicate. *Taqrir al-Ghurfa al-Tijariya etc.* (Alexandria), for the year 1922–23, p. 24.

39. *Taqrir al-Ghurfa al-Tijariya etc.* (Cairo,) for the year 1926–27, pp. 21–2.

40. *Taqrir Lajnat al-Tijara wal-Sina'a* (Cairo, 1925), pp. 2, 194–5. For the ideas of S. Sornaga on industrialisation, see E. R. J. Owen, *Cotton and the Egyptian Economy* (Oxford, 1969), pp. 349–50. *Misr al-Sina'iya*, vol. I, no. 1, (1925), p. 19.

41. F.O. 141/779/9321/106. This factor was regarded by the Egyptian Chamber of Commerce of Alexandria as being the sole cause. See *Taqrir al-Ghurfa al-Tijariya* etc., for the year 1922–23 (Alexandria), p. 17.

42. *Misr al-Sina'iya*, vol. I, no. 1 (1925), p. 15.

43. For instance, Henri Naus was the chairman of the board of the Société Generale des Sucreries; Ernest Trembley, a director of the Société Anonyme des Ciments d'Egypte; A. J. Lowe, a director of the United Egyptian Salt Ltd.; C. W. Crompton, a director of the Filature Nationale d'Egypte, and J. B. Montaner, a director of the Société Egyptienne des Industries Minérales. *Ibid.*, p. 16.

44. *Al-Muqattam*, 9 June, 1922, p. 6.

45. *Misr al-Sina'iya*, vol. I, no. 1 (1925), p. 19.

46. *Sahifat al-Tijara wal-Sina'a*, vol. VI, no. 6, August 1930, pp. 125–6.

47. *Misr al-Sina'iya*, vol. VII, Nos. 2–3 (1932), p. 20.

48. F.O. 371/1553/431/16. 17 January, 1921.

49. F.O. 141/560/1094/2/30.

50. Bank Misr, *Insha' al-Sina'at al-Ahliya etc.*, p. 200.

51. *Ibid.*

52. *Ibid.*, pp. 200–1.

53. *Ibid.*, pp. 62–3.

54. *Ibid.*, pp. 67–8.

55. *Ibid.*, pp. 61–2.

56. Due to the fact that Egyptians preferred to invest their money in land and buildings rather than in companies. *Ibid.*, pp. 212–13.

57. *Ibid.*, p. 211.

58. *Ibid.*, p. 272.

59. *Ibid.*, p. 206.

60. *Ibid.*, pp. 208–9.

61. It was believed by some at the time, 'that the proposed formation of an Industrial Bank . . . [was] receiving careful and sympathetic consideration by the Government'. F.O. 141/624/19990/2.

62. *Sahifat al-Tijara wal-Sina'a*, vol. VIII, no. 6, June 1932, p. 959; *Bank Misr*, *A'mal al-Jam'iya al-'Umumiya al-'Adiya*, held on 27 March, 1932 (Caiιo, n.d.), pp. 19–20.

63. A. A. E. El-Gritly, 'The Structure of Modern Industry in Egypt', *L'Egypte Contemporaine*, vol. XXVIII, nos. 241–2, November 1947, pp. 435–6; Bank Misr, *A'mal al-Jam'iya al-'Umumiya al-'Adiya*, held on 24 March, 1934 (Cairo, n.d.), p. 20.

64. El-Gritly, pp. 435–6.

65. *Sahifat al-Tijara wal-Sina'a*, vol. XI, no. 2, February 1935, p. 475.

66. *The British Chamber of Commerce of Egypt*, vol. XXV, no. 2, February 1939, p. 23.

67. Bank Misr, *Taqrir Majlis al-Idara 'an Sanat 1937* (Cairo, 1938), p. 27.

68. Ḥarb was a member of the board of directors. E. I. Politi (ed.), *Annuaire des Sociétés Egyptiennes par Actions* (Alexandria, 1930), p. 316; E. I. Politi (ed.), *Annuaire des Sociétés Egyptiennes par Actions* (Alexandria, 1932), p. 351; E. I. Politi (ed.), *Annuaire des Sociétés Egyptiennes par Actions* (Alexandria, 1937), p. 128.

69. Both Ḥarb and Sultan were members of its board. *Ibid.*, pp. 128, 147.

70. Sultan was the president of the board of directors. *Ibid.*, p. 147. Yaghan was vice-president of Société Foncière d'Egypte (local Jewish capital) and Ḥarb and Sultan were members of its board. *Ibid.*, p. 151. Ḥarb was also member of Société Anonyme du Wadi Kom-Ombo (mainly Jewish capital) and of the Crédit Foncier Egyptien (French capital). Ḥarb's connection with the first two companies was earlier than the foundation of Bank Misr. He resigned from Kom-Ombo in 1936, but kept his membership in the Société Foncière till the end of his career in 1939. Muhammad Tal'at Ḥarb, *Majmu'at Khutab Tal'at Ḥarb*, vol. III (Cairo, n.d.), pp. 80–1.

71. *The British Chamber of Commerce of Egypt*, vol. XXV, no. 3, March 1938, p. 43; *ibid.*, vol. XXVI, no. 2, February 1939, pp. 23, 25.

72. *Taqrir al-Ghurfa etc.* (Alexandria), for the year 1924–25, p. 44; *Taqrir al-Ghurfa al-Tijariya al-Misriya li Madinat al-Iskandariya*, for the year 1925–26 (Alexandria, n.d.), p. 69.

73. *Taqrir al-Ghurfa etc.* (Alexandria), for the year 1924–25, p. 13.

74. *Taqrir al-Ghurfa al-Tijariya al-Misriya li-Madinat al-Iskandariya*, for the year 1931–32 (Alexandria, 1933), p. 69.

75. *Misr al-Sina'iya*, vol. XI, no. 16, 15 December, 1935, p. 5.

76. See below, pp. 30–1.

77. G. H. Selous, *Report on Economic and Commercial Conditions in Egypt* (London, 1937), p. 89.

78. *Misr al-Sina'iya*, vol. XII, no. 1, 1 January, 1936, pp. 21–33; *ibid.*, vol. XV, no. 12, 15 June, 1939, pp. 25–35.

79. *Misr al-Sina'iya*, vol. XV, no. 1, 1 January, 1939, pp. 4–10, 13–15.

80. *Ibid.*

81. *Ibid.*, vol. XVI, no. 1, 1 January, 1940, p. 3.

82. See Table.

83. E. I. Politi (ed.), *Annuaire des Sociétés Egyptiennes par Actions* (Alexandria, 1931), *passim.*

84. Politi, *Annuaire etc.*, 1937, pp. 111–52.

85. *Misr al-Sina'iya*, vol. XV, no. 5, 1 March, 1939, p. 6.

86. *Ibid.*, vol. XVII, no. 3, March 1941, pp. 9–18.

87. 'Siyasat Misr al-Sina'iya Lima Ba'd al-Harb', *Majallat Ghurfat al-Qahira*, vol. X, no. 5, May 1945, p. 421.

88. Bank Misr, *Qanun Raqm 40 Li-Sanat 1941 Khas bi-Tadakhkhul al-Hukumat*

Li-Da'm Bank Misr, Cairo, 1942, pp. 3–4; Muhammad Husain Haikal, *Mudhakkirat fi al-Siyasa al-Misriya*, vol. II (Cairo, 1953), pp. 167–8.

89. Hafiz 'Afifi, *Bank Misr* (Cairo, 1941), p. 6.

90. *Idem.*, *Misr wal-Taharrur min-al-'Awz wal-Faqr* (Cairo, 1944), p. 10.

91. *Cf.* Issawi, *Egypt: an Economic and Social Analysis*, pp. 150–1. In fact, the law was promulgated on 26 January, 1939, but was retroactively in effect from September, 1938. Majlis al-Shuyukh, *Qanun Raqm 14 Li-Sanat 1939* (Cairo, 1939), pp. 247, 350.

92. *Ibid.*, pp. 222–3, 226.

93. *Misr al-Sina'iya*, vol. XII, no. 1, 1 January, 1936, p. 11. In fact, the Government took strict measures, especially in the early 1930's, against the unemployed rural immigrants to urban centres, whom they regarded as vagrants, by physically transferring them back to their villages, thus trying to alleviate the increasing number of unemployed in Cairo and Alexandria in particular.

94. *Ibid.*, vol. XIV, no. 2, 15 January, 1938, p. 13.

95. *Ibid.*, No. 6, 15 March, 1938, p. 21.

96. Hafiz 'Afifi, *Misr wal-Taharrur min al-'Awz wal-Faqr*, p. 11; *Idem.*, *'Ala Hamish al-Siyasa* (Cairo, 1938), pp. 156–61.

97. *Ibid.*

98. Bank Misr, *Taqrir Majlis al-Idara 'an Sanat 1938* (Cairo, 1939), p. 13.

99. *Majallat Ghurfat al-Qahira*, vol. II, no. 8, October 1937, pp. 9–10, *Ibid.*, vol. III, no. 4, April 1938, pp. 10–11.

100. See, for instance, *Majallat Ghurfat al-Iskandariya*, vol. XIII, no. 148, January 1949, p. 31.

101. *Majallat Ghurfat al-Qahira*, vol. V, no. 6, June 1940, p. 544.

102. *Majallat Ghurfat al-Qahira*, vol. XII, no. 10, December 1947, pp. 1225–6.

103. *Misr al-Sina'iya*, vol. XXIII, no. 4, April 1947, p. 10.

Soviet Central Asia: Economic Progress and Problems

Francis Newton

During the past sixty years the region comprising the four Soviet republics of Central Asia and that of Kazakhstan has undergone an economic transformation. With considerable justification, the Soviet regime claims that these republics now enjoy a level of material well-being which most Third World countries would envy. It glosses over, however, the gap between original goals and attainment, and also some of the means by which rapid economic progress has been achieved. And lest doubt should be cast on the infallibility of scientific socialism (the regime's sole source of legitimacy), it likewise plays down the inevitable economic difficulties and problems which arise under any regime.

The purpose of the present article is to provide a review of economic progress and problems in the five republics, based on a careful reading of the voluminous internal press, which differs in many respects from the Soviet material designed for foreign consumption. It begins with a brief summary of economic development under Tsarist rule, of the great changes under the Soviet regime, and of the nature of the economies of the individual republics.[1] This is followed by an account of the results of the recently completed 9th Five-Year Plan, of the provisional targets of the 10th Five-Year Plan and of current economic problems. Finally, some remarks are ventured on whether the indigenous peoples are really as grateful to their 'Russian elder brother' for their material progress as Soviet publications would have us believe, and whether economic grievances, where they exist, may contribute to the growth of republican national feeling.

ECONOMIC DEVELOPMENT UNDER THE TSARIST AND SOVIET REGIMES

The five republics cover an area greater than that of India but, as they consist largely of arid steppe, desert and high mountains, their population even today is only some 38 million. The traditional activities before the Russian annexation in the eighteenth and nineteenth centuries were irrigated agriculture, handicrafts and trade, which had been carried on for centuries in the large fertile oases by the Tadzhiks and Uzbeks; and nomadic or semi-nomadic pastoralism (sheep, horses and camels) in the steppe (Kazakhs), desert (Turkmens and Uzbeks) and mountains (Kirgiz).

Apart from establishing orderly government in the area and thus creating conditions which favoured economic activity, Tsarist rule brought four important economic changes. Firstly, Russian manufacturers obtained a monopoly of the Central Asian market, trade increased, and local handicrafts declined. Secondly, Russia acquired its own cotton base; the Tsarist government encouraged the growing of cotton, improved American strains were introduced, some irrigation works were undertaken, and cotton acreages and output increased dramatically. Thirdly, the rudiments of industry, in the shape of small primary processing and extractive undertakings, were established, and the foundations of a modern communications system were laid, with the building of railways and telegraph lines. Finally, extensive Russian colonisation took place, and with it the introduction of arable farming and the creation of the first towns in the Kazakh steppe. By the time of the Russian revolution in 1917 there were some two million settlers, mainly in the Kazakh steppe, where their cultivation of traditional grazing lands seriously interfered with the Kazakhs' nomadic economy. In Turkestan, where there was virtually no spare cultivable land available, the settlers found employment on the railways and as white collar and skilled workers in industry. When the Soviet regime took over, therefore, although the indigenous peoples remained backward, the very first steps towards modernisation had been taken, and two features which persist today were already well in evidence, namely, the specialisation of the area in the cultivation of cotton and the presence of a large European settler population.

After the Bolsheviks came to power they nationalised industry and the land. Later, after the country had recovered from the economic chaos of the revolution and civil war, they collectivised agriculture and introduced a planned socialist economy. It is not the place here to argue the merits or demerits of the latter, but when considering the economies of the Central Asian republics it needs to be borne in mind that, although the constituent republics of the Soviet Union are nominally sovereign, their economies are treated as integral parts of the Soviet economy and all economic activity is closely regulated by Moscow. It is Moscow which decides what shall be produced where, determines the allocation of resources as well as prices and wages, and disposes of the republics' output as it sees fit. Its decisions may, of course, be in the republics' best interests. The less-developed republics, and notably the Central Asian and Kazakhstan, have almost certainly enjoyed a higher level of investment than they could have generated from their own resources. But the fact remains that the republics cannot develop their economies as they might choose, and Moscow's directives sometimes run directly counter to local wishes. In the pre-war period, for instance, the Uzbeks were strongly opposed to the further expansion of cotton-growing at the expense of grain, which increased their dependence on the rest of the country for grain supplies, and a dislike of what they regard as the excessive specialisation of their economy in cotton evidently persists. Similarly, the largely pastoral Kazakhs opposed the ploughing up of the virgin lands in the north of their republic in the 1950s and the accompanying renewed influx of Russian settlers.

In respect of the non-Russian republics, the Soviet regime started out with the declared aim of putting an end to Tsarist colonial exploitation. No longer were they to be merely raw material appendages of the metropolis. Industry was to be taken to the sources of raw materials and the consumer, indigenous working classes created, and the economic and cultural inequality of the less-developed peoples eliminated. In practice, limits were inevitably set in the realisation of this policy by (a) local natural resources, (b) the availability of investment funds, and (c) the overriding interest of the metropolis in raw materials for European Russian industries.

Broadly speaking, Kazakhstan has enjoyed a consistently high rate of investment on account of its valuable mineral deposits, but the same is not true of Central Asia. With the exception of Kirgizia's mercury and antimony, the area was not at first known to possess mineral resources of all-Union significance, and in the pre-war period, with capital short, industrialisation was symbolised mainly by the construction of a giant textile mill and an agricultural machinery plant in Tashkent, both initially manned almost entirely by Russians. However, the Soviet Union's desire to be self-sufficient in cotton ensured favoured treatment for Central Asian agriculture. An impetus was given to industrialisation by the wartime evacuation of factories from European Russia; but in the immediate post-war period, priority had to be given to restoring the devastated areas in European Russia, and it was only from the late 1950s that Central Asia enjoyed an above-average rate of capital investment. Development was then greatly assisted by the discovery of natural gas, which much improved the fuel and power situation, and other valuable mineral deposits. Manufacturing industry was developed, massive irrigation works put in hand, and construction started on the first major hydro-electric schemes designed both to produce electricity and to regulate the flow of rivers for irrigation purposes.

All the republics now have a mixed industrial-agricultural economy, but on the whole their manufacturing industry tends to be of local significance, and it is their extractive and primary processing industries and agricultural output which are important in the context of the Soviet Union as a whole. Kazakhstan, the largest and best-endowed of the republics from the point of view of mineral wealth, is a major producer of coal (Karaganda and Ekibastuz), oil and natural gas (the Mangyshlak peninsula), iron ore (Rudnyy and Lisakovsk), copper (Balkhash and Dzhezkazgan), and phosphates (Karatau), and it contains the Soviet Union's most important lead and zinc mines (Eastern Kazakhstan and the Chimkent area) and high-grade chromium deposits.[2] Large quantities of coking coal and iron ore are sent to the Urals, while an important iron and steel industry had been developed in the Karaganda area. In and around Pavlodar, a major industrial complex comprising giant power stations, which will transmit electricity to European Russia, and aluminium, tractor and ferro-alloy plants are being created on the basis of cheap Ekibastuz coal. Manufacturing industry includes agricultural and mining machinery and chemicals, as well as light and food. The ploughing up of the virgin lands in the mid 1950s turned the republic into a sizeable contributor to the Soviet 'bread basket', while cotton and rice are produced on irrigated land in the south. Sheep farming still remains an important activity, with Kazakhstan accounting for nearly one quarter of Soviet wool production.

The most important sector in Uzbekistan's economy is the cultivation of cotton and a series of related industries (cotton ginning, cotton-seed oil, cotton textiles, agricultural, irrigation and textile machinery, and fertilisers). The republic is one of the Soviet Union's major producers of gold, copper, lead and zinc, molybdenum and tungsten, and it accounts for one seventh of the country's natural gas output. The lion's share of the latter is piped to European Russia and the Urals, but it also fuels a series of local power stations and supports a local chemical industry. Agricultural production, apart from cotton, includes rice, karakul skins, silk cocoons, and kenaf.

The contribution of the three smaller republics to the Soviet economy is, on the whole, less significant, though Kirgizia is the Soviet Union's principal producer of antimony and mercury, and one of its main sources of uranium ore, and Turkmenistan's rapidly developing natural gas industry has now overtaken that of Uzbekistan. Kirgizia has coal mines, and a major hydro-electric power station, the 1·2 million kilowatt Toktogul, is nearing completion on the Naryn river in the Tyan'-Shan'. Manufacturing industry is concentrated in the north of the republic, where most of the non-Asian settlers live. Sheep-breeding remains the most important sector of agriculture, and crops include cotton in the south and sugar beet and tobacco in the north. In southern Tadzhikistan, a major industrial complex is being developed on the basis of cheap power from the 2·7 million kilowatt Nurek hydro-electric power station currently under construction on the Vakhsh. It includes an aluminium plant at Regar, the first shop of which is already in operation, and an electrochemical complex. The republic's other industries are mainly light and food with some extractive, but the known mineral resources are often in inaccessible areas. Tadzhikistan produces a major share of the Soviet Union's fine-staple cotton, but in the last decade it has lost its place as the second largest producer of cotton in general to Turkmenistan, where the irrigated area has been substantially increased as a result of the construction of the Karakum canal. Turkmenistan's oil industry, which dates back to Tsarist times, is the only one of any size in the four Central Asian republics proper, but it has been overshadowed by the discovery of a number of major natural gas deposits in the desert in the 1960s. Turkmenistan also produces karakul skins and various chemical salts.

Although it has had its vicissitudes, cotton cultivation has been one of the successes of the Soviet regime in Central Asia, a success that stands out all the more against the generally dismal Soviet agricultural record. The regime's initial aim of becoming independent of imports was achieved in 1932, and the Soviet Union, with an annual crop in the region of eight million tons a year, 94 per cent of which comes from Central Asia, is now the largest producer in the world ahead of the USA, and cotton fibre is an important export. The size of the cotton crop has risen as a result of both higher yields and an increase in the irrigated area, which totalled

6,950,000 hectares in Kazakhstan and Central Asia in 1975. Irrigation works have been and are being carried out on a massive scale and include over 800 km. of the Karakum canal, which will eventually link the Amudar'ya (Oxus) and the Caspian, and in recent years, with power more plentiful, a number of large pump-operated schemes.

The economic achievements have, therefore, been very real. At the same time, it has to be pointed out that the Central Asian republics and, to a lesser extent, Kazakhstan still remain less developed than the Soviet Union as a whole, and the regime's goal of bringing them up to the level of European Russia has still not been realised. In fact, the increase in gross industrial output since 1913 (Table 1) has been proportionately lower than average in Uzbekistan, Tadzhikistan and Turkmenistan, and on a *per capita* basis in Kirgizia as well; and *per capita* national income

TABLE 1

Rate of Growth of Total Volume of Industrial Output 1913–74

	Output in 1974		*Per capita* output in 1974
	1913=1	1940=1	1913=1
USSR	122	16	77·2
Kazakh SSR	196	25	78·7
Uzbek SSR	56	12	18·2
excluding output of cotton ginneries	113		36·8
Kirgiz SSR	265	27	71·0
Tadzhik SSR	111	13	34·9
Turkmen SSR	62	9	26·6
excluding output of cotton ginneries	69		29·6

Sources: *Narodnoye khozyaystvo SSSR v 1974 g.*, Moscow, 1975, pp. 176 and 177; and calculations based on population figures for 1913 and 1 January, 1974 from census results and statistical yearbook.

produced in the Central Asian republics is just over half the national average[3]. It is possible that the way gross industrial output is computed and national income is formed do not adequately reflect the contribution of primary producers such as Uzbekistan to the Soviet economy, and *per capita* national income and industrial output are certainly depressed by the large number of dependents in the population of the Central Asian republics as a result of the phenomenally high rate of natural increase of the indigenous population. None the less, a breakdown of employment by sector (Table 2) shows clearly that a smaller than average percentage of the active population is employed in industry and construction and, in the case of Uzbekistan, Tadzhikistan and Turkmenistan, a very much higher percentage in agriculture. Moreover, with the European population

TABLE 2

Distribution of Population Employed in the National Economy by Sectors (in per cent)

	USSR 1974	KazSSR 1973	UzbSSR 1974	KirSSR 1974	TadSSR 1971	TurSSR 1972
Industry and construction	38	30·9	23·1	28·2	22	23·4
Agriculture and forestry	24	26·4	42·2	32·8	44	38·3
Transport and communications	8	10·5	6·1	7·2	6	8·2
Trade, public catering, material-technical supplies and sales, procurements	8	7·9	6·7	7·1	6	7·0
Public health, physical culture and social security, education, culture, the arts, science and scientific services	16	17·5	16·5	18·2	16	16·4
State administration, administrative agencies of co-operative and public organisations, banking and state insurance	2	2·7	2·1	3·1	3	3·1
Other sectors of the economy (housing and public utilities, services, and others)	4	4·1	3·3	3·4	3	3·6

Sources: *Narodnoye khozyaystvo SSSR v 1974 g.*, Moscow, 1975, p. 547; *Narodnoye khozyaystvo Kazakhstana v 1974 g.*, Alma-Ata, 1975, p. 196; *Narodnoye khozyaystvo Uzbekskoy SSR v 1974 g.*, Tashkent, 1975, p. 243; *Narodnoye khozyaystvo Kirgizskoy SSR v 1974 g.*, Frunze, 1975, p. 213; *Narodnoye khozyaystvo Tadzhikskoy SSR v 1972 g.*, Dushanbe, 1973, pp. 172–3; *Turkmenistan za 50 let*, Ashkhabad, 1974, p. 126.

concentrated in the towns, the indigenous peoples remain overwhelmingly rural. As regards industry, the biggest gap between words and deeds is the failure to develop a cotton textile industry which meets even local needs. Uzbekistan, for instance, which grows nearly two-thirds of the Soviet Union's cotton and has 5·4 per cent of its population, produces only 2·8 per cent of its cotton textiles. Furthermore there is evidence that, in the mid-1960s at least, as in Tsarist times, transport costs were weighted in favour of the mills in European Russia.[4] However, it is also true to say that the existing textile mills in Central Asia have suffered a chronic shortage of labour. This seems to stem largely from Moscow's insistence to date on building giant mills in which the native women dislike working.

In assessing economic progress in Central Asia and Kazakhstan, there are also two other facts which cannot be ignored. Firstly, not only has Moscow pursued its economic policies with little or no regard for the wishes of the local population, but at times unacceptable coercion has been used, particularly during collectivisation and the campaign to settle the Kazakh and other nomads in the late 1920s. Rather than yield, many Kazakhs slaughtered their animals and starved or fled to Sinkiang. As a result, the number of Kazakhs in the Soviet Union dropped from 3,968,300 in 1926 to 3,098,800 in 1939,[5] and the catastrophic fall in livestock numbers took years to make good. The role of forced labour in the development of Kazakhstan's mineral resources should also be mentioned, and according to dissident sources, prison-camp labour is still used to a minor extent where the occupation is hazardous or the locality particularly inhospitable, for example, at the Uzbek gold mines in the Kyzylkum desert.[6]

Secondly, industrial development and the ploughing up of the virgin lands of Kazakhstan have led to an enormous increase in the size of the European settler population. By 1970 the total of non-Asians in the region as a whole was more than eleven million, and they constituted over 30 per cent of the population (nearly 60 per cent in Kazakhstan), a far higher proportion than in Algeria under French rule. While this immigration has been an important factor in the progress made in industrialisation, it has naturally been resented by the local population. More important from the long-term economic point of view, in the Central Asian republics in particular, it has militated against greater involvement of the indigenous population in industry.

9TH FIVE-YEAR PLAN RESULTS

Turning now to current economic performance and the results of the recently completed 9th Five-Year Plan, as can be seen from Table 3, all the republics achieved respectable rates of growth in both industry and agriculture. They did not, however, all reach their plan targets. On the whole the Central Asian republics, whose irrigated agriculture makes them less dependent on the whims of nature, did better than Kazakhstan (and the Soviet Union in general). A series of bumper cotton harvests, achieved with the aid of new wilt-resistant strains, higher procurement prices and an over-abundant supply of labour, helped the three main cotton-growing republics (Uzbekistan, Tadzhikistan and Turkmenistan) considerably exceed their agricultural targets and, as cotton-ginning accounts for an important part of their gross industrial output, also boosted their industrial performance. The excellent cotton results were obtained at some cost, however. Exceptionally low water in the rivers, particularly in the Syrdar'ya basin, in 1974 and 1975 was overcome only by massive emergency measures (concreting canals to reduce losses through seepage, drilling hundreds of artesian wells, and building canals and pumping stations to link irrigation systems with an adequate supply to those without),[7] and by putting all hydro-electric schemes on an 'irrigation regime'. The threat to the cotton harvest was so serious that the extreme measure was resorted to of twice draining the newly-created reservoir of

TABLE 3

9th Five-Year Plan: Increases in Industrial and Agricultural Output, National Income Produced, and Retail Trade Turnover (in per cent)

	Industrial output[a]		Agricultural output[b]		National income produced[a]		Retail trade turnover[b]	
	Plan	Actual	Plan	Actual	Plan	Actual	Plan	Actual
USSR	47	43	23	13	38·6	28	41·8	36
Kazakh SSR	59	42·4	22	14	n.a.	26	44	n.a.
Uzbek SSR	51	51	24	30·8	n.a.	41	52	45
Kirgiz SSR	55	52	20	18·6	n.a.	27·8	51	44
Tadzhik SSR	38	38	28	33·8	n.a.	33	47	44
Turkmen SSR	64	55·7	20	33	n.a.	35	52	45

[a] 1975 compared with 1970.
[b] Average annual 1971–75 compared with 8th Five-Year Plan (1966–70).
n.a. = not available.
Sources: *Pravda* 27 November 1971; Gregory Grossman. 'An Economy at Middle Age', *Problems of Communism*, March–April 1976, p. 22; *Kazakhstanskaya pravda* 5 February, 1976; *Uzbekistan za gody devyatoy pyatiletki* (*1971–75 g.*), Tashkent, 1976, pp. 13–14; *Pravda Vostoka* 8 February, 1976; *Sovetskaya Kirgiziya* 27 January, 1976; *Kommunist Tadzhikistana* 5 February, 1976; *Turkmenskaya iskra* 24 January, 1976.

the Toktogul hydro-electric power station, which had only just started to fill. It is claimed that this action resulted in the power station paying for itself even before it produced its first electricity,[8] but this probably leaves out of account the effect on industry of lost power-output. The priority accorded to the cotton crop resulted in the loss of two million kilowatts of generating capacity at hydro-electric power stations in the area, and led to interruptions in supplies to both industrial and domestic consumers in Uzbekistan.[9]

Temporary loss of generating capacity at Toktogul and further delays at the Nurek hydro-electric power station kept the increase in electricity output well below plan in Kirgixia and Tadzhikistan, but both Uzbekistan and Turkmenistan exceeded their targets.[10] Thanks to the new gas-fired Mary power station, Turkmenistan became self-sufficient in power for the first time, and a net exporter. With natural gas production almost quadrupling, Turkmenistan's share of total Soviet production rose to 18 per cent. But shortfalls in the output of both natural gas and oil were among the reasons why the republic failed to achieve its very high target of industrial growth. The difficulties in the natural gas industry were the usual ones associated with the exploitation of mineral deposits in remote inhospitable areas of the Soviet Union, namely, a chronic lack of skilled workers, a high turnover of labour because of failure to provide tolerable living and working conditions, supply difficulties, and a lack of machinery and equipment adapted to the specific conditions.[11] In the long-established oil industry the trouble lay in the failure to discover new deposits in the

Karakum, and some were now beginning to doubt that they exist.[12] The new oil refinery under construction in Chardzhou and the refinery in Fergana in Uzbekistan, which were to rely solely or largely on Turkmen crude,[13] are now being linked to the West Siberian fields by a 2,700 km. extension of the Omsk-Pavlodar pipeline.[14] In all four Central Asian republics the food industry, reflecting agricultural successes, did relatively well, but light industry, the Cinderella of the Soviet economy, failed by a substantial margin to meet its targets.

Kazakhstan registered sizeable increases in its output of coal, power, oil and natural gas, but major shortfalls in the production of iron and steel, oil, and probably non-ferrous metals as well (for which no figures are published) must have played a large part in the republic achieving only some 70 per cent of its planned growth. Two factors seem to be chiefly responsible for this state of affairs. Firstly, new mineral deposits were apparently not discovered in the quantities anticipated, leading to an under-utilisation of processing capacity,[15] and secondly, there is a chronic lag in capital construction, the creation of reasonable living and working conditions at construction sites and at new undertakings, and the training of skilled workers, for which the blame lies as much with the parent ministries in Moscow as with the republican authorities. At the large Karaganda Metallurgical (Iron and Steel) Works at Temirtau, for instance, whose performance has come in for repeated criticism at the highest level, the main problem appears to be an acute shortage of skilled labour. The works are situated in semi-desert outside Temirtau, and the 15 per cent wages supplement does not compensate for the harsh climatic conditions. Moreover, although the works has been in existence 15 years, no provision has been made for training skilled iron and steel workers locally. As a result, when any new production unit at the works is due to be brought into operation, skilled workers have to be brought in temporarily from other parts of the country. They do a rush job, depart, and leave the relatively unskilled and constantly changing local labour force to cope as best they can.[16]

The important Kazakhstan non-ferrous metals industry evidently ran into serious difficulties in keeping its concentrators supplied with ore during the Plan period. The situation seems to have been most acute in the lead and zinc industry, particularly in East Kazakhstan (although it was claimed at the recent Kazakh Party congress that East Kazakhstan had substantially increased its production of non-ferrous and rare metals).[17] The continued existence of the ore-processing plants in Leninogorsk and Zyryanovsk, and hence the existence of the towns themselves, seems to have been threatened by the closure or imminent closure of open-cast lead and zinc mines in the vicinity. They are now having to resort to more expensive underground mining and are devising new methods of concentration which make it profitable to process tailings and ores previously considered unprofitable.[18] In the 10th Five-Year Plan, three-quarters of the investment in the non-ferrous metals industry are to be devoted to developing the raw material base, and prospecting for extra resources is to be stepped up in East Kazakhstan, the Balkhash area and south Kazakhstan.[19]

As regards agriculture, Kazakhstan did marginally better than the Soviet Union as a whole. But average annual output increased by only 14 per cent compared with the 8th Five-Year Plan, instead of the scheduled 22 per cent, and both arable farming and animal husbandry remain inordinately at the mercy of the weather, in spite of lavish investment. A record grain crop of 29 million tons was harvested in 1972, when the crop failed elsewhere, but in 1975, output plummetted to between 11 and 12 million tons,[20] bringing average annual production down to below 22 million tons instead of the planned 24. Severe drought was the main reason for the 1975 failure, but it was claimed that yields would have been appreciably better if farms in some of the main grain-growing areas had observed proved methods of cultivation and had not abandoned clean fallow in earlier years.[21] According to local officials, grain production is also hampered by a lack of machinery suited to farming in the arid conditions of northern Kazakhstan,[22] and there is still a substantial shortage of labour, in particular, agricultural machine operators.[23]

Inadequate fodder supplies, insufficient attention to the natural pastures, and a shortage of *chabans* (shepherds) are the main factors behind the slow progress of animal husbandry in Kazakhstan, as in the Central Asian republics as well. The number of cattle showed a fairly steady rise,[24] though productivity remains low. But pigs were an immediate casualty of the 1975 grain harvest failure, with the numbers in Kazakhstan dropping from 2,619,000 on 1 January, 1975, to 1,675,100 on 1 January, 1976. (The Soviet regime has still not managed to overcome ingrained Muslim prejudices, and in the Central Asian republics, with their smaller non-Asian population, pig breeding has never developed to any extent.) The head of sheep and goats, which by the beginning of 1975 had more or less recovered from the heavy losses of the severe winter of 1969 and somewhat smaller losses in three of the Central Asian republics in 1972, was also affected, though less severely, by the 1975 drought, and Kazakhstan, with 34,500,000 head, remains a long way from Brezhnev's target of 50 million.[25] In order to overcome the reluctance of the now better-educated younger generation of Central Asians to become shepherds, which still involves continuously moving with the sheep over the desert, mountain and steppe pastures, efforts are being made to organise them into teams with regular working hours and proper amenities, but it remains to be seen if this will be successful.

THE 10TH FIVE-YEAR PLAN

As regards the 10th Five-Year Plan, although the plan period started on 1 January, 1976, so far only provisional targets are available from the 'Main Trends of Development of the National Economy of the USSR 1976–80' adopted at the XXV Soviet Party Congress in March 1976. The plan proper will not be finalised and adopted by the Supreme Soviet until towards the end of the year. The provisional targets (see Table 4) show a marked slowing down in the anticipated rate of industrial growth in four out of the five republics compared with that achieved in the 9th Five-Year Plan. This is in line with the general trend of development of the Soviet economy as a whole.[26] The odd one out is Tadzhikistan, which had a rate of industrial growth well below the average for Central Asia in 1971–75, and is expected to reap the benefits of the long-awaited completion of the Nurek hydro-electric power station and the greater part of the Regar Aluminium Works. Kazakhstan, as usual, has been set a higher than average industrial target. Three of the four Central Asian republics, on

TABLE 4

Provisional 10th Five-Year Plan Targets

	Increase in industrial output 1980 *cf.* 1975 (in per cent)	Increase in average annual agricultural output 1976–80 *cf.* 1971–75 (in per cent)
USSR	35–39	14–17
Kazakh SSR	39–43	14–17
Uzbek SSR	35–39	21–24
Kirgiz SSR	33–37	12–15
Tadzhik SSR	38–42	15–18
Turkmen SSR	30–34	14–17

Source: *Pravda*, 7 March, 1976.

the other hand, have targets the same as or below the average, in spite of the fact that their populations are growing three or more times as fast. This would seem to indicate that the continuing commitment to equalise the levels of economic development of the republics has once again had to take second place to other claims on investment resources. As for the agricultural targets, in several instances they are also well below what was achieved in the 9th Five-Year Plan.

There is no space here to go into details of the plan, but apart from envisaging a general all-round increase in production, particular emphasis is laid on the continued exploitation of the region's mineral and power resources; there are provisions designed to meet specific needs of the economies of the individual republics themselves, for example, a large new coal-fired power station in Uzbekistan to overcome a growing energy gap, and the production of more powerful tractors for the virgin lands in Kazakhstan; and the irrigated area is to be expanded by a further million hectares.[27]

On the evidence of the last Five-Year Plan, the provisional targets should be within reach, particularly in the Central Asian republics, which do not suffer from the same tight labour situation which is one of the major factors slowing down the development of the Soviet economy as a whole. However, the industrial growth target for Kazakhstan was lowered one percentage point and those of Tadzhikistan and Turkmenistan two percentage points between the publication of the draft of the 'Main Trends . . .' in December 1975[28] and the adoption of the final version in March 1976, which suggests that they may be on the optimistic side. Whether the individual republics are happy with the targets is another matter. The Uzbeks, with a major employment problem on their hands, clearly think they need greater industrial development. The Tadzhiks also give the impression that they do not think that the State Planning Commission in Moscow makes enough allowance for the need to employ their rapidly growing labour resources.[29]

The problem of creating jobs for the rapidly growing labour force, almost certainly the most difficult problem facing Uzbekistan, Tadzhikistan and, possibly, Turkmenistan as well, has arisen primarily as the result of the phenomenally high rate of natural increase of the indigenous peoples since the beginning of the 1950s. In the eleven years between the 1959 and 1970 censuses, the average annual rate of natural increase of the titular nationalities of the five republics was between 3·5 and 4 per cent, and since 1959 the populations of Turkmenistan, Uzbekistan and Tadzhikistan have risen 70, 74 and 76 per cent respectively, compared with 22 per cent for the Soviet Union as a whole. (The increase has been somewhat less dramatic in Kirgizia and Kazakhstan, 63 and 55 per cent, because of the much larger European elements in their population.) The results of this demographic explosion have been coming onto the labour market in growing numbers for some time now. Thus, whereas the number of able-bodied in Uzbekistan increased by 25 per cent in the eleven years 1959 to 1970,[30] the republic's labour resources will increase by more than 22 per cent (or well over a million) in the current Five-Year Plan,[31] and continue to rise at the rate of roughly four per cent per annum until at least 1995.[32]

There are two additional factors which aggravate the situation. First, because of the preference of the ministries in Moscow for siting undertakings in large towns, there has long been an employment problem in the smaller, longer-established, predominantly native towns (as opposed to those which have grown up recently on the basis of new mineral workings). Second, and more important, with the increasing mechanisation of cotton-growing, far fewer people are needed on the land. At present, mechanisation is not proceeding as fast as hoped, and the cost of producing cotton is rising rather than falling, because the labour input remains so high.[33] As *Pravda* of 1 June, 1975, said apropos Tadzhikistan, the continuing high proportion of manual labour in agriculture is due largely to the need to find work for the population, and nearly a quarter of the able-bodied could work in other sectors without detriment to agriculture.

Seeing that many industrial undertakings and construction projects in the big cities and new industrial towns are short of labour, it might be thought that this would provide at least a partial solution. But up to now the indigenous peoples have shown a remarkable unwillingness to migrate to the towns, in particular those where a high proportion of the population is European and the language of the factory and the whole ambiance is Russian. This is put down largely to inadequate knowledge of Russian on the part of the rural population.[34] Their resistance to working in Russian-dominated undertakings can be seen from reports of rural youngsters put through trade schools (probably with Uzbek as the language of instruction) attached to big undertakings in Tashkent, who have failed to take up jobs in these undertakings and have returned home.[35]

In an effort to solve the employment problem, strenuous efforts are being made to step up the training of skilled workers locally and also to improve the teaching of Russian, particularly in the rural areas. A start has also been made at last on setting up small industrial undertakings or branches of larger undertakings in the smaller towns, and large rural settlements to absorb some of the surplus rural labour. In agriculture it is planned to develop labour-intensive sectors such as fruit- and vegetable-growing, and the expansion of the irrigated area should help, although the new cotton-growing state farms tend to be highly mechanised. There is also scope for increased employment in the service industries. But whether sufficient job opportunities can be created in the region in the short term, even if all the vacancies in industrial undertakings are taken up, seems extremely doubtful.

Because of the reticence of the Soviet press on the subject, it is difficult to judge exactly how acute the employment problem is at present, but from the fact that it has figured more and more prominently in the public statements of leading republican Party and government officials, it is obvious that it is a matter of major concern. One of the clearest indications of this came at the December 1975 USSR Supreme Soviet session, when the chairman of the Uzbek Council of Ministers, N. D. Khudayberdyyev, stated that '*the rapid growth in number of the population and labour resources* [emphasis added] and also the existence of rich sources of raw materials puts forward the need for a further acceleration of the development of the [Uzbekistan] economy, particularly industry', and implored the USSR State Planning Commission and the relevant all-Union ministries to study carefully the republic's proposals on the provisional 10th Five-Year Plan with this in mind.[36] As far as one can tell, he elicited no positive response. Given that there is under-utilisation of capacity at many existing undertakings in Uzbekistan, this is perhaps not surprising. But under-utilisation would not have occurred to the same extent if the ministries in Moscow had not ignored the local situation and failed to take industry to the labour resources.

Another problem which has loomed large recently, particularly following two years of severe drought, is the growing shortage of water in Central Asia, which could in the future be a constraint on the development of both agriculture and industry. The question of water resources and their management is one of enormous importance for the area, and merits special study. Suffice it to say here that already so much of the flow of the Syrdar'ya and Amudar'ya rivers is being used for irrigation, that the Aral Sea is shrinking fast, and is in danger of disappearing in the not-too-distant future, unless radical measures are taken. In the short term, there is considerable scope for saving irrigation water, much of which is wasted, leading to unnecessary salination and bogging.[37] But the long-term solution is seen in the diversion of part of the flow of the Siberian rivers into the Aral basin, which would not only prevent the undesirable consequences which would be likely to follow the drying up of the Aral, but would also assist the expansion of both industry and agriculture in Central Asia and Kazakhstan. This has long been mooted, but after pleas from both the Uzbek and Kazakh First Secretaries at the recent Soviet Party Congress, specific provision was made for research to be carried out on the project and preliminary proposals to be drawn up during the current Five-Year Plan.[38] The cost of the project would be such, however, that its realisation probably lies well in the future.

GRATITUDE OR GRIEVANCES?

It is often considered, and not only in Soviet pronouncements, that the indigenous population of Central Asia and Kazakhstan both should be and are grateful for their material progress, if not to the Russian people, then at least to the Soviet regime. But as a rule, subject peoples have not been particularly grateful for the material benefits bestowed on them by their alien rulers, and the tributes paid by Central Asian and Kazakh Party leaders on every possible occasion to the 'great Russian people' for what they have done for the indigenous peoples lack the ring of authenticity. The continual harping in the Soviet press on how backward the natives were before the coming of the Russians and the revolution is obviously hurtful and seems to have led only to an exaggerated pride in the achievements of their peoples before the Russian contact. Moreover, in drawing up the balance sheet of economic progress not everything is on the credit side, and while the sufferings of collectivisation and the settlement of the nomads may not be very real to the younger generation, this is not true of the large influx of Slav and other non-Asian settlers. The fact that the Kazakhs, who have suffered most from in-migration, have not seemed particularly keen on further industrialisation, would suggest clearly that they, at least, see a very clear connection between the two,[39] and there is no doubt that the Slav presence is widely resented.

Unfortunately it is impossible to gauge accurately from Soviet publications the temper of local officialdom, but the inevitable tensions between the central government and the regions over economic policy in any country are almost bound to exacerbate national feeling where the administrative set-up is based on the national principle. That such tensions exist between Moscow and the Central Asian republics is perfectly evident from the Soviet press. For instance, as already mentioned, the Uzbeks have not always been entirely happy with the specialisation of their economy on cotton. They have also felt that less of their natural gas should be piped to European Russia and more retained for the needs of the republic itself.[40] This inability to dispose of their natural resources as they see fit must be something that particularly rankles. Do the Uzbeks, one wonders, not wish that they could raise the price for their natural gas to the consumer in European Russia in the same way that their fellow-Muslims in OPEC have raised oil prices in the last two or three years? As for their gold, the very fact that no output figures are published is likely to give rise to inflated ideas of the quantities mined, and it would be understandable if the Uzbeks, whose cotton and karakul exports also contribute handsomely to the Soviet balance of payments, should resent their gold being used to buy the grain the Russian farmer failed to produce.

Another problem which seems almost certain to cause racial tensions in the future is the employment problem. These tensions could result either from competition between natives and the settler population for jobs within Central Asia or, if the indigenous peoples found themselves forced to migrate in large numbers to parts of the Soviet Union where labour is short, from their having to accept the least-skilled jobs and with them the lowest place in society. The nearest parallel would probably be with the influx of blacks from the south of the United States into its northern cities, following the mechanisation of cotton-growing. The Soviet authorities are fully aware of the problem, and one reason for the increased effort being put into improving the teaching of Russian to non-Russians seems to be to ensure that the non-Russians, and in particular the Central Asians, can be more easily integrated into the mainstream of the country's economic activity, but one has the impression that events will almost certainly overtake them. As regards possible competition for jobs within Central Asia, it would seem strange in the circumstances that a stop has not been put to continuing Slav migration to Central Asia, particularly as much of it comes from labour-deficit areas like Siberia. The main reason is probably that Moscow is not anxious to see the Slav proportion of the population, which is already declining in spite of inmigration, reduced and its hold on the region thus weakened. It also seems likely that one reason that the authorities might be chary of increasing their investment in Central Asia and so creating more jobs on the spot could be fear of possible instability in an area bordering on China.

APPENDIX

Contribution of Kazakhstan and Central Asian republics to Soviet economy as a whole in 1974 in per cent

	Total Kaz. and CA	Kaz.	Uzb.	Kir.	Tad.	Tur.
Area	17·8	12·1	2·0	0·9	0·6	2·2
Population	14·8	5·6	5·4	1·3	1·3	1·0
Industry						
Electricity	9·3	5·0	3·1	0·4	0·4	0·4
Oil (including gas condensate)	8·8	4·9	0·3	0·05	0·05	3·5

Appendix (contd.)

	Total Kaz. and CA	Kaz.	Uzb.	Kir.	Tad.	Tur.
Industry						
Natural gas	31·7	2·1	14·2	0·1	0·2	15·1
Coal	14·1	12·7	0·7	0·6	0·1	—
Iron ore	9·0	9·0	—	—	—	—
Pig iron	3·4	3·4	—	—	—	—
Steel	3·8	3·5	0·3	0·0	0·0	—
Finished rolled metal	4·4	4·0	0·4	—	—	—
Mineral fertilisers (in conventional units)	14·8	6·6	7·2	—	0·5	0·5
Chemical fibres and threads	3·9	1·9	2·0	—	—	—
Metal-cutting machine tools	3·6	1·2	0·1	1·0	1·3	—
Tractors (in physical units)	9·6	5·5	4·1	—	—	—
Agricultural machinery	10·3	6·1	2·7	1·3	0·2	—
Excavators	7·0	3·4	3·6	—	—	—
Motor vehicles	0·9	—	—	0·9	—	—
Oil apparatus	0·9	—	—	—	—	0·9
Paper	0·7	0·2	0·5	—	—	—
Cement	10·9	5·6	3·0	0·9	0·9	0·5
Bricks	10·9	4·5	3·6	1·2	0·8	0·8
Cotton fibre	94·1	4·2	63·9	2·9	10·4	12·7
Cotton textiles	6·3	1·2	2·8	0·6	1·4	0·3
Woollen textiles	3·5	2·0	0·1	1·3	—	0·1
Silk textiles	10·4	0·0	6·0	0·6	3·4	0·4
Hosiery	8·7	4·4	2·4	0·7	1·9	0·3
Leather footwear	10·6	4·3	3·5	1·4	1·0	0·4
Domestic refrigerators	4·2	—	1·7	—	2·5	—
Domestic washing machines	9·9	5·0	—	4·9	—	—
Furniture	6·5	3·2	1·7	0·8	0·5	0·3
Animal fats	5·6	3·8	0·7	0·7	0·2	0·2
Vegetable oils	18·9	2·4	11·8	0·6	2·7	1·4
Tinned food	9·2	2·7	3·7	0·9	1·6	0·3
Wine	12·2	5·7	3·8	1·0	1·2	0·5
Agriculture						
No. of tractors (in physical units)	19·5	9·5	6·3	1·1	1·2	1·4
Sown area:						
Total	19·2	16·2	1·7	0·6	0·3	0·4
Grain crops	21·7	20·0	0·9	0·5	0·2	0·1
Industrial crops	20·6	2·5	12·0	0·9	1·9	3·3
Potatoes and vegetables	5·8	3·1	1·5	0·5	0·3	0·4
Fodder crops	16·3	14·0	0·9	0·8	0·3	0·3
Crops:						
Grain:	10·9	9·5	0·6	0·6	0·1	0·1
Cotton	93·7	4·0	63·4	2·5	10·5	13·3
Sugar beet	4·9	2·6	—	2·3	—	—
Potatoes	3·0	2·1	0·3	0·4	0·2	—
Vegetables	12·5	3·9	5·3	1·4	1·1	0·8
Livestock holdings:						
Cattle	12·6	7·3	2·9	0·9	1·0	0·5
Cows only	11·8	6·5	2·9	0·9	1·0	0·5
Pigs	4·9	3·6	0·5	0·4	0·2	0·2
Sheep and goats	40·5	23·4	5·7	6·5	1·9	3·0

Appendix (contd.)

	Total Kaz. and CA	Kaz.	Uzb.	Kir.	Tad.	Tur.
Agriculture						
Livestock products:						
Meat (dead weight)	10·6	7·0	1·7	1·0	0·5	0·4
Milk	7·9	4·6	1·9	0·7	0·4	0·3
Eggs	8·4	4·8	2·3	0·6	0·4	0·3
Wool	39·6	23·2	5·3	6·8	1·1	3·2

Source: *Narodnoye khozyaystvo SSSR v. 1974*. Moscow, 1975, pp. 90–5.

NOTES

1. A detailed and authoritative account can be found in Dr. Violet Conolly's *Beyond the Urals* (Oxford University Press, 1967).
2. For details of mineral resources, see Theodore Shabad, *Basic Industrial Resources of the USSR*, Columbia University Press, 1969.
3. *Per capita* national income produced in the Central Asian republics was 62 per cent of the all-Union average in 1965 (A. I. Vedischev, 'Soizmereniye urovney khozyaystvennogo razvitiya ekonomicheskikh rayonov SSSR', *Ekonomicheskiye problemy razmescheniya proizvoditel'nykh sil SSSR*, Moscow, 1969, p. 82), and the gap has widened still further since then (calculations based on population figures and increase in national income given in *Narodnoye khozyaystvo SSSR v 1974 g.*, Moscow, 1975, p. 574), although in absolute terms *per capita* national income produced has risen by about 40 per cent.
4. Violet Conolly, pp. 33 and 182.
5. Figures quoted by Geoffrey Wheeler in *Racial Problems in Soviet Muslim Asia*, 2nd edition, Oxford University Press, 1962, p. 28.
6. Il'ya Lyuksemburg, 'Novyy Vavilon na beregakh Syrdar'i', *Posev*, 1973, no. 9, pp. 35–6.
7. *Pravda Vostoka*, 6 February, 1976.
8. *Sovetskaya Kirgiziya*, 28 December, 1975.
9. *Pravda Vostoka*, 4 December, 1975 and 15 January, 1976.
10. Comments on 9th Five-Year Plan results are based on a comparison of 1970 output and 1971–75 plan targets given in *Gosudarstvennyy pyatiletniy plan razvitiya narodnogo khozyaystva SSSR na 1971–1975 gody*, Moscow, 1972, and 1975 plan results in *Kazakhstanskaya pravda*, 10 February, 1976, *Pravda Vostoka*, 1 February, 1976, *Sovetskaya Kirgizia*, 6 February, 1976, *Kommunist Tadzhikistana*, 4 February, 1976, and *Turkmenskaya iskra*, 3 February, 1976.
11. *Pravda*, 25 April, 1975 and 13 January, 1976.
12. *Izvestiya*, 15 February, 1976.
13. Shabad, pp. 311, 322.
14. *Izvestiya*, 25 March, 1976.
15. *Izvestiya*, 7 February, 1976.
16. *Pravda*, 21 April, 1975, *Izvestiya*, 23 September, 1975.
17. *Izvestiya*, 7 February, 1976.
18. *Izvestiya*, 22 February, 1976.
19. *Izvestiya*, 10 April, 1976.
20. Computed from figures for 1971–74 crops given in *Narodnoye khozyaystvo SSSR v 1974 g.*, Moscow, 1975, p. 355, and 1971–75 total in *Kazakhstanskaya pravda*, 10 February, 1976.
21. *Izvestiya*, 17 January, 1976.
22. *Ibid.*, also *Pravda*, 7 February, 1976 and 27 March, 1976.

23. A. Altynov, V. Dunin, 'Resursy truda: povysheniye effektivnosti ispol'zovaniya', *Voprosy ekonomiki*, 1976, no. 3, pp. 156–7.

24. Remarks on head of livestock in this paragraph are based on the figures given in the statistical yearbooks and the 1975 plan results.

25. *Pravda*, 16 March, 1974.

26. See Gregory Grossman, 'An Economy at Middle Age', *Problems of Communism*, March–April 1976, pp. 18–33.

27. *Pravda*, 7 March, 1976.

28. *Pravda*, 14 December, 1975.

29. For example, the Tadzhik First Secretary Rasulov in his remarks on the need to improve planning at the Soviet Party congress in February–March 1976 (*Pravda*, 28 February, 1976).

30. *Itogi vsesoyuznoy perepisi naseleniya 1970 goda*, Tom II, Moscow, 1972, pp. 28–9.

31. *Pravda Vostoka*, 5 February, 1976.

32. *Pravda Vostoka*, 30 April, 1976.

33. *Pravda Vostoka*, 25 January, 1976 and 11 May, 1976.

34. Galetskaya R., 'Demograficheskaya politika: yeye napravleniya', *Voprosy ekonomiki*, 1975, no. 8, p. 152.

35. *Pravda Vostoka*, 2 November, 1975.

36. *Pravda Vostoka*, 5 December, 1975.

37. V. Zhamin, 'Ekologiya i ekonomika', *Voprosy ekonomiki*, 1975, no. 7, p. 99; V. Kovalev, 'Kak poddershat' Aral?', *Ekonomika i zhizn'* 1976, no. 3, pp. 59–62.

38. *Pravda*, 26 and 27 February, and 7 March, 1976.

39. Violet Conolly, p. 360.

40. *Ibid.*, p. 137.

Recent Economic Growth in Iran

Hossein Askari and Shohreh Majin

I. INTRODUCTION

Iran, one of the larger countries of the Middle East, has been considered historically a less-developed country. In recent years, however, Iran appears to have been achieving tremendous economic progress. In 1972, Iran's gross national product increased to 1,186·4 billion rials (from 412·9 billion rials in 1964); the average annual real rate of growth of G.N.P. (since 1965) has been a phenomenal 10·4 per cent; and *per capita* G.N.P., despite Iran's considerable population growth, has expanded at a real rate of 7·2 per cent.

At the same time, Iran has experienced high levels of oil exports which, combined with increasing oil price, have provided a substantial amount of revenue. There is no doubt that the proportion of total revenue attributable to petroleum-related factors is responsible for a significant share of Iran's increasing national income and high rate of growth. In this paper, the question is asked whether the great economic strides achieved by Iran are largely the result of expanding oil revenues. In other words, has the rate of growth been directly influenced by increasing oil revenues or also indirectly—that is, have increased oil exports financed significant growth in other sectors? To analyse this issue, we will examine other characteristics of the Iranian economy, such as changes in real sectoral product, economic structure and employment, level of education, social welfare, and so on. Our purpose is to survey these factors, and to determine the extent to which Iran's growing national income is due primarily to increased oil revenues as opposed to overall economic development.[1]

II. THE RATE OF GROWTH IN RECENT YEARS

As was mentioned before, Iran has achieved a substantial growth rate of G.N.P. (and G.N.P. *per capita*) in recent years. The movements of G.N.P., G.N.P. *per capita* and their rate of growth for the period 1960–72 is given in Table 1. This rapid rate of growth is partly due to a continuous increase in revenues received from petroleum exports. Share of oil income in total national income has increased from 10·6 per cent in 1959/60 to 19·5 per cent in 1972/73; oil revenues in 1974 amounted to over 20 billion dollars. One may conclude that the rapid rate of growth of national income in Iran is largely the result of the G.N.P. accounting method resulting in rapid increase of oil income; in the remainder of this paper, we shall determine the validity of this statement.

TABLE 1

Gross National Product in 1971 Prices

Year	Total GNP (millions of $)	Rate of Growth	*Per capita* GNP	Rate of Growth
1960	5,040	—	234	—
1965	6,970	7·7	281	4·0
1966	7,510	7·7	294	4·6
1967	8,390	11·7	319	8·5
1968	9,200	9·6	340	6·6
1969	10,020	8·9	359	5·6
1970	11,150	11·3	389	8·3
1971	12,750	14·3	428	10·0
1972	14,400	12·9	470	9·8

Source: National Publications, U.N. 'Yearbook of National Accounts Statistics', and reports from A.I.D. missions and U.S. Embassies.

III. PRODUCTION

A. *Agricultural Production*

The index of agricultural production for the period 1960–72 is presented in Table 2. Total agricultural production has increased very slowly, and *per capita* product has increased by an even smaller amount. Furthermore, the annual rate of growth of total and *per capita* production has exhibited large annual variations during this period. This indicates that production in this sector is still subject to a number of varying factors. It is, therefore,

TABLE 2

Index of Agricultural Production
(1961–65=100)

Year	Total Production	Rate of Growth	*Per capita* Production	Rate of Growth
1960	88	—	96	—
1965	105	+3·9	99	+0·6
1968	133	+8·9	115	+3·0
1969	128	−3·7	108	−6·1
1970	133	+3·9	109	+·9
1971	119	−10·5	94	−13·8
1972	133p	+11·7	102	+8·5p

Note: p = preliminary.
Source: Data prepared by Economic Research Service of the U.S. Department of Agriculture for A.I.D.

clear that agricultural production has not contributed to the recent Iranian economic growth. In fact, the agricultural sector has performed rather miserably, and the success of agrarian reform is not supported by at least the output figures.

B. Industrial Production

The industrial sector in Iran, on the other hand, has shown a very rapid rate of growth. In Table 3, we present the overall index of industrial production, the index of production in mining, manufacturing, electricity and gas for the period 1960–71. Industrial production has increased substantially at an average rate of growth of 15·3 per cent. Among the three minor sectors, electricity and gas have the highest rate of growth, while manufacturing has grown least rapidly. The overall high rate of growth in the industrial sector, and the new industries recently developed (producing automobiles, buses, trucks, refrigerators, other consumer goods, and some investment goods), indicate that Iran has developed to a large extent in this sector, and industry is an important contributor to recent economic growth. However, the increase in industrial production does not, *per se*, indicate success; clearly, as this import substitution may be at very high cost and may not necessarily be in an area in which Iran has a long-run comparative advantage. The possibility may be casually confirmed by the high price of domestically produced items.

IV. STRUCTURAL CHANGES

In a developing economy, during the first stages of growth, some changes in the structure of the economy are usually necessary. Increasing the level of production in appropriate areas, reallocation of resources into more efficient sectors, the movement of labour from low to high productivity sectors, higher level of investment as opposed to increasing consumption expenditures (especially consumption of luxuries), and redistribution of income aiming at more equality are examples of changes in a rapidly developing economy. The contribution of major sectors of the economy to national income is one possible criterion for judging whether the economy is moving in the right direction.

The contribution of major sectors and their trends, for 1959–72, are given in Table 4. The share of agriculture has decreased to less than half (from 34·3 per cent to 16·0 per cent) during this period, while the shares of the industrial sector (manufacturing and mining) and oil have almost doubled (share of manufacturing and mining has increased from 8·7 per cent to 16·5 per cent and that of oil has increased from 10·6 per cent to 19·5 per cent). These results are not surprising, and were, in fact, expected from above—namely, a very small increase in agricultural production and an increasing output with a high rate of growth for the industrial sector. And clearly the increasing share of oil in G.N.P. again indicates that recent economic growth is in large part due to increased oil revenues.

TABLE 3

Index of Industrial Production (1963 = 100)

Year	Industrial Production	Rate of Growth %	Mining	Rate of Growth %	Manu-facturing	Rate of Growth %	Electricity and Gas	Rate of Growth %
1960	75	—	76	—	75	—	65	—
1965	127	13·9	127	13·4	125	13·3	143	24·0
1967	170	16·9	177	19·9	157	12·8	199	19·6
1968	196	9·4	195	10·2	174	10·8	194	−2·5
1969	229	23·1	246	26·1	195	12·1	285	46·9
1970	251	9·6	263	6·9	218	11·8	381	33·7
1971	299	19·1	314	19·4	256	17·4	496	30·2

Source: U.N. Statistical Yearbook and U.N. Monthly Bulletin of Statistics.

TABLE 4

Contribution to GNP by Major Sectors

Year	Agriculture and Livestock	Manu-facturing and Mining	Oil (Iranian Share)	Construction	Water and Electricity	Services	Net Income From Abroad	Non-Oil GNP
1959/60	34·3	8·7	10·6	5·2	·7	40·5	—	89·4
1963/64	25·3	11·2	20·8	4·2	1·2	37·3	—	79·2
1967/68	23·5	14·4	14·3	6·2	1·1	40·5	—	85·7
1968/69	21·3	10·5	25·1	5·5	2·1	35·5	—	74·9
1969/70	19·3	13·6	26·2	3·8	2·2	34·9	—	73·8
1970/71	19·9	15·6	18·7	4·2	2·5	41·6	—2·5	81·3
1971/72	16·5	16·0	20·0	4·2	2·6	42·9	—·1	80·0
1972/73	16·0	16·5	19·5	4·2	2·7	43·5	—2·4	80·5

Source: Central Bank of Iran, Annual Report.

The rate of growth for each sector for the same period is given in Table 5. We observe a low and varying rate of growth of agriculture, and a high and increasing rate of growth of oil and industry.

V. EMPLOYMENT

Employment and the allocation of the labour force between different sectors can also be crucial in the process of development. Unfortunately, there are not enough data available in this case. The only figures obtainable were the results of the 1966 census and 1971 sample survey, which are presented in Table 6. According to this table, around 42 per cent of the total labour force was employed in the agricultural sector. Considering the low level of productivity in this sector, and its decreasing share in the national income, the portion of the labour force active in this area is excessive—indicating the possible existence of a large pool of disguised unemployment. The industrial sector, on the other hand, has employed only 17 per cent of the total labour force. Movement of labour from the agricultural to the industrial sector seems necessary, since it will lead to a higher productivity of labour and a higher rate of growth through more industrial production. However, in order for the labour force to enter the industrial sector, a minimum level of skills, and in some areas a particular type of skill, is required. Shortage of skills (or at least specific skills) seems to be one of the obstacles to labour mobility and, thus, more efficient usage of resources in Iran. The lack of labour mobility can also be seen from Table 6, since the allocation of labour among different sectors changed very slightly between 1966 and 1971. The rate of unemployment (around 10 per cent), while large shortages in skilled categories exist, also indicates the inappropriate training and use of the labour force. Providing a higher level of education, a nationwide minimum level of education and the training of the indigenous labour force seem to be needed and necessary for Iran's continuing economic growth.

VI. EXPENDITURES

A growing economy requires a higher level of domestic production which, in turn, requires a higher level of investment. The portion of national income which is allocated to capital formation determines the level of domestic products in the future, and thus is very important in terms of future economic growth. In Table 7, we present the portion of the gross national product which is consumed by the private sector, by the public sector, the proportion which is invested, and the trend for each for 1959/60 to 1972/73.

The ratio of private consumption to gross national product has decreased from 70·4 per cent to 56·6 per cent, while this ratio for government consumption has increased from 10·2 per cent to 23·1 per cent during this period; on the other hand, the total consumption (private and public) ratio has not changed significantly. At the same time, the ratio of

TABLE 5

Contribution to GNP by Major Sectors
(Rate of Growth)

Year	GNP (Factor Cost)	Agriculture and Livestock	Manu-facturing and Mining	Oil (Iranian Share)	Construction	Water and Electricity	Services	Net Income From Abroad	Non-Oil GNP
1959/60	—	—	—	—	—	—	—	—	—
1963/64	5·7	—2·2	14·6	35·3	—·2	27·5	3·3	—	2·3
1967/68	10·2	+7·6	20·4	—·9	+27·4	9·5	13·2	—	13·1
1968/69	9·6	—·6	—20·4	+92·4	—3·0	94·8	—3·7	—	—4·2
1969/70	16·0	+4·9	+51·6	+20·9	—19·6	23·9	13·6	—	14·3
1970/71	2·2	+5·5	+16·1	—26·7	+12·8	15·7	21·9	—	12·5
1971/72	16·8	—5·0	+16·9	+21·8	+13·6	19·7	18·1	—	15·6
1972/73	10·7	+10·0	+17·0	+10·7	+12·9	17·5	14·5	—	10·8

Source: Central Bank of Iran, Annual Report.

TABLE 6

Economically Active Population

	1966 (Census)		1971 (Sample Survey)	
		%		%
Agriculture, Forestry, Hunting and Fishing	3,168,515	41·8	3,410,400	42·2
Mining and Quarrying Manufacturing	1,293,912	19·1	1,391,800	17·2
Construction	509,778	6·7	508,900	6·3
Electricity, Gas, Water Supply	52,858	·7	100,400	1·2
Commerce	552,023	7·3	642,500	8·0
Transport, Storage and Communications	224,086	2·9	277,200	3·4
Services	929,685	12·2	833,300	10·3
Others (not-adequately described)	127,539	1·7	78,900	1·0
Total in Employment	6,858,396	90·4	7,243,400	89·6
Unemployed	725,689	9·6	836,900	10·4
Total	7,584,085	100·0	8,080,300	100·0

Source: Europa, The Middle East and North Africa.

gross capital formation to G.N.P. has increased from 16·2 per cent to 23·8 per cent.[2] In essence, there has been a transformation of relative shares of private consumption to government consumption and investment. As noted above, a higher level of investment leads to increasing future output and, as such, it is desirable for a growing economy, especially if there is increased investment in areas of high productivity. Clearly, Iran has at least not squandered her oil revenues for financing rapidly growing levels of consumption.

In the case of increasing government expenditures as opposed to private consumption, one should look at the different types of government expenditures. Higher government consumption would be desirable if a relatively high proportion of these expenditures were allocated for economic and social services and less were spent on military defence services. This, however, has *not* been the case. In 1960, military expenditures represented 4·2 per cent of G.N.P., but by 1972, this percentage had increased to 8·7 per cent—more than a 100 per cent increase in its share over a twelve-year period.[3]

VII. COMPOSITION OF IMPORTS

The Iranian trade surplus has been decreasing over the period 1959/60–1972/73 (although, since 1973, Iran has had enormous monthly surpluses), due to the increase in imports rather than decreasing exports. A deficit in the balance of trade or the excess of imports over exports is not necessarily undesirable for a developing country, *if* the imported goods are used for increasing the level of domestic production. Thus, one should consider the composition of imports to determine the role of foreign trade in economic development.

The composition of imports for Iran, over the period 1965/66–1972/73, is given in Table 8 (the major shifts in broad categories is given in Table 9). The ratio of imports of capital and intermediate goods, such as machinery, electrical items, chemicals, iron and steel, road vehicle parts, and probably tyres and tubes, to total imports has gone up in most cases (with the exception of chemicals)[4] over this period; with the remainder of imports, such as sugar, tea and those items which are not mentioned in the Table, being consumer goods (including luxury items). Because the ratio of the imports of capital and intermediate goods to total imports has increased over the period 1965/66–1972/73, the ratio of consumers' goods and luxuries to total imports has been decreasing. The main industries in Iran, such as food manufacturing, textiles, clothing, rubber and rubber products, chemicals, base metals, electrical and non-electrical machinery and so on, most of which have been established recently, are producing the consumer goods (and, in some cases, investment goods) which were previously imported.

Therefore, to the extent that the higher level of imports is, in fact, due to an increase in imports of capital and intermediate goods used to increase domestic production (and given that these are areas of Iranian

TABLE 7

Expenditure on Gross National Product
(Per cent)

Year	Private Consumption	Government Consumption	Total Consumption	Gross Capital Formation	Net Exports
1959/60	70·4	10·2	80·6	16·2	+3·2
1965/66	66·0	12·1	78·1	17·1	+4·8
1967	58·7	12·2	70·9	20·3	+8·8
1969	61·2	18·1	79·3	21·5	—·8
1969/70	61·6	17·5	79·1	22·6	—1·7
1970/71	60·8	18·5	79·3	22·4	—1·7
1971/72	59·3	19·1	78·4	21·0	+·6
1972/73	56·6	23·1	79·7	23·8	—3·5

Source: Central Bank of Iran, Annual Report.

TABLE 8

Main Imports as a Percentage of Total Imports

Year	Machinery, including Electricity	Iron and Steel and Manufactures	Chemicals and Pharmaceuticals	Electrical Items	Road Vehicles Parts	Tyres and Tubes	Sugar	Tea	Total
1965/66	20·5	12·2	7·8	6·0	3·3	1·7	2·9	1·9	56·3
1966/67	22·7	11·2	8·6	6·8	3·6	1·6	1·8	1·2	57·5
1967/68	24·3	15·6	7·9	7·0	2·9	1·0	1·0	·8	60·5
1968/69	23·6	18·2	8·3	7·9	6·2	2·0	·7	·7	67·6
1969/70	25·4	19·3	8·6	10·7	4·3	2·6	·4	·7	72·2
1970/71	21·9	18·2	7·6	9·8	4·0	1·9	·4	·6	64·4
1971/72	21·4	18·6	6·6	12·3	4·7	1·8	·5	·6	66·5
1972/73	23·7	15·8	7·1	10·0	5·0	2·2	1·0	·6	65·4

Source: Foreign Trade Statistics of Iran.

TABLE 9

Iran: Percentage Distribution of Export and Import Categories

	0	1	2	3	4	5	6	7	8	9
1955	6·09	—	9·98	73·57	·01	1·08	4·13	—	—	—
	20·75	—	·52	1·25	—	5·22	34·01	16·25	·49	
1960	2·74	—	5·03	86·20	—	·56	3·23	—	—	—
	10·98		·19	·74	1·77	7·18	29·60	27·63	·06	
1963	3·28	·01	6·42	86·59	·07	·61	2·96	·03	·02	—
	10·82		5·84	·64	2·60	13·12	33·44	29·58	3·91	·03
1965	3·39	·01	5·44	86·72	·02	·57	3·76	·02	·06	·01
	13·22	·03	4·86	·21	2·84	10·34	29·55	35·65	3·26	·04
1972	2·28	—	4·25	88·26	—	·71	3·20	—	·98	—
	8·01		4·91	·43	2·28	9·26	28·73	42·83	3·37	

Totals:	*1955 rials*	*1960 rials*	*1963 rials*	*1965 rials*	*1972 dollars*
	X=12783·7	X=61750·2 M	X=69667·7 M	X=98709·4 M	X=3811595 K
	M=8286·6	M=50467· M	M=39223·7 M	M=65152·3 M	M=2592973 K

Source: *Yearbook of International Trade Statistics*, United Nations, Various Issues.

comparative advantage), this observed shift has been a positive factor in Iran's economic growth.

VIII. ROLE OF GOVERNMENT

The influence of the Iranian government on economic development has become increasingly important in recent years. As noted in Table 7, the ratio of government consumption to G.N.P. has been increasing over the period 1965/66–1972/73. In Table 10, the details on government revenues and expenditures are shown for the years 1970, 1971 and 1972.

IX. DEVELOPMENT PLANS

The Iranian government has contributed to the economic growth through several economic plans during the post-war period. A series of five economic development plans has been authorised under a semi-autonomous plan organisation established in 1948. The first development plan was a seven-year plan, 1949 to 1955, and resulted in a total investment of 14,100 million rials. The second seven-year plan covered the period

TABLE 10

Budget

	1970 %	1971 %	1972 %
Revenue:			
Direct Taxes	6·1	5·3	5·3
Indirect Taxes	10·2	0·4	8·7
Monopolies, Government Undertakings	21·6	26·8	27·1
Government Service Revenues	3·0	2·6	2·4
Loans, Aids	13·3	10·5	12·1
Profit-Making Enterprises	5·8	7·1	7·3
Commercial Agencies	38·5	36·9	35·8
Social Welfare Institutions	1·5	1·4	1·3
Total	100·0	100·0	100·0
Expenditures:			
General Services	6·0	5·7	5·3
Defence and Security	13·2	13·6	14·5
Social Services	11·2	11·4	11·9
Economic Services	20·9	20·4	19·8
Debt Repayments	2·9	3·6	4·1
Profit-Making Enterprises	5·8	7·0	7·3
Commercial Agencies	38·5	36·9	35·8
Social Welfare Institutions	1·5	1·4	1·3
Total	100·0	100·0	100·0

Source: Europa, The Middle East and North Africa.

TABLE 11

Expenditure Under the Development Plans
(in Billions of Rials)

	First Plan		Second Plan		Third Plan		Fourth Plan	
		% of Total		% of Total		% of Total		% of Total
Agriculture/Irrigation	5·7	40·4	17·4	20·9	47·3	23·1	41·2	8·1
Industry/Mines	4·1	29·1	7·0	8·4	17·1	8·4	113·1	22·3
Transport/Communications	3·5	24·8	27·3	32·8	53·8	26·3	71·4	14·1
Social Services	·8	5·7	9·3	11·2	43·1[a]	21·1	73·5[a]	14·5
Power and Fuel	—	—	—	—	32·0	15·6	79·7	15·7
Total	14·1	—	83·2	—	204·6	—	506·8	—

Note: [a] = Health, education and housing.
Source: Central Bank of Iran, Annual Report.

1955–62 and a total investment of 83,200 million rials was achieved. The third five-year plan covered the period from September 1962 to March 1968. This plan was designed to raise national income by a 6 per cent annual rate of growth. The early years of this plan showed only a slow rate of development expenditure, but extremely rapid growth was attained in later years of the plan period. Total actual expenditure during the entire plan period was 204,600 million rials, which was 88·9 per cent of the total planned expenditure. During the fourth five-year plan, from 1969 to 1973, total expenditure was 557,000 million rials, which was 20·5 per cent above the original allocation. This was made possible by rising oil revenues during this plan period.

The actual allocation of expenditures under the first four plans is given in Table 11. Agriculture received 40·4 per cent of total expenditures, but this ratio drops for the second and third plans, and only 8·1 per cent of total expenditures was allocated to agriculture during the fourth plan. Transport and communications received between 20 and 30 per cent of total expenditures during the first three plans, which is reasonable, since, during the early stages of development, transport and communication facilities will encourage market economy, thus increasing total production through incentives for market production. The bulk of funds were directed to industry during the fourth plan. Power and fuel were also emphasised during the third and fourth plans.

The allocation of expenditure during the third and fourth plans is shown in Table 12. Primary emphasis was to be on agriculture and transportation; secondarily on industry, power and fuel. Agriculture received less attention during the fourth plan, while it seems that it should have been more emphasised, considering the low rate of growth of production in this sector. But increased emphasis was placed on industry, transport, and power and fuel.

Education, health and manpower training have not been stressed during any of these four plans, while a higher level of education, better health and, especially, skilled labourers are critically important during periods of rapid economic growth. Iran is currently suffering from this lack of foresight. And by and large, the current shortage of skilled manpower is a direct failure of the so-called plans, which were not even consistent.

X. THE FIFTH PLAN

The fifth Plan is the current five-year plan. Starting in 1973, original estimates of state investments during the plan period were set at 1,299 billion rials, but this was increased to 2,847 billion rials in August 1974. For the plan period, it is forecast that G.N.P. will grow from 1,547 billion rials to 3,866 billion rials or at an annual average rate of growth of 25·9 per cent. It is also predicted that during this plan period, oil's contribution to G.N.P. will increase to 48·7 per cent, while the share of industry and agriculture are expected to drop to 16·1 and 8 per cent, respectively. However, this is due to the substantial increase in the oil

TABLE 12

Sector Allocations of Third and Fourth Plans
(in Billions of Rials)

	Third Plan September 1962– March 1968		Fourth Plan March 1968– March 1973	
		% of Total		% of Total
Agriculture/Irrigation	49·0	21·3	65·0	13·5
Mines/Industry	28·6	12·4	125·3[a]	26·1
Power and Fuel	36·5	15·8	86·5[b]	18·0
Transport/Communications	59·5	25·9	100·3[c]	20·9
Education	18·1	7·9	35·0	7·3
Health	13·5	5·9	13·8	2·9
Manpower/Training	3·2	1·4	—	—
Urban Development	7·5	3·3	7·6	1·6
Statistics	1·7	·7	1·0	·2
Housing	12·4	5·4	24·0	5·0
Others	—	—	21·5	4·5
Total	230·0	100·0	480·0	100·0

Notes: [a] = Inc. Rls 26,334 mn for petroleum and natural gas.
[b] = Inc. Rls 48,500 mn for water development.
[c] = Inc. Rls 20,330 mn for telecommunications.
Source: Central Bank of Iran, Annual Report.

revenue and *not* a decrease in production in other sectors. The annual growth rate for industries and mines is expected to be 18 per cent, 7 per cent for agriculture, and 51·5 per cent for oil and gas, during the plan period.

The allocation of fixed investment during the fifth plan is given in Table 13. The bulk of investment is to be directed to industry and oil production, while agriculture will receive only 6·2 per cent of the total expenditures, and only 6·6 per cent of the total fund is allocated to education, health and social welfare. Considering the failure of the agricultural sector to keep up with the overall economic growth of the country, and the importance of a higher level of education, an increase in the supply of skilled labour, and better health for a developing country, it seems that even now not enough attention has been paid to these sectors in allocating funds for the fifth plan.

However, owing to the recent increase in Iran's oil revenue, from $6·5 billion in 1973 to over $20 billion in 1974, the fifth plan was revised upward in 1974. The revised plan is almost double that of the original plan in 1973, calling for about $70 billion worth of public and private investment. Housing is the largest single non-military expense in the fifth

TABLE 13

Fixed Investment During the Fifth Plan
(in Billions of Rials)

	Public Sector	Private Sector	Total	% of Total
Agriculture	102·6	50·0	152·6	6·2
Water	109·0	4·0	113·0	4·6
Industry	175·6	326·8	502·4	20·4
Mines	44·8	5·2	50·0	2·0
Oil	190·4	139·7	330·1	13·4
Gas	84·5	47·0	131·5	5·3
Electricity	118·8	—	118·8	4·8
Communications	53·4	—	53·4	2·2
Transport	187·3	4·0	191·3	7·8
Rural Development	36·0	2·5	38·5	1·6
Urban Development	61·0	—	61·0	2·5
Government Buildings	90·8	—	90·8	3·7
Housing	94·0	308·8	402·8	16·4
Education	125·9	2·6	128·5	5·2
Culture and Arts	5·0	·4	5·4	·2
Tourism	3·9	12·2	16·1	·7
Health	20·0	9·2	29·2	1·2
Social Welfare	5·5	—	5·5	·2
Physical Culture and Scouts	8·7	—	8·7	·4
Statistics and Studies	·7	—	·7	—
Others	30·1	—	30·1	1·2
Total	1,548·0	912·4	2,460·4	100·0

Source: Fifth National Development Plan, The Plan Organisation.

plan, which seems reasonable for this country (a survey made at the beginning of the plan showed that, nationwide, the average housing unit held 1·4 families and in urban areas, the average rose to 1·8 families). The current five-year plan calls for an expenditure of \$13·7 billion on housing by 1978, with the private sector providing two-thirds of the investment.

Iran will spend about \$11·7 billion on industry during this plan, with the goal of doubling industrial production, while the private sector will provide two-thirds of this investment. The largest investment in the industrial sector will be in chemicals and petro-chemicals (\$2·4 billion), and in metal and steel (\$3·4 billion). During this five-year plan, \$4·6 billion will be invested on power generation, which will lead to an increase in *per capita* consumption of electricity to 891 kwh, which is more than three times that of the 1973 level.

This plan calls for an expenditure of about \$2·5 billion to build dams, irrigation networks, water supply systems, sea water desalting plants, and flood control and hydropower generation. Water supply dams begun in the previous plan and completed in the current plan will add about 8·3 million acre-ft. of regulated water annually. Water regulated under dams begun in this plan will amount to about 17 million acre-ft. Out of a total $70 billion expenditure of the fifth-plan, $9·2 billion will be spent on the oil industry, $7·3 billion on transportation (of which $2·3 billion will go for roads, $2 billion for ports, $1·2 billion for railways, and $400 million for airports), and almost $1 billion for the expansion of mining operations that produce copper, iron, chromite, gold and coal.

XI. CONCLUSION

Gross national product and *per capita* income in Iran have been increasing at very rapid rates in recent years. Iran's performance compares favourably with Venezuela's *per capita* annual growth rate of 1·1 per cent for 1965–72; Iraq's 1·8 per cent, Algeria's 3·5 per cent, and Libya's 8·1 per cent.[5] However, industrial production, which has been increasing at a substantial rate, and the Iranian government's attempts at rapid development in some sectors, have also contributed to the recent economic growth of Iran. Real industrial output has increased. Transport and communications have been greatly developed. There have been some desirable structural changes, such as a diversion of resources to the industrial sector, which has a higher productivity than the agricultural sector, a higher rate of investment, and changes in the composition of imports towards more capital and intermediate goods.[6] All of these factors have been clearly beneficial to growth. However, real output in the agricultural sector has not increased fast enough, and agricultural output *per capita* has hardly changed in the last decade.

Further, the allocation of the labour force between different sectors and, in particular, between agricultural and industrial sectors, is not desirable, and further diversion of labour to the industrial sector seems to be necessary. The level of education has to be improved—this has not received sufficient allocations in development plans—large skilled-labour bottlenecks have already appeared. Because of this current technical manpower shortage, the Iranian government has resigned itself to importing foreign manpower; for example, it is expected that Iran will import 3,800 civil engineers and architects and 270,000 skilled construction workers. The level of health care is backward and the government should emphasise health programmes in the development plans.

Thus the Iranian government, through its expenditures, has largely stressed infrastructure and industrial development but has neglected, or at least it has been very unsuccessful in, the agricultural, social services and skilled manpower training areas. However, even its apparent success cannot yet be certified if the areas selected for industrialisation prove to be sectors where Iran does *not* enjoy a long-run comparative advantage; thus, the success or failure of import substitution (industrialisation) will have to await further time and analysis. But at least Iran's recent overall economic performance compares favourably with other OPEC nations.

On the other hand, future success is not in any way guaranteed; skilled labour and foreign exchange constraints have already converged in 1975. The shortage of technical and professional manpower is partially the result of inconsistent plans and also the rapid expansion of expenditures. And the foreign exchange bottleneck is clearly due to both the rapid expansion of military expenditures and the desire to go ahead with many unplanned projects (and possibly with very low rates of return) in order to spend all of the oil revenues. Iran would clearly do much better by making investment expenditures at a rate where the marginal product is reasonable and *not* at a rate dictated by oil revenues—only time will tell the waste that is possibly occurring.

NOTES

1. Because of data limitations, our study cannot go beyond 1973, a time of dramatic change in Iran resulting from the phenomenal increase in oil revenues. For economic development in Iran since 1900, see Julian Bharier's *The Economic Development of Iran: 1900–1970*, Oxford, 1971.
2. China in the 1950s had about a 25 per cent figure and the Soviet Union during its great surge forward had a ratio of about 30 per cent.
3. SIPRI Yearbook 1975.
4. A reason for this is the rapid increase in the Iranian chemical industry.
5. *The U.S. and World Development, Agenda for Action: 1975*, overseas Development Council.

Labour and Trade Unionism in Turkey: The Eregli Coalminers

Delwin A. Roy

The Eregli Coal Basin[1] is located in the province of Zonguldak, which is in northwestern Turkey bordering the Black Sea; within its boundaries lie virtually all of the known deposits of bituminous coal. This extremely mountainous area is the centre of Turkish heavy industry; besides coal, Turkey's two steel plants are located in this province—one at Karabuk and the other at Eregli.

The coal deposits are wholly owned by the state and operated by the Eregli Komürü Işletmesi (EKI), the Eregli Coal Administration, one of the more important state enterprises. Employing close to 50,000 workers, EKI and the basin itself have in recent years witnessed increasing labour difficulties and violence. The most major event, one with far-reaching implications and consequences, took place in March 1965.[2] Beginning as a somewhat localised event and ultimately spreading throughout the region and involving almost the entire labour force, this wildcat strike culminated in several coalminers being shot by Turkish marines in a midnight clash. Since then, the area has been plagued by spontaneous outbursts and demonstrations, wildcat strikes and violence. In most instances it has been directed against both management and the union, but not infrequently against the latter solely.

At the centre of these recurring disputes has been the largest local union in the area—for that matter, in Turkey—the Zonguldak Maden Işçileri Sendakasi (ZMWU), the Zonguldak Mine Workers' Union. All of the workers at EKI—some 47,000—are members, and it has exclusive representational rights with respect to collective bargaining for the mine workers. It is one of the most financially sound unions in Turkey, and the pattern which it sets in its collective agreements often serves as a model of demands in other sectors of the economy.

The labour movement in the basin is complex, involving as it does a heterogenous labour force in both cultural and educational terms. It comprises, in essence, some 30,000 workers who are not totally committed to an industrial way of life, and some 20,000 who are. It is in many ways a labour force in transition, moving slowly away from its agricultural orientation and increasingly being forced to rely on industrial employment for its livelihood. Caught clearly between two ways of life, the majority of the workers in the coal mines are frustrated and confused, given to emotional and uncontrolled outbursts against those features of their working lives which they feel impinge upon them but which they feel helpless to counter.

It is the problems with which the nascent labour movement is beset, when confronted by a culturally and intellectually disparate labour force, with which this article is concerned. While it deals directly with the situation of the coal miners of the Eregli Coal Basin and their union, the ZMWU, it is apparent that other locals in Turkey have experienced the same difficulties. While hard and fast parallels may be difficult to draw, it is clear that the Turkish labour movement as a whole has not been able to come to grips with its responsibilities to educate its workers in trade unionism, nor have they particularly concerned themselves with the special problems of the peasant as he moves toward industrial employment.

PART I

THE LABOUR FORCE OF THE COAL REGION

Table 1 indicates the size of the labour force at EKI according to its basic components for selected years. The totals shown for each year are somewhat understated because of the peculiar practice of using temporary workers systematically on a mass scale. Hence, while at any one time 34,000 (1965 approximate) workers are actually present at the coal works, 13,000 more who are in the villages awaiting their turn to work in the mines must be counted in the labour force as well; the total, then, is 47,000. These are the 'rotational workers', often termed the 'exchange, or reserve' workers.

This segment comprises the majority of the labour force, although in any given month they are in the minority at the workplace. They are divided into two groups, A and B, of approximately 13,000 each. Group A, for instance, will work for one month; the majority of these workers live, eat and relax in facilities provided them by the management of EKI. Upon completion of their tour of work, they are transported (by management) back to their villages, and Group B replaces them; this cycle is repeated throughout the year. This practice of rotation has been a characteristic of coalmining in this region since 1860 (with variations in the length of the working period). As such, the rotational workers cannot truly be considered a permanent industrial labour force, and they do not consider themselves so; rather, they are 'farmers who supplement their income by working in the mines'.

The balance of the labour force is comprised of permanent workers—approximately 20,000 (1965) including managerial personnel. They derive their entire income from industrial employment and usually reside in the immediate area of the coal works in either company housing or rentals from private citizens. Even this portion of the labour force is not truly permanent in its entirety. Many of those workers considered to be permanent may work for a continuous period of six months, a year, or possibly longer, and then return to the place (village or town) from which they originally came for one or two months. Later they return to EKI and repeat the cycle. They are, in essence, semi-permanent workers, but because they come and go on an individual basis and stay longer than rotational workers, they are considered to be permanent. EKI management, until recent years (i.e. up to 1961), has readily rehired these workers

TABLE 1

Structure of the Labour Force, 1942–1965

Year	Hewers	Total Underground[a]	Direct Surface[b]	Washeries	Other Services[c]	Total Surface	Cadre	Grand Total
1942	2,554	9,701	1,581	1,105	8,719	11,405	1,101	22,267
1945	3,743	14,876	2,302	1,648	10,095	14,045	1,868	30,787
1948	3,902	14,242	2,034	1,095	8,681	11,810	1,706	27,758
1951	4,181	14,160	1,886	976	8,496	11,358	1,620	27,138
1954*	5,092	16,520	1,718	1,329	10,952	13,999	1,482	32,001
1957*	4,739	17,856	2,762	1,910	10,488	15,207	1,397	34,460
1960	4,342	17,859	3,555	1,675	12,599	17,829	1,625	37,313
1963	3,100	16,107	2,714	906	9,811	13,485	1,572	31,164
1965*	3,185	16,643	2,542	915	10,341	13,798	1,516	31,957

Note: Figures reported are averages for the year indicated; employment levels may vary from day to day and month to month.

[a] This figure includes the number reported under 'Diggers'.

[b] These are personnel directly assigned to the various districts in a surface capacity.

[c] Includes all surface activity such as central services, washeries operations, and district service personnel. After 1960 it also includes personnel working in the Briquet factory.

* Election years.

Source: *TKI, Istatistik Servisi, Eregli Kömür Havzasi Istatistikleri, 1941–1961, 1963 and 1965*, Ankara.

whenever they chose to return; hence, although this practice was never officially condoned or adopted, by tradition it had in effect the characteristics of a systematic arrangement.

The labour force of EKI, then, is composed of two basic elements: temporary workers who are rotated on a systematic basis, and permanent and semi-permanent workers who, with the qualification noted above, are totally committed to the industrial labour force. Besides these, there is the office and administrative staff, which includes clerks, engineers and managers (above the foreman level).

WORK PATTERNS AND THE LABOUR FORCE

The basic division of the labour force noted above is reinforced by the nature and type of work performed by each group. Although there are some exceptions, generally the rotational workers are confined to performing tasks associated with actual production work. This, in turn, means that they perform their labour underground and at the coal face. At Kozlu District, for instance, out of a total labour force of 6,500 (1965), 4,500 work underground—1,700 in actual production work. There are 3,100 rotational workers, all of whom work underground; of the 1,700 directly involved in coal production, all are rotational workers. At Karadon District there are 10,900 workers (1965); of these, 3,500 are surface and 7,400 are underground workers, with 1,272 actually working the face. Of the total number of underground workers, 70 per cent are rotational; of those involved in working the coal seams, 100 per cent are rotational. In both districts rotational workers are only given surface jobs when they become too ill, or too old, to continue to work underground. These underground positions usually require considerable physical exertion and very little in the way of skill.[3]

Conversely, permanent workers hold jobs on the surface; if they work underground, they work in exploration and development of new production areas, as first-level foremen, or on transportation or technical jobs. They do not, and in fact refuse to, work in actual production, even though in recent years this has meant that they have had to go without employment. Only about 25 per cent of the permanent workers actually perform their tasks underground—the rest occupy a variety of surface positions (there are some 432 different jobs at EKI), most of which require a greater degree of skill than that required of the average production job.

According to the type of work, then, we find that the labour force is, in effect, divided into two distinct groups. Rotational workers perform the more physically taxing, dangerous and less skilled jobs and must work underground, while the permanent workers hold the more skilled positions which require their presence primarily, but not exclusively, on the surface. Permanent workers clearly do not aspire to hold production jobs; it is not unusual, however, to find that rotational workers prefer to work on the surface.

CHARACTERISTICS OF PERMANENT AND ROTATIONAL WORK GROUPS

One would expect that these characteristics of labour-force structure and job orientation would be rooted in factors other than merely that indicated so far, i.e. managerial policy. To some extent this is the case; cultural factors appear to have a great deal to do with the fact that one man is an unskilled rotational worker while another is not, why one refuses to work on a strenuous, dangerous job while another accepts this as 'his lot in life'. Cultural characteristics, then, also lead to a reinforcement, and in fact are a partial cause, of the diversification in the labour force noted so far.

The rotational workers of EKI are drawn from some 377 villages located throughout the province of Zonguldak and, as already noted, they are first and foremost peasants. In most instances, the jobs in the mines are handed down from father to son, with the father retiring from the job when his sons are old enough to replace him; usually this is between the ages of 40 to 45.[4] Working in the mines is a family tradition, often resulting in all of the male members of a family working in the mines. These workers live in a typical rural setting in the Turkish sense,[5] and seemingly do not wish to lead any other type of life. They are passive, obedient, rely heavily on anyone in authority to help mitigate their problems, and are somewhat fatalistic, trusting in their religion to take care of the exigencies of their lives.

The literacy rate of this group is estimated to be somewhere between 20–25 per cent.[6] Table 2 gives data on the literacy rate for Zonguldak Province. Several things are immediately apparent when one examines the data. First, there is a substantial discrepancy in the literacy rate in urban areas as opposed to rural. Secondly, the literacy rate of the rural male age six and over is increasing, which means that EKI can expect an increasingly more literate rotational labour force as this group attains employment age (18 years of age). Thirdly, note that the literacy rate after 1955 has declined in rural areas; the decline in urban area between 1950 and 1955 is no doubt due to the influx of people from rural areas.

The illiteracy rate is indicative of the extent of formal education which the average peasant of Zonguldak receives. Zonguldak Province ranks below the national average in terms of various educational factors, as can be seen from the data included in Table 3. While the trend for the past decade has been for a higher proportion of the eligible population to receive some form of schooling, in recent years this pattern has shown signs of reversing itself in several provinces; Zonguldak has tended to follow this pattern, particularly in rural areas (see Table 2).

In the author's own survey[7] of rotational workers, 45 per cent reported having received no formal education whatsoever; 55 per cent reported having received from one to five years of education, with the majority of these having had two years on the average. Over 60 per cent indicated that they are literate, with 15 per cent of these having received no formal education; in most instances, they received training while in the Army.

TABLE 2

Literacy Rate for Male Population Age 6 and Over for Zonguldak Province, 1960–1960

Male Population	1950[a]	(Thousands) 1955[b]	1960
Zonguldak Province (overall)			
Literate	85·4	110·7	125·2
Illiterate	99·0	89·0	109·9
Total	184·4	200·1	235·1
Literacy Rate	46·3%	55·3%	53·3%
Localities with 10,000 or more inhabitants			
Literate	39·2	38·7	53·4
Illiterate	13·9	16·3	20·3
Total	53·0	55·3	73·7
Literacy Rate	73·9%	70·0%	71·9%
Localities with fewer than 10,000 inhabitants			
Literate	50·4	72·0	71·8
Illiterate	81·0	72·8	89·7
Total	131·4	144·8	161·4
Literacy Rate	38·3%	49·5%	44·4%
Turkey (overall)			
Literate	4,091·0	5,478·7	6,157·8
Illiterate	4,853·0	4,292·1	5,324·4
Total	8,944·0	9,819·6	11,491·2
Literacy Rate	45·7%	55·6%	53·6%

Notes: Discrepancies in total figures are due to rounding off and use of an 'Unknown' category by Census Office.
[a] Figures reported for this year are for 'over age 5' and for 'localities with more, and less, than 5,000 inhabitants'.
[b] The Census Office used a 'Read Only' column category for this year; the amounts reported are insignificant, and have been counted in the illiteracy figures.
Source: T. C. Başbakanlik, Devlet Istatistik Enstitüsü, *Genel Nüfüs Sayimi: Türkiye Nüfüsü, 1950, 1955 and 1960*, Yayin Nos. 359, 399 and 444, Ankara.

The relatively high percentage indicating literacy was due to the inability to distinguish differing levels of proficiency; clearly, some of those interviewed could not read or write, but were embarrassed to admit this fact. Almost all of those between the ages of 20–25 indicated that they had not attended school. Judging from the data published by the Census Office and the Ministry of Education, it would appear that the literacy rate of the rural population is about 40 per cent; it could possibly be lower for the rotational workers as a whole, depending on the age distribution of the labour force (unfortunately, there are no data on this).

The rotational system of employment has slowed down the rate of

TABLE 3

Educational Factors for Zonguldak Province and Turkey, 1960 (Percentages)

Educational Factors	Zonguldak	Turkey
Villages with schools	65·1	66·6
Persons between ages 6–10 enrolled in schools	63·8	78·3
Persons between ages 11–13 enrolled in schools	9·5	11·7
Persons between ages 14–16 enrolled in schools	5·0	6·5

Source: T. C. Milli Egitim Bakanligi, *Turkiyede Okullarin Mevcudiyet ve Yeterligi, 1964*, Test ve Araştirma Burosu, Ankara.

rural-to-urban migration in Zonguldak Province, although there has been a tendency for those in the extreme southern region of the province to move closer to places where industrial activity is located. As will be seen later this has led to the majority of the population being concentrated in the rural areas immediately adjacent to such centres of industrialisation. It has also allowed the workers to maintain their rural way of life and value system.

The permanent workers possess characteristics in sharp contrast to those who work on rotation. This segment of the labour force comes from all over Turkey, but the majority come from an area known as the Black Sea Region, primarily from the provinces of Trabzon, Giresun, Artvin and Rize (located in the northeastern-most portion of Turkey). To have workers coming from this region has also been a matter of tradition,[8] for there is little land available in this area nor is there any other means of earning a livelihood. Tables 4 and 5 illustrate the pattern of immigration into Zonguldak Province. On average, 63 per cent of those migrating to Zonguldak have been males; 18·6 per cent of the immigrants have settled in rural areas.

Semi-permanent workers come from provinces in the Black Sea Region

TABLE 4

Immigration to Zonguldak Province, 1935–60

Year	Total Population	Persons Residing in District but Born Elsewhere	Per cent of Total Population
1935	322,108	21,383	6·63
1945	383,481	45,413	11·84
1950	426,684	34,355	8·05
1955	491,147	59,284	12·07
1960	569,059	75,472	13·26

Source: T. C. Imar ve Iskân Bakanligi, Plânlama ve Imar Genel Müdürlügü, *Zonguldak Bölgesi Ön Plâni*, Ankara, 1964, p. 25.

TABLE 5

Immigration by Province of Origin, 1960

Province	Immigrants from Province	Per cent of Total Immigrants
Trabzon	15,692	20·79
Kastamonu	8,720	11·55
Çankiri	6,854	9·08
Giresun	5,872	7·78

Note: All other provinces contributed less than 5 per cent.
Source: T. C. Imar ve Iskân Bakanligi, Plânlama ve Imar Genel Müdürlügü, *Zonguldak Bölgesi Ön Plâni*, Ankara, 1964, p. 26.

as well as from the provinces of Kars and Van. As heavy snows cover much of the land in the latter, there is little work for the farmers of this area to do—particularly during the period from October to April. Hence, many of them travel to Zonguldak for employment through the winter, returning to their farms in the spring.

The workers from the Black Sea Region are generally considered to be more aggressive, better educated and more literate; this is reflected in the type of jobs which they fill and, as we shall see, their influence and participation in the labour movement in the coal basin. This region is the land of the Lâz—a people known historically for their fierce and aggressive manner. Table 6 gives data on literacy for four provinces in the Black Sea Region from which substantial numbers of permanent workers come (compare with data in Table 2). The most significant contrast is in the literacy rate for those living in rural areas in the Black Sea Region; in most instances, these rates are considerably higher than those for Zonguldak Province. This can partly be explained by the fact that a greater percentage of the population attends school and the proportion staying in school is higher than in Zonguldak. Table 7 gives data on educational factors in this region (compare with Table 3). With the notable exception of the province of Giresun, the data show that the other Black Sea provinces rank above Zonguldak in terms of the educational factors listed.

In interviews with surface workers, it was found that almost all of them were literate and considerably more aware of a broader range of matters—particularly those things which affected them—than rotational workers. This relatively 'educated' position of the permanent worker is due, as we have seen, to his having received more education on the average; it is also due to the fact that workers from the Black Sea Region are generally more travelled than are those from Zonguldak.[9] The villagers usually know only their villages and the coal mines; they have little occasion or desire to travel elsewhere. Besides being physically more mobile, permanent workers are occupationally more mobile as well. Over half the merchant

TABLE 6

Literacy Rates for Male Population Age 6 and Over in Four Provinces in Black Sea Region, 1950–1960 (Percentages)

Provinces	1950[a]	1955	1960
Literacy Rate (overall)			
Artvin[b]	—	—	60·8
Giresun	41·7	49·8	45·4
Rize	50·9	66·3	63·3
Trabzon	40·5	53·9	51·3
Literacy Rate (localities with 10,000 or more)			
Artvin	—	—	80·0
Giresun	70·0	81·2	80·0
Rize	70·2	75·3	75·3
Trabzon	72·1	75·0	77·7
Literacy Rate (localities with less than 10,000)			
Artvin	—	—	60·0
Giresun	40·0	56·2	43·2
Rize	48·2	60·5	61·6
Trabzon	39·1	50·9	54·4

[a] Data for this year are for 'Male Population over Age 5' and 'Localities with more, and less, than 5,000'.
[b] No data indicated prior to 1960.
Source: T. C. Başbakanlik, Devlet Istatistik Enstitüsü, *Genel Nüfüs Sayimi: Türkiye Nüfüsü, 1950, 1955, and 1960*, Yayin Nos. 359, 399, and 444, Ankara.

TABLE 7

Educational Factors for Selected Black Sea Provinces and Turkey, 1960 (Percentages)

Educational Factors	Artvin	Giresun	Rize	Trabzon	Turkey
Villages with schools	95·1	54·7	72·8	68·2	66·6
Persons aged 6–10 enrolled in schools	81·2	43·8	66·8	42·7	78·3
Persons aged 11–13 enrolled in schools	15·1	9·5	10·6	11·5	11·7
Persons aged 14–16 enrolled in schools	5·3	3·0	6·7	7·5	6·5

Source: T. C. Milli Egitim Bakanligi, *Türkiyede Okullarin Mevcudiyeti ve Yeterligi 1964*, Test ve Araştirma Burosu, Ankara.

class in the city of Zonguldak has come from the Black Sea Region, many initially working at the mines.

The cultural differences of these two groups—permanent and rotational workers are significant in many respects; we have already seen that it is reflected in the type of jobs to which they aspire and will accept. One of the most significant results is that it has meant that management has developed (not necessarily in the official sense) two sets of labour policy for the problems which they encounter with each group, and the way that they have to be handled differs substantially.

RECRUITMENT OF THE LABOUR FORCE

Recruiting that portion of the labour force involved in performing surface tasks has not proved to be difficult over the years. The well-established tradition of men coming from the Black Sea Region and other areas of Turkey to the coal basin, as noted above, has resulted in an ample supply of workers for these jobs. If anything, particularly in the past five years, there has been an excessive supply of workers available for surface or non-production jobs.[10]

With respect to rotational workers, the situation is somewhat different. Historically, it has been difficult to get adequate numbers of workers on a consistent basis to work in the mines; lately, this shortage has been somewhat alleviated by the increasing rate of mechanisation of coal production processes and the implementation of a policy of economic rationalisation, particularly since 1960. Prior to this, the rotational labour needs of EKI were recruited in three ways: (1) relying upon tradition and the worker's own desire to supplement his income by working in the mines; (2) using local party leaders and village officials as labour contractors who were paid bonuses according to the number of workers they recruited; and (3) occasionally resorting to the use of forced labour. These practices have not been used separately but simultaneously, with an emphasis upon whatever method proved most successful or necessary at any given time.

Under normal conditions, tradition and custom has usually led to an ample supply of rotational labour being available. However, there are times—particularly during religious holidays and harvesting time—when the supply has been insufficient; at such times the firm has relied heavily on local village officials and party leaders acting as labour contractors.

The firm itself maintains labour bureaux in several of the main population centers of the province such as Devrek, Bartin and Caycuma, and the officials who staff these often are required to travel throughout the villages encouraging the men to come to the mines. Presthus noted in this respect that

> If an insufficient number of miners show up at the time of recruitment it is the duty of the district labor officer to persuade others to come. He gets the help of the muhtars[11] and of the town political chief in this process. Both function as recruiting agents for EKI.[12]

At times, the Director of the labour office himself has found it necessary to travel throughout the province encouraging workers to come to work.

It is the 'muhtarlik system' that is one of the most interesting facets of the recruitment process. The muhtar, as the village headman, is the most influential man in the villages and towns; he may be the religious as well as the political head. The practice has been to use the muhtars and the local party leaders (of the party in power) to encourage workers to come to the mines. This system, of course, has not been without its problems, for there is evidence that these officials often used the stature of their office and other pressures to force the workers to work. Because rotational workers are strictly temporary, i.e. they sign on for only one period at a time and the employment relationship is severed if any one of them fails to show up within two days of the beginning of the next applicable tour of work, recruitment is a continuous process and, thus, a lucrative source of income for these agents. This system was abandoned in 1961 owing to the aforementioned reduction in employment levels at EKI, and so far has not been reinstituted.

Forced labour has been resorted to at various times in the history of the coal basin. When coal exploitation first began in 1848, most of the workers had to be imported from the Balkans—Montenegro and Croatia—because the local population refused to work underground. As the coalworks expanded and production increased, however, local peasants began to turn to the mines for employment, but still in insufficient numbers, given the labour requirements. In 1865, the mines in the basin came under the jurisdiction of the Office of Naval Administration; in that same year the Dilaver Paşa Regulations[13] were adopted. These regulations provided for forced labour in the mines:

> According to the regulations regarding employment, the male peasants of the Province between the ages of 13–50 were forced to work 15 days in the mines, spend 15 days in the village, and then return to the mines.[14]

The penalties for failing to report for work were usually to double the amount of time the errant worker had to spend in the mines. The practice of forced labour was abolished in 1882.

Forced labour was again resorted to during World Wars I and II. The latter instance is especially important, since many of the rotational workers still employed in the basin began working at that time. Under the forced labour provisions, a worker could conceivably become involved in criminal prosecution should he repeatedly violate these regulations by absenting himself from the workplace or failing to report at the proper time.

The workers, while submitting to such practices in most instances, regard being forced to work as an infringement of their personal dignity. Several workers interviewed indicated that most of their friends, and they themselves, disliked being forced to work; some stated that during the strike a rumour was circulating to the effect that forced labour was going to be reinstated once again.

Since 1961, EKI has relied largely on the worker's own willingness and desire to work. The reversal in employment trends has resulted in an ample number of workers being available and, hence, allowed the firm to rely on this more desirable method of recruitment. More recently, since the fall of 1965, employment levels have once again begun to rise, and

EKI may find that it will have to reinstitute some of the past practices or develop new methods of recruitment.[15]

WORKER ATTITUDES

Rotational workers are not emotionally or socially committed to the concept of industrial employment; they look upon mining as an unpleasant, temporary expedient rather than as a career. These workers themselves refer to their working in the mines as 'yatmaga gitmek', meaning literally 'going to lie down'. The attitudes which they hold embody several contradictions that are at one and the same time conducive and detrimental to the efficient performance of their jobs.

On the one hand they are obedient, passive, respectful of authority and willing to do what they are told without question. As an ex-district manager put it, 'they are the best people I have ever seen in a coal mining operation; I have been to Germany, Belgium and the United States and they are the finest . . . they do what they are told'. The rotational worker seldom complains[16] about the job that he must do or the conditions under which he must work; it is seldom, if ever, that he openly complains of his superiors and the treatment they give him. Yet, he dislikes working in the mines and is ill-motivated on his job.

In interviews with rotational workers, when asked 'Would you prefer permanent employment at EKI?' fewer than 20 per cent responded in the affirmative; 45 per cent indicated that they would prefer permanent employment at any other place other than EKI. When asked 'Would you prefer employment elsewhere (either temporary or permanent)?' 65 per cent responded affirmatively.[17] Generally speaking, most of those interviewed displayed mixed feelings—apathy and indifference not only toward their jobs, but toward EKI management and its policies as well as the policies and leadership of their own union. At the same time, they stated that there was little else they could do; there was nowhere else to earn money (or the same amount of money). They did not wish to appear disrespectful of their supervisors or indicate that they were ungrateful for having a job, and yet they were clearly resentful of the fact that they indeed had to work in the mines in order to subsist.

This heterogeneity in rotational worker attitudes has had a variety of consequences. Managers and engineers at EKI tend to hold a low opinion of them.

> Miners and workers at this level do not attract much sympathy from their superiors. They are regarded as 'lazy', 'they lie, they cheat'. They are 'dirty' and 'careless in their living habits'.[18]

This managerial attitude has led to administrative policies and practices that are often arbitrary and inconsistent—and regarded as somewhat unfair by the workers. Historically, this has not led to active resistance, but worker resentment has expressed itself in other ways—absenteeism, complaining, refusal to change methods of work and the like. It expresses the same kind of passive attitude with which the rotational worker approaches the whole idea of employment in the mines.

In sum, then, the attitudes which the worker holds are not likely to prove to be a source of positive motivation. He works at EKI because he feels he must; he does not like it and, apparently, when he feels he no longer needs the income he severs the relationship as quickly as possible. This attitude manifests itself in low productivity, and indifference mixed with resentment and animosity.

Permanent workers seem to hold more positive attitudes regarding their work. As has already been noted, they hold jobs requiring greater skill and in some cases a degree of authority and responsibility; hence, they occupy positions of higher 'status', deriving more satisfaction therein. They are career workers in that they derive their sole income from industrial employment; because they live in urban areas, their attitudes tend to be industrially oriented or 'progressive'.

Those who hold technical jobs, generally electro-mechanical workers, seem particularly proud of their position. They note that there are few technically skilled workers in Turkey and that they are 'more valuable' to EKI (and to Turkey in general).

As positive as their attitudes may be, this has not meant that permanent workers are necessarily more productive. Surface jobs, usually held by permanent workers, are often created solely for the purpose of extending favouritism or paying off political debts or insuring a favourable 'political climate' prior to an election.[19] Hence, a good deal of excessive employment occurs in this category of jobs. As well, efficiency and higher productivity have not been high-priority goals of the management in the past, and this has led to an atmosphere hardly conducive to high productivity. Even if a worker wanted to produce, he might find this attitude inimical to his own interests. Given the extreme arbitrariness and presence of favouritism regarding promotions, merit raises and transfers, being productive or non-productive may be of little or no consequence.

Permanent jobs are more highly valued than rotational work and as such absenteeism, complaining and other forms of worker unrest and dissatisfaction are not as prevalent. Workers who fill these positions are generally better educated and more aggressive; this has led management to treat them with greater deference, hence there has been little occasion for permanent workers to complain.

The attitudes which each group—i.e. permanent and temporary—hold toward one another are also important. Permanent workers, while they obviously feel superior in ability, skill and status to rotational workers, do not look down upon them as such but, rather, 'respect them for their bravery'. As one worker put it, 'Why should we feel angry toward one another—the country is ours'. Given the nature of his position, the permanent worker in fact has little cause to feel animosity toward the rotational worker.

The attitude of the rotational workers in this respect is more difficult to ascertain. As has been noted already, they are at one and the same time submissive and resentful. They do not display overtly this resentment—and not toward the permanent workers. They are aware that there are differences between them, that permanent workers are perhaps more favoured by management and have easier and better jobs; this is often expressed in rather oblique ways. For instance, one worker who was asked whether he had voted in the last union election said, 'Yes, but I didn't vote for the Lâz—I voted for the Turk'. The 'Lâz' was an obvious reference to a permanent worker from the Black Sea Region who was running for a union office; the 'Turk' was a rotational worker from Zonguldak Province. When a major strike did occur in 1965, it was the permanent workers who protected the officials and managers, who kept the pumps going and who, generally, refrained from participating in the demonstrations and tried to calm those who were; it was the rotational worker, goaded as he may have been, who was most active in this event. Basically, it would appear that there is some animosity toward the permanent workers from the point of view of those who are temporary, but they don't seem to recognise it as such and believe that it is not the case.

THE ROTATIONAL WORKER AND THE AGRICULTURAL ECONOMY

One final aspect of the labour force must be considered here in order to have a basic understanding of many of the points made so far regarding the exchange workers; this is the economic nature of the agricultural sector from which most of these workers are drawn.

It is almost axiomatic that the worker who finds that he must work in the mines in order to supplement his income would be basically involved in subsistence farming. The size of the land holdings are, on the average, quite small, the methods of farming crude and primitive, with agricultural production varying according to the weather and little else. In addition to these factors, which in their own right severely limit the livelihood which one could expect from the land, there are three major problems which currently affect the agricultural sector of Zonguldak Province and, hence, those who depend upon the land for part of their income: 1. Population density, particularly on land that is most suitable for agriculture, is higher than in most other regions of Turkey, and is increasing. 2. The amount of arable land in the province is decreasing at an increasing rate due to severe soil erosion. 3. The *per capita* agricultural income is lower than in most other regions of Turkey, and is declining. These problems and their various manifestations need to be examined in greater detail in order to understand adequately the current economic situation.

The province of Zonguldak is, generally speaking, mostly mountainous, with 67 per cent of the total land area (863,200 hectares or 8,627 sq. km.) comprised of slopes inclining 20 degrees or more. The result is that most of the land is not suitable for agriculture. As of 1960, approximately 299,000 hectares, or 34·8 per cent of the land area, were under some form of cultivation, even though agricultural experts deem only 118,000 hectares as actually suitable for agriculture.[20] This means that most of the land being used for agriculture is marginal. Of the land under cultivation, including that which is most suitable, most is located in the Bartin-Çaycuma-Devrek region, where it is relatively level.

Population density is, of course, directly correlated to the pattern of agricultural activity. Table 8 gives the population of Zonguldak Province

TABLE 8

Rural and Urban Population of Zonguldak Province, 1940–1960

Year	Total Population	% Change	Urban	% Change (Thousands)	Rural	% Change	Density (population/km²)
1940	349·8		49·6		300·1		—
1945	383·5	9·6	60·5	21·9	323·0	7·6	—
1950	426·7	11·3	63·1	4·0	363·6	11·1	57
1955	491·1	15·1	95·3	51·0	395·9	8·9	58[a]
1960	569·0	15·8	123·1	28·8	446·0	12·6	66

Notes: The area of the province in 1950 was 7,449 km.²; 1955–58, 483 km.²; 1960–68› 627 km.².

[a] In some census tables this is listed as 57.

Source: T. C. Başbakanlik, Devlet Istatistik Enstitüsü, *Genel Nüfüs Sayimi: Türkuye Nüfüsü*, 1950, 1955 and 1960, Yayin nos. 359, 399, and 444, Ankara.

according to location and the overall population density. Population projections for the province indicate that it will increase at a rate of 3 per cent per year for approximately the next twenty-five years; by 1980, then, the population of the province would be in excess of 1,000,000.[21]

The rate of rural-to-urban migration has not been consistent, increasing sharply in the period 1950–55 and declining in the same manner in the period 1955–60. This can be partially explained by (1) the fact that a new iron and steel mill was completed at Karabük in 1951, and (2) employment was increasing in the coal basin. In addition, there have been some shifts of the population within Zonguldak Province; notice that (see Table 9) in the sub-provinces of Bartin, Çaycuma and Devrek, the population density has increased markedly in 1955–60 (the land area of these sub-provinces remaining relatively stable). The sub-provinces of Safranbolu and Karabük, on the other hand, have experienced a declining rate of population increase and, hence, a slower rate of increase in population. (Note that in the case of Karabük, the majority of the population increase has occurred in urban, not rural, areas.) As noted above, there has been a tendency for the population to locate more closely to centres of industrial activity; also, the land in the sub-provinces actually losing population is quite mountainous, and particularly unsuitable for farming.

Soil erosion has proved to be a problem which has compounded that of over-population on arable land and on marginal agricultural land.

TABLE 9

Population Density by Sub-Province, 1950–60

Sub-Province	1950 Area	1950 Density	1955 Area (sq. kilometers)	1955 Density	1960 Area	1960 Density
Center	717	121	607	181	637	207
Bartin	1,115	69	1,403	59	1,266	67
Çaycuma	757	61	494	102	490	118
Devrek	1,554	42	1,858	29	1,222	51
Eflani	—	—	654	33	619	35
Eregli	996	62	1,134	59	1,132	67
Karabük	—	—	659	75	1,376	48
Kurucaşile	—	—	—	—	159	58
Safranbolu	1,593	40	962	25	1,013	27
Ulus	717	36	712	38	713	45

Source: T. C. Başbakanlik, Devlet Istatistik Enstitüsü, *Genel Nüfüs Sayimi: Türkiye Nüfüsü*, 1950, 1955 and 1960, Yayin nos. 359, 399 and 444, Ankara.

Extensive erosion has been observed in areas comprising some 13 per cent (97,300 hectares) of the total land area of the province. The prime cause of deterioration of the land in this area has been the planting of previously virgin regions. Other causes are the cultivation of steep and inclined land, improper methods of tillage, the planting of inappropriate crops, animal grazing (particularly goats), and the practice of leaving the land bare for the greater part of the year.[22] Erosion is most prevalent in those areas where farming activity is being conducted. The result has been that agricultural productivity has either declined or, at best, remained constant in an effort to maintain output, more marginal land is brought under production, which often only serves to aggravate the problem of erosion, since it is usually mountainous land which must be tilled.

These two major factors—increasing population concentration and the erosion of farm lands—coupled with a primitive agricultural technology have resulted in a relatively (compared with the overall average of Turkey) low and declining level of agricultural income for the region. Table 10 shows the output for various major crops of the region for the years 1959 to 1963.

The pattern of production, area sown and productivity indicated in the years included in the Table is relatively the same for years prior to this. It is evident that, while the area sown is somewhat stable from year to year for most crops, production and productivity fluctuate rather sharply. Note particularly that in those years in which the area sown has increased, production has not necessarily increased; in some instances it has actually declined (e.g. wheat, 1961 62; barley, 1960–61; maize, 1961 62; etc.). Climatic variations have far more to do with the amount of production than any other variable.

TABLE 10

Agricultural Production of Zonguldak Province, Selected Crops, 1959–63

Type of Crop	1959	1960	1961	1962	1963
Wheat					
Area sown (hec.)	69,600	71,950	73,850	67,000	67,175
Production (tons)	51,620	74,730	63,080	60,170	61,860
Kg./hectare	741	1,038	854	895	920
Kg./hec. (Turkey)	1,042	1,097	907	1,083	1,273
Barley					
Area sown	21,150	23,525	25,075	22,770	23,965
Production	19,110	30,253	26,162	24,347	29,060
Kg./hectare	903	1,285	1,043	1,069	1,212
Kg./hec. (Turkey)	1,200	1,304	1,058	1,250	1,504
Maize					
Area sown	60,000	62,000	62,400	61,950	63,900
Production	79,060	86,567	72,235	71,075	66,500
Kg./hectare	1,247	1,396	1,157	1,147	1,041
Kg./hec. (Turkey)	1,428	1,568	1,442	1,199	1,477
Dry Beans					
Area sown	2,130	2,154	2,153	2,299	2,000
Production	2,766	2,690	2,702	2,770	2,490
Kg./hectare	1,298	1,248	1,254	1,205	1,245
Kg./hec. (Turkey)	1,371	1,304	1,175	1,089	1,266
Potatoes					
Area Sown	2,345	2,132	2,215	2,120	1,910
Production	16,815	12,920	10,995	12,510	12,700
Kg./hectare	7,170	6,060	4,963	5,900	6,649
Kg./hec. (Turkey)	10,135	8,750	9,591	10,869	11,428
Grapes					
Area sown	2,550	2,521	3,242	3,242	3,295
Production	5,497	3,536	6,631	11,131	11,242
Kg./hectare	2,155	1,402	2,045	3,433	3,411
Kg./hec. (Turkey)	4,189	3,549	4,115	4,375	3,391
Other Fruits[a]					
Area sown	1,452	1,430	1,767	1,784	1,837
Production	26,163	20,882	25,147	18,123	23,842
Kg./hectare	18	15	14	10	13
Kg./hec. (Turkey)	17	13	18	16	16

Note: [a] Area sown refers to numbers of trees in thousands; production refers to number in thousands.

Source: T. C. Başbakanlik, Devlet Istatistik Enstitüsü, *Zirai Bünye ve Istihsâl*, 1959–61, 1961–63, Yayin nos. 445 and 455, Ankara.

The technology of farming in this region is, in the majority of cases, quite primitive. Mechanisation is not possible, owing to the pattern of land ownership and the topography of the region, as well as the low income of the average peasant. Even where technical changes could be made, there has not been widespread utilisation, or acceptance by the farmers. This is partly due to the fact that it is the women who perform the agricultural tasks, not the men, and they have little interest in, or understanding of, new methods. Although the premise has been that rotational workers work the land when they are not in the mines, this has not proved to be the case; they rest and/or frequent the coffee houses, leaving the farm work to their wives and daughters.

Of the workers interviewed, 90 per cent reported that they owned land, with 83 per cent indicating that their land holdings ranged in size from one to five dönüms (1 dönüm = $\frac{1}{4}$ acre). When asked if they derived any cash income from their land, all of them replied that they did not, and that their land barely fed their families. In 1960, even though 70 per cent of the population of the province was committed to agriculture, it accounted for only 18·2 per cent of the total GNP of the region. Disguised unemployment is obviously quite high; some estimates indicate that 75 per cent of those on the land are non-productive.

With the erratic nature of agricultural production, owing to inadequate technology and the other factors noted above, given a population increase, it is axiomatic that agricultural income is declining. Although it is impossible accurately to estimate what the average income is, or has been, one might reasonably infer that the land cannot support an increasing population and that economic pressures are becoming more severe.

Agricultural co-operative programmes providing seed, fertilisers and loans exist in the area, but their effect has been negligible. Since ownership is often difficult if not impossible to prove, many cannot qualify for loans. Those who do, use the money for a variety of things, many of which are totally unassociated with increasing agricultural production. When the loans fall due, they borrow money from a local usurer, pay off the balance of the loan, get a new one which allows them to pay back the usurer and possibly have some left over for themselves; this cycle is repeated year after year. Commercial or cash crops are almost non-existent in the region and transport difficulties preclude any farmer from marketing his products on all but a local basis, if in fact he has anything to sell.

To summarise then, the land is poor and in some areas is getting poorer; subsistence farming is, by far, the most prevalent characteristic of the agriculture. The economic pressures resulting from the factors noted above have become particularly severe in the past 7–8 years—exactly at the time that EKI undertook a policy of reduced employment. The result has been that the rotational worker, already somewhat resentful of his situation, has become increasingly frustrated by the problems with which he is confronted; more important, he cannot see any way of alleviating the conflicts which he encounters.

EKI has, in essence, two rather distinct labour forces, each embodying its own peculiarities. The rural mentality of the rotational worker, his agricultural orientation, and his dislike for the rigours of industrial employment in the mines, coupled with a managerial policy which calls upon him to make only a partial commitment to industrialism, create obvious problems. Conversely, permanent workers, with their sharply contrasting attitudes and 'urban frame of reference', present yet another type of problem. Perhaps the most significant consequence has been that the groundwork has been laid for what one might call 'quasi-exploitation' of one group by another. The fact that permanent workers are totally committed to industrial employment means that they have a greater interest in certain types of policies and institutions being developed; the relatively passive attitude of the rotational workers has (1) allowed the permanent workers, as a minority, to pursue their own interests with some success, and (2) allowed management to cater to the interests of this minority with little fear of repercussions arising from adopting a differential labour policy. This divisive character of the labour force, while it has not led to open conflict between the two groups, has led to the formation of labour organisations which mirror the peculiarities and attitudes of each, a circumstance which has increasingly given rise to situations where conflict might well arise.

PART II

THE LABOUR MOVEMENT IN THE COAL BASIN

The organised labour movement in the Eregli Coal Basin had its beginning, to all intents and purposes, with the passage of Law 5018 on 26 February, 1947.[23] Prior to this, the Law on Associations, passed in 1938, precluded the formation of any organisation along 'class lines' which in practice prevented the formation of trade unions. A unique case has prevailed in the coal basin, however, in that, through special legislation enacted in 1921, a 'quasi-union' was allowed to come into existence; this is the 'Amele Birligi' (Labour Federation), which is basically a mutual aid society. It continues to exist to this day, although it has not undertaken any other functions than those originally stipulated. Article 3 of Law 5018 stipulated that:

> An employee who is employed in different types of work may join one or more of the trade unions corresponding to the said types of work.
>
> Two or more trade unions may be formed in a single branch of activity.[24]

In the coal basin, this has led to the development of no fewer than 20 unions (excluding the Labour Federation), which have memberships ranging in size from 15 to 47,000. The largest of these is the Zonguldak Mine Workers' Union which, according to the Trade Unions Act and Collective Agreements, Strike and Lock-out Act (Laws 274 and 275) passed in July, 1963, has sole collective bargaining rights for the labour force at EKI.[25] It is a general union, comprising workers from the some 432 occupations performed in the industry.

The other 19 organisations, which are known as 'locals', are, in effect, mutual aid societies; they do not have any collective bargaining rights.

Besides these locals and the ZMWU, there is the Maden-Iş Federasyonu (WIF), the Mine Workers' Federation, to which most of them affiliate; it, in turn, is affiliated with the major labour conferation, the Türk-Iş Confederasyonu (TLC), the Turkish Labour Confederation.

The multiplicity of unions has meant that most workers in the basin belong to at least two unions; not an insignificant number belong to three or four. Because of this rather prolific state of labour organisations, the labour movement in the basin is complex, characterised by conflicts of interest and inter-organisational friction. In order to clearly understand the nature of this conflict, as well as the overall context and characteristics of the labour movement in this region, the following factors will be considered: (1) the development and growth of the ZMWU; (2) the structure and orientation of the locals and their relations with the ZMWU; (3) rank-and-file participation in union activity; and (4) the relationship between the ZMWU and the Mine-Workers' Federation and the TLC.

BRIEF HISTORY OF THE ZONGULDAK MINE WORKERS' UNION

The ZMWU was founded in 1946 by eleven permanent workers; initially it was known as the Zonguldak Mine Workers' Society.[26] When the law was amended in February 1947, it then took the name 'union'.

There have been three rather distinct periods in the history of the ZMWU: (1) the period from October 1946 to April 1947, when it was a workers' society; (2) the period from April 1947 to July 1963, characterised by legal limitations on the performance of contemporary trade-union functions; and (3) the period from July 1963 to the present, during which it has begun to develop and exercise its newly won rights.

From 1946 to 1947, as a workers' society, it served few if any significant functions. It had no official relations with EKI management, few members, and provided financial aid of limited scope to the workers where and when it could. When the law was amended in 1947, the functions which it could perform, and the methods by which it could perform them, were clearly stipulated.[27] These functions fell, roughly, into three categories: worker representation in disputes and arbitration proceedings; provision of mutual aid and assistance to the workers; and the organisation of social and educational activities. The constitution of the ZMWU, adopted in 1957, duly reflected these legally acceptable functions:

> The Union has been founded for realisation of the following purposes:
>
> (a) To provide unity and order among workers working in occupations indicated in Law 151 and related interpretations of the Grand National Assembly (Parliament).

(b) To sign collective contracts in the name of its members.
(c) To help in the solution of job conflicts that may arise between employers and workers or their organisations and to take measure, within the framework of the law, to protect the rights of workers in case there are attempts to decrease wages by employers or their associations.
(d) To make contacts with other occupational organisations provided there is no legal prohibition against doing so.
(e) To arrange conferences and publications to increase the occupational knowledge and culture of its members.
(f) To establish consumer, production, credit and housing-construction co-operatives and similar organisations and to co-operate with them.
(g) To establish health and sport activities. No commercial interests are intended in the development of these.[28]

From 1947 to 1963, when Laws 274 and 275 became effective, the union was, in essence, confined to performing mutual aid and assistance and social functions; the provisions regarding collective bargaining and worker representation in disputes remained decidedly underdeveloped and somewhat unattainable.[29] One of the founders and past presidents of the ZMWU notes:

> The period from 1947–63 was mainly characterised by unilatera decisions being made by management. If the problems were serious enough, the union would go to appropriate ministries and ask for help. If the government said OK then the problem was solved—if not, there was nothing to be done. It was not until after 1963, and Laws 274 and 275, that the trade union movement, in the democratic and European sense, started.

This relationship between management and the union was not hostile; rather, it was paternalistic—this was to prove decisive in the events and changes that conspired to breed misunderstanding between the two after 1963. This attitude of paternalism arose out of the attitude of the politicians who drew up, and passed, the 1947 law; it did not grant the unions the right to strike, it precluded political activity on the part of the labour unions, and did not include any mechanism by which to conduct collective bargaining. This, then, was not simply a problem for the ZMWU, but for the Turkish labour movement as a whole. What developed were labour organisations which were primarily mutual aid societies and, in some instances, 'company unions'. In this respect, the ex-union president noted:

> We used to present management with a list of things that we wanted; often they would accept some of our demands and reject others. This situation arose because of the nature of the organisation [i.e. it was a state-owned enterprise]. Management would help us get the things that were within their power to grant. Concerning those matters

outside their province, they told us that we would have to go to higher authorities. They [management] have been helpful in trying to solve our problems. This relationship has changed since 1963 because, after that year, the union has had more power to demand things and the wherewithal to base these demands on fact. Prior to this it was a dependency relationship; now it is a matter of independence.

Even with the limitations imposed upon it by law, and to some extent culture and tradition, the ZMWU was able to make some progress in the years between 1947 and 1963. According to union officials, the following major accomplishments can be credited to the union:

(1) Underground workers involved in actual production are exempted from paying income tax.
(2) Permanent workers receive 10 TL per child.
(3) All of the workers are supplied with suits of work clothes and shoes annually.
(4) Workers travelling to the workplace by train pay reduced fares.
(5) Workers can ask for advances on their wages twice a month.
(6) Union can send inspectors to the working place to check the dining halls and menus.
(7) Permanent workers can receive an amount of money equal to the food which they would consume if they ate at company dining halls.
(8) Underground workers are supplied with a dry breakfast.
(9) The first Housing Co-operative was established and 146 houses were built and occupied by the workers [permanent].
(10) Ambulances were supplied for the regional dispensaries.
(11) Minimum wages were increased to:[30]
1951—2 TL
1953—3 TL
1955—4 TL
1957—5·25 TL for underground
4·50 TL for surface
1959—6·50 TL for underground
6·00 TL for surface
1961—8·50 TL for underground
7·50 TL for surface
(12) The union has purchased two buildings.

It is, of course, difficult to ascertain to what degree the union was instrumental in bringing about the majority of these, particularly changes in wages; to the extent that they were willing, and did, go to Ankara to press for changes, one might conjecture that they were a precipitative factor. Political factors and considerations, however, cannot be discounted and, traditionally, these have been more important than union agitation.[31]

From the beginning, the financial position of the ZMWU was guaranteed in one sense; Law 5018 provided for the 'check-off' system of dues collection. This has had both positive and negative effects historically. On the one hand, it has permitted the union to operate from a position of relative financial solubility through time, thus insuring, to an extent, its perpetuity and allowing it to focus upon worker problems; also, it has allowed it to carry out its mutual aid and assistance functions on a fairly consistent basis. On the other hand, it has established a tradition of little contact between the leadership of the union and the rank-and-file—a tradition which manifests itself in many ways and persists to this day. Dues payments were, initially, 1 TL per month; later this was increased to 2 TL per month, and still later, in 1961, to $1\frac{1}{2}$ per cent of the workers' monthly wages. Prior to 1961 the rotational workers, if members of the ZMWU, were required to pay dues monthly even though they actually worked only six months per year.[32] Since the last increase in dues, however, they are required to pay only for the months when they actually work.

Membership growth for the period 1947–63 is shown in Table 11;

TABLE 11

Membership of the ZMWU, 1947–63

Year	Total Labour Force[a]	No. of Members
1950	38,000	9,000
1951	37,000	9,100
1952	37,500	10,100
1953	39,900	10,500
1954	39,800	14,500
1955	44,000	16,000
1956	43,500	18,000
1957	50,000	22,000
1958	51,000	25,000
1959	50,000	28,000
1960	48,000	29,600
1961	46,000	31,000
1962	45,000	34,000
1963	44,600	35,000[b]

Notes: [a] Figures include all rotational workers and are approximate.
[b] Figure for period up to June 1963 only.

unfortunately, there is no breakdown of rotational and permanent members. Although the figures are somewhat inflated,[33] the union experienced steady growth up to 1963; after this date all workers had to belong to the ZMWU in order to become eligible for any benefits negotiated by the union; hence, membership is 100 per cent. The obvious appeal of the union as far as the workers were concerned was the right to receive benefits if they became ill, retired or died—when the money went to their family. Organising efforts, such as they were, consisted largely of informing workers as to what the benefits would be if they joined. There is some indication that some were coerced into joining; in other instances, workers who had and later tried to withdraw seem to have been told that they could not even though the law clearly states that they can. In almost all such cases which the author encountered, the workers were rotational.

The leadership function was initially performed by the original founders of the union; since that time, although some of them continue to be active in the union, union leaders have come from the ranks of those who were not instrumental in bringing the union into existence. Up to 1960, even though the union held elections once a year as required by law, few changes occurred; since 1960, however, they have been more frequent. Table 12 indicates the names of the individuals who have held office, the job which they held at EKI, period in office and province of origin.

TABLE 12

Leadership of the ZMWU, 1946–65

Name	Office	Position at EKI	Province of Origin
Memduh Suer*	Pres. (11/46–4/47)	Şefporyon	Trabzon
Hayri Oguz*	VP (11/46–4/47)	Foreman	Trabzon
Mustafa Kocer*	Pres. (4/47–10/50)	Chief miner	Trabzon
Omer Karahasan*	VP (4/47–2/54)	Foreman	Trabzon
Necati Diken	Pres. (10/50–2/54)	Foreman	Unknown
Omer Karahasan	Pres. (2/54–1960)	Foreman	Trabzon
Mehmet Alpdündar	VP (1958–59)	Gas Station Attendant	Zonguldak
Niyazi Yildiz	Pres. (1960)	Foreman	Unknown
Fasim Girgin	Pres. (1960)	Chief miner	Bolu
Mzaffer Yilmaz	Pres. (1961)	Chief miner	Trabzon
Mehmet Alpdündar	Pres. (5/61–6/64)	Gas Station Attendant	Zonguldak
Hasan Ulubay	General Secretary (5/61–6/64)	Unknown	Unknown
Osman Ipekçi	Pres. (6/64–present)	Chauffeur	Trabzon
Ahmet Baş	General Seçretary (6/64–present)	Chief foreman	Trabzon

Note: * Founders.

Several things are important to note with respect to the leadership, past and present, of the ZMWU: (1) almost all of them come from the Black Sea Region; (2) all of them have been permanent workers (although not necessarily surface workers); and (3) more recently (since 1960), they have all been surface workers.

This domination of permanent workers can be seen as well in other positions of leadership and control in the union. The delegates to the General Assembly[34] who elect the union officers have predominantly been permanent workers; fewer than 10 per cent have come from the ranks of the rotational workers. All of the key committees whose membership is drawn from the election delegates have historically been totally comprised of permanent workers.

Up to 1962, the leadership was non-salaried and part-time; the officials would work on their jobs during the day and meet at the union in the evening to conduct their business. With the advent of collective bargaining, it was felt that the union needed full-time professional leadership. The current president received 2,500 TL net per month; the general secretary and chief accountant 2,000 TL net per month. In addition to his salary, the president has at his disposal a 1,000 TL per month expense account.

While the leadership had not been compensated in the earlier years, they did have, and continue to have, other benefits associated with being a union leader. Several past presidents—Mustafa Kocer and Necati Diken—have, after serving in the union, served in the Turkish Parliament;[35] Omer Karahasan was selected to the Constituent Assembly after the revolution in 1960, and ran in the parliamentary elections of October, 1965. Mehmet Alpdündar, although deposed from the office of president in June 1964, also ran in the 1965 elections; Osman Ipekçi wished to run but was not accepted by his party. There is higher status and certain privileges (such as travel to the U.S. for union training and attending international labour conferences) attached to key leadership positions. This has made them highly valued and a position to which to aspire—particularly since 1962. Union leadership positions, then, have been convenient stepping stones to higher-level jobs.

In summary, the period from 1947 to 1963 was one in which the ZMWU, although seriously hampered and restricted, began to develop the characteristics of trade unionism as it is now practised. The period from 1963 to the present, precipitated as it was by the passage of Laws 274 and 275, has substantially changed the power position of the ZMWU and the labour movement of Turkey as a whole; it is this period to which this article will now turn for examination.

CURRENT UNION ORGANISATION AND ADMINISTRATION

The passage of 1963 labour laws brought about a number of changes for the ZMWU; of specific concern here are those of an organisational and administrative nature.

The organisation of the ZMWU, prior to 1963, was basically simple and highly informal. Although the law of 1947 required that certain committees be formed, prescribed election procedures be followed, and the like, the nature of the functions, and the degree to which the union was allowed to perform them, in effect limited the responsibilities and duties of the leadership as well as the various other administrative organs. The gaining of collective bargaining rights of a more systematic nature than those stipulated in Law 5018 has given the leadership more power and created the necessity of performing new functions. New responsibilities and duties must now be undertaken by administrative organs; the result is that the organisational structure, although basically the same as before 1963, has become more formalised.

Figure 1 shows the current organisational structure of the ZMWU. A brief examination of each of the administrative bodies will prove useful in understanding the internal authority and power system of the union.

The General Assembly is elected by the membership at large and, as stipulated in Law 274, convenes at least once every two years to elect new officers;[36] previously, elections were held annually. It is the controlling body of the organisation, although control is not exercised by the delegates as a whole but through three committees—the Honorary Committee, the Auditors' Committee, and the Management Council. Typically, until the 17th General Assembly held in September 1964, there has been little turnover in those who serve as delegates—less than 25 per cent. Their sole function, save for those who serve on the various committees, is to convene, render judgment on past decisions and policies and elect officers and committee members for the next administrative period; they do not perform any representational functions at the workplace.

The Honorary Committee, consisting of five members elected from among delegates to the General Assembly, handles matters of internal discipline; the Auditors' Committee, consisting of five members selected in the same manner, has investigatory powers regarding the use of union funds, embezzlement and the like.

The Management Council, consisting of 21 members (24 including union officers) elected from the delegates, is the second-ranking administrative body of the union and is more actively involved in the administration of the union. Meeting once a month, they have a variety of duties, chief among them reviewing major decisions of the union officers; they must also pass on any contract negotiated between EKI and the union and select union representatives to administer the contract at workplace level.

The Executive Committee comprises the union officers—the President, the General Secretary, and the Chief Accountant. Although presumably possessing more power and authority than the President alone, in effect it is dominated by him.

The office of president of the union is, according to the constitution, a position which, in terms of authority, ranks after the General Assembly, the Management Council and the Executive Committee; however, it has been and continues to be the most powerful position in the union—this will more clearly be seen below.

The Joint Disciplinary Committee is composed of three members of the union and three members of EKI management and is the final step prior to top management consideration of workers' grievances; it reports directly to the president of the union.

Under the president is a staff of advisers; prior to 1963 some of these had existed, although not on so formal a basis as is currently the case. The advent of collective bargaining necessitated the addition of a technical

FIGURE 1 *Organisation of the ZMWU*

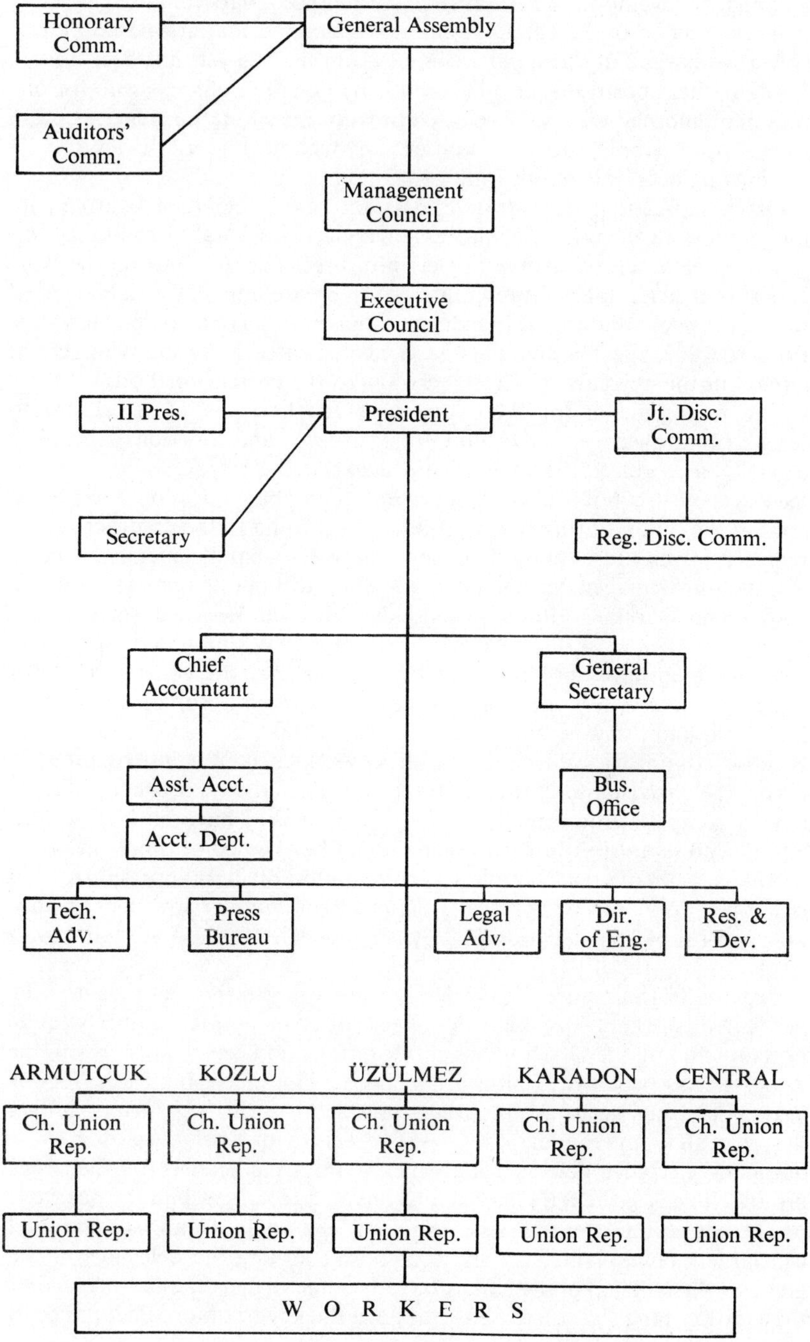

adviser to handle matters of mine safety, a director of education and training to develop union training classes and seminars (required by law), and an adviser on research to handle economic matters pertaining to collective bargaining demands (this position has, as yet, not been filled). To date, these positions have been filled by ex-union officials who for one reason or another were not re-elected or who chose to retire. The exception to this is, of course, the legal adviser. The technical adviser is an ex-EKI mining engineer and engineering consultant.

Office staff and administrative assistants are either men who can no longer work in the mines, or professional clerks—a total of 15 altogether.

The level which ostensibly comes into direct contact with the workers is that of district union representatives. These are unpaid officials selected by the president and the Management Council to serve as union stewards. Prior to 1963, these individuals were elected directly by the members at large, but the new law required a change to the current method.

The requirements for these positions are basically (1) a 'desire to serve', (2) knowledge of the union, its purposes and functions, and (3) a capacity to regulate the relationship between the workers and management. They are not full-time representatives, but work on their jobs, serving the union during when off-duty. According to the contract, union representatives are supposed to get time off to handle members' complaints, but management has been unwilling to honour this. They are all permanent workers, although these are divided between surface and underground—i.e. surface workers are served by union representatives who are themselves holding jobs on the surface; the same is true for underground workers. Because the ratio of workers to union representatives is so high, that is, one for every 800 to 1,000, it has not been a very effective administrative tool for handling workers' complaints or administering the provisions of the contract; most rotational workers, if they have a complaint, go directly to the union, as they have no idea what a union representative is, or who theirs might be. These positions have been useful as 'listening posts', and in keeping union officials apprised of what is happening at the workplace. Keeping their number low also ensures that control of any situation largely remains with the top administrative levels.

Because of the nature of the election process and the fact that it is the permanent workers who control 95 per cent of the union's administrative posts (including the General Assembly itself), and because turnover in the delegates has been low, a number of power blocs have built up over the years. Each man who aspires to be president has his supporters among the delegates, and among those who are instrumental in getting those delegates elected, such as foremen and informal leaders of the work groups; if he is elected, then most likely his supporters will fill the positions on the key committees and lesser offices of the union. Changes since 1962 can largely be explained by shifts of power among the delegates to the General Assembly. As the stakes have become higher, the importance of these power blocs has increased—they are the key to union office; once in office, they are the key to controlling the union—and staying in office. The result is that it is the position of president that is the most important in the entire union structure—and the most powerful.

The formulation of collective-bargaining demands within the union structure is perhaps the best example of the extreme centralisation of power in the union—specifically in the office of the president—and the desire and/or necessity of maintaining strict control over the membership. The following excerpt from an interview with the president will serve to illustrate this:

Q. How are union demands formulated?
A. Those things to be demanded are formulated scientifically. Technical matters are studied by the Technical Director; less important matters are settled by EKI management and the union.
Q. Who decides as to what will be demanded?
A. The overall demands are determined by the Executive Committee, the Director of Education and the Technical Director, a committee of five altogether.
Q. If there is a conflict within this committee over what is to be demanded, how is it resolved?
A. Majority rules.
Q. Can workers have a voice in what is to be asked from management?
A. No.
Q. Are proposed demands in any way transmitted to anybody within the union for approval?
A. No.
Q. Who performs the negotiations for the union?
A. Myself, the Technical Director, the Director of Education, the General Secretary and two members of the Management Council.
Q. Who must approve prospective terms of the contract prior to signing?
A. Discussion is held between EKI and the union representatives on each article. If both parties agree, then it is immediately signed.
Q. Does the new agreement concluded have to be ratified by any administrative body within the union?
A. Yes, the Management Council has the right to accept or reject the contract.
Q. Has this body ever rejected any of the terms of a contract?
A. No. Disagreement has occurred once, however; two members did not want to accept the wages as they were too low. I explained the situation to them and told them that *I* wanted an absolute majority on this clause. They concurred and withdrew their votes against it.
Q. Is the proposed contract, prior to submission to the Management Council, communicated to the workers?
A. No, not until after the decision of the Council.

Q. Do the workers ratify the contract?
A. No.
Q. Does any single member of the union have the right to protest against any clause, or part, of the contract?
A. No, he has no such right. Even if there were such a right, it would not be taken into consideration in formulating the demands.

This desire for control seems to arise from a number of factors. It stems from the overall policy of the TLC, of which the ZMWU is an active supporter, aimed at attaining total unity in, and control over, the labour movement of Turkey; by unity they mean 'one union for one industry'. In this way they hope to achieve complete solidarity. For the ZMWU this has meant adopting a policy of centralisation of power, not only within the union but with respect to the other unions of the basin as well.

In addition to this mania for unity in the labour movement, there is the obvious problem of trying to control, and work with, a rank-and-file that is basically illiterate and historically somewhat uninterested in the labour union. If the right to strike is going to mean anything at all to the union—if it is to be a weapon with which to counter managerial resistance—then it behoves union leaders to develop the wherewithal to control its membership. Unfortunately, the response of the ZMWU, until recently, was to keep the majority of the membership ignorant of what was going on in the union; the only time that contact was made extensively was just prior to union elections. Hence, presumed indifference on the part of most of the membership of the ZMWU has been countered with indifference of the leadership toward the majority of the workers—primarily the rotational workers. This can be seen most clearly in terms of the communications media used by the union.

The union publishes a union newspaper weekly. It is distributed free, but only 5,000 copies are published for some 47,000 members and a number of these are given to local government offices, EKI management and other officials in the area. There are 7,000–8,000 copies of the collective agreement printed; none are given to the workers—there are no abstracts of major clauses printed and distributed, nor are they posted on bulletin boards. Each union representative in the district has a copy, but the rest are distributed among the union and management hierarchy.[37] The union officials contend that the workers learn about the contract provisions through educational seminars, but these were not conducted for the membership at large until November 1965; as of March 1966, only 1,500 had attended such seminars, and they were all concentrated in the Kozlu District.

Other than the printed media which, in the light of the literacy problem, would have limited use in any case, word of mouth is used as the primary means of communicating with the membership. This is done through the union representatives (somewhat ineffectively, as already noted), the delegates to the General Assembly and members of the Management Council. In addition, occasional visits are made to the workplace by union officials or special committees; this is most often done when a 'crisis' occurs. Oral communication is, however, a highly selective and totally unsystematic communications device as used by the ZMWU; it also lends itself to considerable distortion, which may serve to attain certain objectives.

Law 274 stipulated that it was the duty of the trade unions to educate the membership at large. At the ZMWU, as has been the case with other unions in Turkey, this has been done only in terms of the leadership; that is, union leaders and representatives are trained, but there is no systematic training of the rank-and-file (with the exception noted above). Of course, it is obvious that one needs an educated cadre with which to approach the problem of educating so large a number of workers, but even allowing for this and the fact that Law 274 has only been in effect since 1963 (although a similar provision existed in Law 5018), there is a decided reluctance on the part of union leaders to educate their members. This tendency is noticeable in the ZMWU; it does not appear to be a conscious policy, but has been more an assumption that most of the membership—particularly the rotational workers—are totally indifferent to union matters; hence, why try and train them?

The ZMWU is one of the most financially sound unions in Turkey. Dues payments currently net the union about 250,000 TL per month; 50 kuruş (6c) per worker per month is paid to the Mine Workers' Federation—25 kuruş to the TLC.

In addition to the dues, the leadership can levy assessments under special circumstances, such as national disasters and the need to develop special funds. For instance, each year a 2 TL per worker assessment is made to finance the scholarship fund for workers' children; in September 1965, a total sum of 100,000 TL was assessed for the Cyprus problem (workers paid anywhere from 5 TL to a day's wages) and in November 1965, a 5 TL per worker special assessment was made in order to form a strike fund.[38]

There are no provisions in the constitution regarding such assessments; they have been a matter of custom, and whenever the leadership felt that one was necessary, they had only to notify the accounting office of EKI. No contact has been, nor needs to be, made with the workers in this respect.

Administrative salaries are also a matter for the Management Council to decide; no referendum need be submitted to the General Assembly or the membership at large.

There are internal and external mechanisms for conducting audits in order to guard against misuse of ZMWU funds; however, because the president sits on the key committees, which may request the appropriate committees to conduct an audit, and because he controls the union, such checks have not always proved effective.

The period since 1963, then, has been a period of reorganisation of the union and formalisation of the union structure; it has also been a period when control has been a primary goal, especially in light of the power which unions have obtained as a result of the new laws.

Several key characteristics of the ZMWU, both in the historical and contemporary sense, might now be noted:

(1) It has been a trade union which was largely conceived by, and has been and is controlled by, permanent workers with many of the key founders and officials coming from the Black Sea region.

(2) The leadership pattern is changing from a non-professional basis to a professional basis with surface workers predominantly filling the role of the 'professional'.

(3) The organisational structure, of necessity, is becoming more formal, and has had to undertake new functions since Laws 274 and 275 were passed.

(4) The locus of power rests with the president; although constitutionally limited by a number of checks and balances, in practice, 'one-man rule' is the operating principle.

(5) Little, or no, contact is maintained with the large bulk of the membership, particularly the rotational workers.

(6) Since the advent of new labour legislation in 1963, the relationship between EKI and the ZMWU has changed. EKI now expects the union to control its members and to settle all differences as a price of collective bargaining gains.

The ZMWU has, since 1963, embarked upon a period of 'sophisticated' trade unionism with a membership—the majority of whom have little knowledge of or, presumably, interest in, trade union matters—largely isolated from the mainstream of the labour movement. It has, in essence, become a highly particularistic type of labour organisation, even though it is officially the sole representative of the total labour force. The power structure has been self-selecting and self-sustaining; it has, as such, become a labour movement largely serving the interests of only a portion of its membership. Given the aspirations of its leaders, it has, in some ways, become a 'middle-class' rather than 'working-class' movement.

THE LOCAL UNIONS

There are 19 local unions in the coal basin; they are organised either according to occupational or skill orientation, or according to geographical location. The following list indicates those currently in existence:

(1) Chief Mine Foremen's Union
(2) New Sailors and Ship Personnel Union, Zonguldak Branch
(3) Mine Clerks' Union
(4) Armutçuk Mine Workers' Union
(5) EKI Motor Transport, Drivers, Repair and Maintenance Union
(6) EKI Skilled Technical Workers' Union
(7) EKI Central Workshops and Maintenance Workers' Union
(8) EKI Cargo Handlers, Communications and Washery Workers' Union
(9) Turkish Mine Explosive Handlers' Union
(10) Railroad Workers' Union

(11) EKI Surface Workers' Union
(12) Zonguldak Washery Workers' Union
(13) EKI Üzülmez District Mine Workers' Union
(14) Central Washery Workers' Union
(15) EKI Health and Social Workers' Union
(16) Kozlu District Mine Workers' Union
(17) Karadon District Mine Workers' Union
(18) EKI Railroad Maintenance Service Workers' Union
(19) Electro-mechanical Equipment Repair and Washery Workers' Union

They vary in size, the smallest having 15–40 members, the largest, over 6,000. The locals have a number of similarities to the ZMWU and to each other, since it was the 1947 law which formed the basis for their constitutions. Thus, election procedures, functions, dues collection and the like all tend to be the same. The main difference, besides size and financial status, arises from two factors: (1) the locals make their basic appeal only to a segment of the labour force; and (2) they have no right to conduct collective bargaining for their members; they must depend upon the ZMWU in this respect. It is this which leads to the more serious difficulties that take place between these various locals and the ZMWU.

The locals, like the ZMWU, started out as mutual aid societies, and have remained basically such since they are precluded from other functions. They tend to be more cohesive organisations, with greater membership participation, than the ZMWU; this is by virtue of the nature of their limited appeal, and skill and geographical orientation. An examination of the characteristics of several of these locals will prove useful in understanding the inter-relationships among the unions which comprise the labour movement of the basin.

The Chief Mine Foremen's Union (CMFU) was formed in 1946 at the same time as the ZMWU; it is the oldest of the locals. Its membership consists of the 820 chief mine foremen of EKI, all of whom are permanent workers. Their primary function is providing social aid and benefits for their members. Largely financed by dues—15 TL per month (collected by a check-off system)—they have the following benefits: retirement—1,000 TL (lump sum payment); rest and recuperation—3 TL per day for a period not exceeding 60 days; death—1,000 TL (lump sum payment) to survivors; retirement due to illness—1,000 TL (lump sum payment).

Their election procedures and organisational structure are quite similar to those of the ZMWU, although far less formal. There is approximately a 50 per cent turnover in delegates to their General Assembly and an 80 per cent turnover in leadership; the latter is largely due to the fact that they receive no pay and must work at their jobs during the day and conduct union business in the evening. As their current president puts it, 'One year is enough'.

The union maintains representatives at the workplace who handle members' complaints. As there tends to be some overlap here, that is, all of their members also belong to the ZMWU, an artificial division of authority has taken place with respect to member complaints. If the complaint is one of a technical nature, then the member works through the grievance procedure of the CMFU. If the complaint arises out of a contract violation, then the member must work through the ZMWU.

One other facet of the complaint procedure is most interesting. If a complaint develops involving a worker and a chief foreman, it is handled entirely within the structure of the two unions even though, technically, the foreman is a member of management. The president of the CMFU notes in this respect:

> If two workers leave work early and are subsequently punished by their foreman and they appeal to the Disciplinary Council [comprised of EKI and ZMWU officials] then the matter is often solved between our union and the Mine Workers' Union.

EKI management has, in fact, used this as a method of avoiding worker problems and complaints themselves. They contend that 'since they are members of the same union, they should solve the complaint'.

This situation has created a degree of conflict and frustration between the CMFU and the ZMWU. The CMFU president notes:

> We don't have any complaints about the work, EKI or the Mine Workers' Union—we do have complaints regarding Laws 274 and 275 because these do not differentiate between workers and foremen; that is, we don't have collective bargaining rights.
>
> Also, we consider ourselves as part of management. The Mine Workers' Union cannot deal with the foremen over worker problems even though we are part of management because we ourselves, of course, are members of their union as well. This creates trouble and frustration; we are management and yet are members of the workers' union.

The result has been that the CMFU has been trying to find ways to obtain collective bargaining rights for their union. They dislike having to rely on the ZMWU in order to get their demands; the president noted:

> Up to now everything has been all right—I don't know about the future. The current relationship is not the best for us. They speak for us, but it is not as effective as if we could speak for ourselves. The new premium system is currently being negotiated; we have given our demands and we will see what happens.

With respect to the other local unions in the area, the CMFU maintains informal and infrequent contact. About 10 per cent of their membership belongs to various other unions. While they do not have any direct affiliation with the ZMWU, the CMFU is directly affiliated with the Mine Workers' Federation.

One of the most influential and powerful locals is the EKI Skilled Technical Workers' Union (STWU), with some 2,500 members. Most of the members are skilled electro-mechanical workers at EKI; all of them are permanent workers. While they have the purpose of providing social benefits to their membership, they have a broader, and perhaps more important, goal: 'to preserve and promote the value of their occupation and skills in the eyes of management'.

The social benefits, as in the case of the CMFU, are financed by dues payments of $5\frac{1}{2}$ TL per month, for which their members can expect to receive the following: rest and recuperation—4 TL per day for a maximum of 60 days; retirement—2,000 TL (lump sum payment); and in the case of death—2,000 TL (lump sum payment) to survivors.

The union's election procedures and organisational structure is similar to the other unions already discussed; almost 100 per cent of the membership vote in their elections, and membership participation is quite active throughout the year. The union maintains representatives in the workplace whose function it is to pass on information and handle worker complaints and problems. With respect to complaints, a similar pattern has developed as noted in the case of the CMFU. If the complaint involves a contract violation, then the member refers it to the ZMWU; if it involves anything else, then he comes to the STWU and they deal directly with management.

Unlike the foremen's union, which feels the necessity of separation from the ZMWU but has been unable to make much progress in this respect, the STWU has taken a more adamant stand and has a stronger 'separatist' tendency. The basic issue is that they are skilled workers and, as such, are more valuable to the firm than unskilled workers; yet, they receive less pay than unskilled rotational workers. Their president commented in this respect:

> This was one of the reasons that this union was founded. Most of the members argue this way: 'I am acquiring a skill which must be maintained through time—but as long as my wages don't increase, why should I wear myself out?'

Recently, the STWU disaffiliated itself from the Mine Workers' Federation. The following reason was given by the president:

> We were affiliated with the Federation but because they tried to influence the ZMWU with respect to signing a contract which was unfavourable from our point of view, we withdrew. We are now working on a proposal that will affiliate us with another federation which will be more agreeable to work with.

When asked as to what the basic problem was, he responded:

> Our main goal is to achieve the right to bargain collectively for our members through legislation. Now we have no such rights, but we believe that if our members are separated from the ZMWU and the MF and our union affiliates with another federation, we stand a better chance of getting these.

The issue with the STWU, then, is basically the same as it was for the CMFU—they want to operate as a separate entity. With respect to their relations with the ZMWU, the president stated:

> They can't really serve the interests of our membership because they don't understand the nature of our problems. Our contact with them is confined to union matters; because we are essentially right in our demands, the ZMWU cannot be against us. We don't have any conflicts with the current administration; as long as they don't try to hinder our work there will be no conflict.

About 15–20 per cent of the membership of the STWU belongs to other locals; although their relations with other locals have been infrequent, they are often asked to help these because of their influence in the area.

The largest of the regional unions is the Karadon District Mine Workers' Union, which has a membership in excess of 6,000 workers—both rotational and permanent. Like the other locals, they are confined to the provision of social benefits and they maintain the most comprehensive and extensive programme of all of the locals. By paying 4 TL per month in dues, a member can expect the following: 50 TL when called up for military service; 50 TL for every new birth in his family; if unemployed owing to illness—25 kurus per union member (e.g. 25 krs × 6,000) paid in a lump sum; retirement—1 TL per union member (lump sum payment); severance due to ill health or other reasons—1 TL per union member (lump sum payment); rest and recuperation—2 TL per day for a maximum of 120 days; and death—1 TL per union member (lump sum payment) to survivors. Also, loans without interest are given to workers under special circumstances.

The union maintains representatives in the workplace, but these have no authority to represent workers if complaints arise. Unlike the other locals already discussed, they do not handle any member complaints—it is a matter of union policy.

The relationship between this union and the ZMWU are somewhat strained. Several leaders of the KDMU had been arrested in connection with the strike in 1965; this obviously had something to do with the character of the relationship between the two.[39] This is all the more surprising when one considers that the president and vice-president of the KDMU are members of the Management Council of the ZMWU. Excerpts from an interview with the president of this local will indicate the nature of this conflict:

> Q. Does your union maintain good relations with the ZMWU?
> A. We are not affiliated with either that union or the Mine Workers' Federation.
> Q. Do you co-operate with them regarding the formulation of collective bargaining demands?
> A. They don't ask our opinion on such matters and they don't listen to what we say regarding any other matters.

Q. Do any members and/or officers of this union serve in any offic ia capacity in the ZMWU?

A. There are four officers of this union, including myself, who serve on the Management Council of the ZMWU.

Q. Is there any conflict between your union and the ZMWU?

A. Yes—there are many; unfortunately, representation in the form of KDMU officers serving on the Management Council of the ZMWU does little to alleviate these conflicts.

The dispute between this union and the ZMWU appears to be more a matter of personality conflict between leaders of the two than a desire to be separated from them and to have collective bargaining rights. The president of this union, in fact, ran against the current president of the ZMWU in the last union election.

With respect to membership in other locals, about 10 per cent of those belonging to the KDMU are involved.

It is obvious that there is conflict between the locals and the general union, the ZMWU. Almost 80 per cent of the total labour force belongs to at least one local; overlapping of functions, specifically worker representation, and jealousies inevitably occur. However, conflict has not been confined to this. Under the leadership of ZMWU president Mehmet Alpdündar (1961–64), relations between that union and the locals deteriorated to an all-time low; the issue was the negotiation of the first collective agreement, and Alpdündar's desire to exclude any local participation in that process. He was not interested in what the locals had to say and, in fact, actively sought their dissolution. In his report to the 16th General Assembly of the ZMWU in 1963, Alpdündar stated that, in order to derive more income and thus insure the ability of the ZMWU to benefit by the new laws, there must be an 'end to union inflation' (that is, so many unions).[40] In another section of this report he made an obvious reference to the discord between himself and the locals:

> Your leaders have faced various attacks since May, 1962 when they came into office. Some of these attacks were internal, some external . . . We expected the attacks from the outside, but we never even considered those of an internal nature as possible . . . Your leaders were able to cope with these internal attacks.[41]

The fight between the locals and Mehmet Alpdündar came to a head in June 1964; at that time the locals supported those who wished to oust him from office and who were, in the end, successful. But, the conflict has not totally resolved itself, for the current president of the ZMWU wishes to abolish all of the locals and form instead regional departments of the ZMWU. As he has not actively sought this, there exists now somewhat of an impasse—but should an attempt be made to abolish them, it is obvious that it would meet with a great deal of resistance.

The conflict has been somewhat mitigated by what might be described as the unconscious and unintended formation of 'interlocking directorates'. Many officers of the locals also serve, or have served, in some official capacity in the ZMWU. Osman Ipekçi, the ZMWU president as of 1968, was, until March 1966, the head of the Armutçuk District Mine Workers' Union;[42] Ahmet Baş, the General Sectetary of the ZMWU (1968), had also served as the president of the Foremen's Union. Many have served and are serving on the Management Council.

It should be noted that this has only been a limited means by which to avert actual or potential inter-organisational conflict, for local officials use the voting power of their membership as a means to higher office in the ZMWU; it has been a reinforcing factor in the formation of power blocs among the delegates to the General Assembly as well as within the Management Council itself.

In a sense, the problems of the ZMWU—and, in a sense, the response by way of the formation of locals with more specific appeal—are characteristic of a general union. The locals serve two functions which the ZMWU, because of its size and membership base, cannot: (1) they provide an opportunity for involvement with those with whom a worker of a particular skill or occupation has more in common; and (2) they provide a vehicle by which to advance the specific aims and interests of occupational or regional groups of workers. Irrespective of whether workers are interested in locals for these reasons, there exists yet another, which perhaps makes membership in a local imperative; a worker can receive considerable monetary benefits for a modest investment in the form of dues.

Whatever advantages are had by the existence of local unions in the basin, they constitute a further divisive force which creates conflicts within the labour force and, in some respects, within the ZMWU. They have acted as agents for their memberships with respect to collective bargaining; to the extent that the ZMWU can satisfy all of the diverse wants of various occupational and regional groups, there is no problem. However, should they be unable to do this, the locals are in a position to attempt to unseat the leadership or, at least, create difficulties.

One final organisation must be considered here before turning to the question of rank-and-file participation in the labour movement; this is the 'Amele Birligi'—the Labour Federation. This is an association of workers established by the 1921 law in order to abolish employer abuses regarding the deductions from workers' wages to cover the cost of providing medical care and facilities.

Initially, the worker contributed one per cent of his wages and the employer contributed an additional one per cent; currently the figure is $1\frac{1}{2}$ per cent for each. The main functions of the Federation are to: (1) finance in part the medical facilities of EKI; (2) advance money to qualified workers in need; and (3) provide certain safety inspections at the workplace.

The governing board is composed of workers (elected by the labour force) and members of management in equal proportion, who then elect an executive committee of five from among themselves. This committee administers the organisation; the State Regional Labour Director acts as the president of the federation.

Historically, this organisation has been racked by problems of mismanagement, embezzlement and misuse of funds. While it has little or nothing to do with worker representation and collective bargaining, it has, nevertheless, been singled out upon occasion by ZMWU officials as being 'inimical to the workers' interests':

> This organisation has the name Labour Federation, but it has the purpose of destroying the unity of the workers rather than supporting it . . . The Labour Federation, which was perhaps the first important organisation in Turkey founded with the purpose of protecting social rights, is, unfortunately, in a regrettable situation . . . Embezzlements exceeding 100,000 TL . . . meetings attended by yellow-dog unionists and the decisions made therein are entirely to the disadvantage of the workers . . .[43]

Thus, even this organisation enters into the general atmosphere of conflict that attends the labour movement of the coal basin.

RANK-AND-FILE PARTICIPATION IN THE LABOUR MOVEMENT

The rotational workers were not instrumental in initiating the union, nor have they been active in perpetuating it either in spirit or intent. One of the founders recalls:

> There was no desire for such things on the part of these workers mainly because they were involved in earning a living from day to day. The main incentive for formation of the union came from the intellectuals who knew the conditions under which the workers worked and lived and wanted to change these.

There was, in essence, no pressure from the rotational workers for the formation of a trade union; hence, the pattern of indifference of this segment of the labour force was established at the very outset.

The failure of rotational workers actively to support the union did not mean, however, that they did not join the ZMWU or other union organisations—they did, in significant numbers as time passed. As we have already noted, some joined because they were told to; others because they wished to get the social benefits. But they took little interest in the internal politics or policies of the unions; this was reciprocated by the union taking little interest in them, neither educating nor informing them of such matters. This was not done out of malice, nor necessarily as a conscious attempt to keep them ignorant, but because the leaders felt that any efforts of this nature would have accomplished little; thus they made their appeal to that segment of the labour force which, at least in part, supported the union and looked to it for help—the permanent workers.

Oddly enough, this did not mean that rotational workers did not benefit by the union's presence or that the union ignored their problems. Several of the accomplishments noted earlier clearly benefit the rotational worker; others clearly do not. This was partially due to the fact that many of the founders of the union, as well as those in positions of leadership, were in fact themselves permanent underground workers. On balance, it is apparent that the permanent workers have enjoyed a wider range of tangible benefits such as child benefits, housing, a shorter working week, and the wage differential has not been substantial between themselves and rotational workers (when bonus, merit increases and other payments are taken into consideration), even though most of them hold considerably easier jobs. As the leadership pattern has begun to change, especially since 1960, in that the top leadership positions of the ZMWU have been filled primarily by surface workers, the orientation has shifted somewhat.

Even though the rotational workers have benefited from the union, they know little about it, or what unionism means to them. Some policies of the union preclude any opportunity for involvement, if they happened to be interested. For instance, when delegate elections are held, 13,000 rotational workers are in the villages and cannot vote unless they wish to travel to Zonguldak at their own expense which, of course, few, if any, are willing to do. Of the 34,000 or so at the workplace, only about 60 per cent vote,[44] which reduces the active participation rate in elections to approximately 20,000, or less than 45 per cent of the total membership. Although there are no concrete data upon which to rely, it is apparent that it is the permanent workers who most frequently participate in these elections.

After 1963, there are signs that the rotational workers have been taking an increasing interest in the union; the attaining of collective bargaining rights was accompanied by much publicity, the fight for control of the ZMWU in 1964 created a great stir, and those vying for power bombarded them with verbal and written propaganda in an effort to win their support; the shift in employment policies of EKI has perhaps been responsible for this. By this time, however, the pattern of behaviour of the leadership had been set; hence, they knew little of, nor cared about, this changing attitude on the part of the rotational workers.

A review of some of the results of the 300 interviews with rotational workers conducted by the author will serve to illustrate several of the points made above:

Question	*Response*
1. Are you a member of the ZMWU?	100% responded that they were.
2. Do you belong to another union?	25% indicated that they did.
3. What is the name of the ZMWU president?	44% responded with the correct name.
4. What is the name of the union representative serving your workplace?	80% indicated that they did not know.
5. Do you know what a collective bargaining contract is?	91% stated that they did not.
6. Who got your last wage increase for you?	77% indicated that the union had.
7. How do you know this?	All responded that a 'union man told them'.

Question	Response
8. How much do you pay in union dues to the ZMWU?	42% had no idea; 24% gave a figure that was approximately correct (given their wage level); 34% gave an incorrect figure.
9. Have you ever heard of Laws 274 and 275?	95% indicated that they had not.
10. Have you ever seen any document telling you what you are entitled to under the terms of a contract?	91% indicated that they had not.
11. Have you ever been contacted by a union representative?	93% had not.
12. Have you ever attended a union meeting of any kind?	85% had not; 15% had attended union training seminars.
13. What is the name of the General Secretary of the ZMWU?	95% did not know.
14. Did you vote in the last delegate election of the ZMWU?	61% indicated that they had.[45]
15. What is the function of the General Assembly of the ZMWU?	76% did not know; 24% gave incorrect answers.
16. Why do you belong to the ZMWU?	52% responded that 'they had to'; 13% didn't know; 17% responded that 'they protect us'.
17. What is the main purpose of the ZMWU?	20% did not know; 61% responded that 'they protect labour's rights'.
18. If you don't think that the ZMWU is serving your interests what can you do about it?	43% responded 'nothing'; 25% said 'quit the union'; 15% said 'vote for someone else'.
19. If you are punished by your supervisor what rights do you have?	50% said 'appeal to the union'; 28% said 'appeal to management'; 21% said 'none'.
20. Do you care about what goes on in the ZMWU?	60% said 'no'; 22% indicated that they did; 18% had no opinion.
21. What has the union done for you?	50% said 'raised wages'; 45% said 'nothing'.
22. Would you like to have more contact with your union and union officials?	80% indicated that they would.
23. Do you know how much leaders of the union earn?	98% did not.
24. Would you like to know?	90% indicated that they would.

The pattern of the responses was clearly mixed and, in some cases, contradictory. While almost all of those interviewed knew very little about the union, they wanted to know more. One interesting fact is that they all seemed to have an idea of what the union was for—'to protect labour's rights'[46]—even though they could not remember where they had learned this. Many of those who responded that they had voted in the last delegate election indicated that they had done so because their foreman had insisted, saying that 'my candidate had better win or else no more work'; others said that their foreman gave them a list of individuals for whom they were to vote. Only a few actually knew the individual for whom they had voted.

In sum, then, there were very few answers which indicated knowledge of the union or its policies; where knowledge or participation was indicated, those responding appear to have been 'manipulated' in one way or another.

The air of indifference and lack of knowledge was often mixed with animosity and mistrust of the interviewer's purpose. If a worker was reluctant to answer a question, his friends would encourage him by saying, 'Can't you see he is trying to help us'. They know that the union should be doing something for them; some felt that the union was using them and were very cynical about the prospects of the situation ever changing.

Although these interviews were conducted with specific reference to the rotational workers' knowledge of, and contact with, the ZMWU, it was apparent that the same lack of knowledge and indifference were present with respect to the locals (if they belonged to one); they belonged 'because we get social benefits'. This tended to be the extent of their knowledge about these union organisations.

The attitude of permanent workers is, of course, substantially different, as has been indicated already. Although not all of the permanent workers are active in union affairs or have knowledge of the purpose and value of trade unionism, the majority of them do. They have traditionally controlled the ZMWU and continue to do so. Many of the locals are specifically designed to appeal strictly to permanent workers; control here is a foregone conclusion. The difference in attitudes stems mainly from the difference in commitment to the industrial labour force; permanent workers must look to the union for economic and social gains in order to change their income level. Conversely, rotational workers look to industrial employment only for a supplement to the income they derive from the land; they have not been socially, mentally or economically oriented toward industrial employment.

The situation is changing; as the land becomes more crowded and less productive, the rotational workers will have to look to industrial employment more and more as a means of earning a living. Perhaps this is happening already; if and as this happens, the rotational worker will find that in order to effect changes in his earnings and working conditions, he must rely upon his union.

RELATIONSHIP BETWEEN THE ZMWU AND THE TLC

The relation between the ZMWU, the Mine Workers' Federation and the TLC has been conditioned by certain aspects and provisions of the Trade Union Acts of 1947 and 1963 as well as certain operating policies. The Federation[47] was, in fact, founded by several officials of the ZMWU, in conjunction with other mine worker unions. Because it is the largest union affiliated with the Federation, it exerts a good deal of influence over that organisation's internal policies; oddly enough, this operates in the reverse order as well.

The TLC, rather than being a loose-knit organisation of locals, nationals and federations, has exerted a good deal of influence with respect to its affiliates. Prior to 1959, it was a relatively weak organisation, but once designated as the officially recognised confederation and made the recipient of sizeable amounts of foreign aid funds, its stature and power changed considerably. Although there have been several attempts to form rival confederations,[48] these have never posed any threat to the solidly entrenched position of the TLC. It was instrumental in bringing about the new laws primarily by exerting influence in the Constituent Assembly formed to write a new constitution after the revolution. It was able to get certain guarantees for labour and trade unions written into the constitution.

Once having gained the right to bargain, the Confederation wanted to control its affiliates in terms of the provisions of the law—that is, calling strikes, formulation of wage and other demands. It has been rather successful in accomplishing this and, particularly with respect to matters regarding collective bargaining, power has gradually become centralised in the TLC. It approves wage demands, its representatives actively participate in bargaining sessions, and it exercises certain sanctions with respect to what it considers errant behaviour of the leadership of its affiliates. Its guiding principle in the past few years has been unity and, although less obvious and not stated as a matter of policy, control over the entire labour movement of Turkey.

They have been able to accomplish this in several ways. The ultimate sanction is to throw an affiliate out of the confederation which, in essence, denies it access to foreign aid and other funds. Because the TLC does exert influence in political circles, this can be a fairly serious matter from the point of view of lesser union organisations. Also, it is in a position to deny membership to union organisations of which it does not approve; it has done this on several occasions. A second device is an extension of the 'interlocking directorates' already noted in conjunction with the ZMWU and the locals in the basin. Presidents of the larger unions and federations often sit on the Management Council of the TLC; this is not surprising, considering the fact that the leadership of the TLC is elected by a General Assembly whose delegates come from the affiliates on a 'proportional representative' basis.

The ZMWU has, itself, gone along with the principle of control, and through the Mine Workers' Federation and contact directly with the ZMWU, the TLC has exercised influence and control over it. While this influence is apparent in many facets of the activities and policies of the ZMWU, it was most blatantly so after the strike. In May 1965—shortly after the strike—the president of the union, Osman Ipekçi, was called before the Management Council of the TLC to explain what happened and why—and, in essence, to exonerate himself of any responsibility in the matter. It is interesting to note that no such explanation was ever given to the membership at large. On other occasions this relationship has also been apparent; when Alpdündar was removed from office in 1964, a team of accountants from the TLC audited the union's books; after the strike, the TLC publicly reprimanded the leadership of the ZMWU.

The policy of unity of the TLC is clearly the impetus for the ZMWU's attempts to abolish the locals and establish complete control over the labour force of EKI.

The net effect of this semi-dependent relationship between the ZMWU, with its resultant vestige of ZMWU's prerogatives in higher union organs, has been further to remove the decision-making and policy formulation from the rank-and-file. This has significantly decreased the likelihood that the union will ever—under its current form and structure—operate from a democratic base. Perhaps more significantly, it has decreased the 'desirability' of extensive rank-and-file participation, lest such participation challenge the *status quo* in terms of the leadership and operating policies.

What is most obvious, not only with the leadership of the ZMWU but also with that of the TLC, is that it has become enamoured with its own ability and 'know-how' to the extent that it adopts an attitude toward the workers that one normally associates with management. It is a paternalistic-authoritative relationship: the 'enlightened leadership' must care for the 'uneducated, illiterate rank-and-file'. There are many instances in which this is the obvious premise and it translates itself into operating policy.

Such an attitude, however justified under the current circumstances, renders the notion of a democratically based and independent union more a myth than a fact. It is unfortunate to see some union leaders evince more scorn for the worker than is usually shown by management.

CONCLUSION

The labour movement in the coal basin has not been a 'grass-roots' one; it has not been this for the labour movement of Turkey as a whole. Although the permanent workers of EKI have more actively participated in the union movement, it has not been able to maintain definitive control over the leadership; there are 'power élites'—pockets of members who rally around one aspirant for power or another—but aside from this, the administration of the union has increasingly become isolated from the membership at large. The result is that there is little understanding between the leadership and the workers—most particularly the rotational workers. Traditionally, there has been mutual indifference between the two.

The vying of different power blocs within the structure of the ZMWU, and the squabbling between it and the other union organisations in the area, have hardly served to mitigate a situation already made difficult by an illiterate and uneducated membership; it merely compounds an already difficult situation.

There is perhaps no clearer evidence of this than the strike in 1965 and subsequent disturbances. At times when the union needed to exert control, its leaders found themselves totally isolated from that element of the labour force actively involved in the demonstrations, lacked an understanding of what was happening and why, and found themselves just as much a target for the workers' frustration and scorn as management.

Post-strike events have more clearly underscored the almost complete rupture of communications between the leadership of the ZMWU and its ability to control the rank-and-file. Disputes involving dissatisfaction of a group of rotational workers are not infrequently settled by the dissidents electing a representative from among their number, who then meet ZMWU leaders to resolve their grievances. When spontaneous outbursts (in essence, wildcat strikes) have occurred and union leaders have been called in to control their members, they have often found themselves the object of abuse or outright physical attack. Inevitably, they have found it necessary to leave the area for fear of personal harm.

The ultimate consequences for the labour movement in this region are not clear. However, it is apparent that further schisms are most likely to occur. Particularly, as the rotational worker, however reluctantly, finds that he must increasingly rely upon his industrial income, he will become more aware of the value of having certain policies and institutional arrangements develop that benefit him. Confronted with a labour union leadership that is basically unresponsive to their needs, the rotational workers have evinced—in recent years—an understanding, albeit rather crude, of what unions are for. Resort to popular election of representatives from amongst their number to deal with either ZMWU officials and management, or both, as grievances occur, may in fact represent the initial stages of a 'workers' movement' at the grass-roots level.

NOTES

1. The region is divided—administratively and geographically—into five districts: Karadon (or Gelik), Uzulmez, Kozlu, Zonguldak Central and Armutcuk. Arranged around the city of Zonguldak in an arc, each region operates semi-autonomously from the Central Administration and has its own labour force.

2. See Delwin A. Roy, 'The Zonguldak Strike', *Middle Eastern Studies*, vol. 10, no. 2 (May 1974).

3. Diggers, or hewers, are often skilled in the sense of technique; such skills, however, are only useful in mining operations and are non-transferable to other industrial jobs.

4. In interviews with various workers, they indicate that a man's useful productive years are generally over by the time he is 40; by then, he is in ill-health or cannot maintain the pace of work. In outlying districts, it was not unusual to run across large numbers of workers, aged 40 and over, who were disabled in one way or another and unable to continue working.

5. There are several works dealing specifically with Turkish village life: Paul Sterling, *Turkish Village*, Weidenfeld and Nicolson, London, 1965; Dr. Ibrahim Yasa, *Hasanoglan: A Socio-Economic Structure of a Turkish Village*, Yeni Matbaa, Ankara, 1957; Faculty of Architecture, Middle East Technical University, *Yassihöyük: A Village Study*, Ankara, 1965; and Daniel Lerner, *The Passing of Traditional Society*, Free Press, Glencoe, Ill., 1963. It should be noted that none of these studies specifically covers the Black Sea Region or Zonguldak Province; as there are regional variations in village life, some aspects of village characteristics noted in these studies may not apply.

6. This estimate was given by the Director of the Labour Office of EKI. No specific data exist as to the literacy of the labour force; hence, this is purely an estimate.

7. There are certain matters which should be noted with respect to these interviews. The author was unable to obtain the co-operation of the union and EKI management

in administering it; hence, it had to be conducted *sub-rosa*. As such, it could not be very scientific from a statistical point of view. The results derived have been used largely to substantiate certain facts and attitudes already known to exist and as a vehicle for getting the workers to discuss certain 'sensitive issues'. The selection of interviewees was random and unstructured. Three teams of interviewers travelled to the sub-districts of Bartin, Ulus and Çaycuma; rotational workers were sought out and, when willing to co-operate, interviewed in depth. Even though they have little statistical validity, it is believed that the results are indicative of the situation as it exists among the majority of the rotational workers.

8. Ahmet Naim Çiladir, *Uzun Mehmet'ten Bu Yana Zonguldak Havzasi*, Istanbul, 1940. Workers first came from this region in 1882; prior to this, only those from Zonguldak Province were permitted to work in the mines.

9. T. C. Imar ve Iskân Bakanligi, *loc. cit.* Many of those emigrating from the Black Sea Region use employment in Zonguldak as a stepping stone, moving to Ankara or Istanbul at some future date.

10. The director of the Labour Office indicated that, while no data exist on the number unemployed during this period, he believed that there were no fewer than 4,000 seeking jobs.

11. These roughly correspond to mayors, and are elected to office.

12. R. Vance Presthus and Oguz Ari, *An Administrative Study of Eregli Kömürleri Işletmesi*, Public Administration Institute for Turkey and the Middle East, Ankara, 1955, p. 16.

13. Çiladir, *Uzun Mehmet'ten . . .*, *op. cit.* Dilaver Paşa was an official of the Naval Administration sent to Zonguldak to administer the mines.

14. *Ibid.*

15. Levels of employment have risen recently, owing to the new practice of giving rotational workers one day off per week; also, the policy of the newly elected political leaders (October 1965) has been to increase employment. A plan recently under consideration would develop a new production area in the vicinity of Amasra (located northeast of Zonguldak); if this were done, 5,000 additional workers would be needed.

16. He does, however, complain that others are being treated better than him. Because work groups are usually formed according to villages, i.e. at least some of the workers from one village work together, there is squabbling over who works in what area. Also, there are complaints about the food, living quarters and other non-production aspects of the job. Management does not consider these complaints as requiring formal handling or processing through the grievance machinery but, rather, as 'grousing'. They are, in fact, complaints; however, the workers have not usually been adamant with regard to their complaints, and go back to work whether management attempts to remove the source of their irritation or not.

17. Almost all of these wished to go to Germany to work.

18. Presthus, *loc. cit.*

19. See Table 1.

20. T. C. Imar ve Iskân Bakanligi, *op. cit.*, p. 42.

21. *Ibid.*, p. 30.

22. *Ibid.*, p. 43.

23. See Int. Labour Office, 'Turkey 1, Act: Trade Unions', *Legislative Series*, 1947–Tur. 1. (Sept.–Oct., 1949).

24. *Ibid.*, Art. 3.

25. Article 7, Section 1, of Law 275 states that:

> The Workers' Federation, which represents the majority of the workers in a branch of industry, has the authority to conclude collective agreements covering the workplaces in that branch of industry.
>
> A trade union which represents the majority of the workers working in one or more workplaces has the authority to conclude collective agreements for that or those workplaces.

For a full text of Laws 274 and 275, see International Labour Office, 'Turkey 1, Act: Trade Unions', *Legislative Series*, Tur. 1 (September 1963).

26. The first instance in which labour unions could organise came with the amendment to Law 3512 (1938), the Law on Associations, in 1946, to allow for the formation of organisations along class lines. Several of the early union organisations began to indulge in political activity (since it was not illegal at this time) and some became associated with the Left. The Trade Unions Act of 1947 was passed to rectify the situation—and prohibit trade unions from indilging in political activity.

27. Article 4 of Law 5018 states that:

In addition to the powers possessed by them as bodies corporate in virtue of the general provisions, employees' and employers' trade unions may:

(a) enter into collective contracts in the name of their members;
(b) submit their views on any labour disputes which may arise between employees and employers to the arbitration bodies or other competent authorities, and offer suggestions as to their settlement;
(c) apply to the authorities or arbitration bodies competent for dealing with collective labor disputes in the event of any combination of employers' or employees' trade unions against workers seeking employment with a view to reducing wages below the current level (in such cases, the provisions relating to collective labour disputes shall apply);
(d) establish mutual assistance funds and enter into contracts of insurance on behalf of their members to provide against sickness, unemployment, invalidity and death;
(e) provide legal assistance in cases relating to employment contracts for members bringing claims and for the heirs of members having claims; and represent members or the heirs of members as plaintiff or defendant in cases arising out of collective employment contracts and relating to the common interests of the occupation, and in connection with insurance rights;
(f) send representatives to any organisations formed under the provisions of the Workers' Insurance (Administration) Act, the Employment Exchange Department (Establishment and Powers) Act and the Ministry of Labour (Organisation) Act;
(g) organise lectures and courses to improve the vocational and general education of their members, and enable proper use to be made of leisure;
(h) undertake and assist in the formation of production, consumption, credit and housing co-operative societies;
(i) establish and conduct health and recreational organisations not having commercial objects.

28. ZMWU, *Constitution of the Zonguldak Mine Workers' Union*, art. 5.

29. For fuller discussion of this point, see Sumner Rosen, 'Turkey', in Walter Galenson, *Labor in Developing Economies*, University of California Press, Berkeley, 1962, pp. 264–272.

30. Prior to 1958 the exchange rate was 2·73 TL per $1.00; currently it is 9 TL per $1.00.

31. This is a difficult point with respect to the attitude of trade union leaders. While they are quick to take credit for any changes that benefit the workers, they readily admit that no changes would come about if the political party in power didn't want them. They see no inconsistency in this and believe themselves quite powerful and skilful, even though it is apparent that this power exists only at the discretion of the politicians. The president of the TLC noted in this respect, 'We don't care how we get it as long as we get it'.

32. The working period, of course, varied during this time.

33. The union has been rather lax in keeping records, and many have been destroyed. They readily admit that these figures are probably incorrect, particularly for the earlier years.

34. Because the union is so large, delegates are elected by the membership at large and these in turn elect officers. Proportional representation was used according to the following rules:

Up to 5,000 members; 1 delegate/25 members;
Up to 10,000 members; 1 delegate/50 members;
Up to 25,000 members; 1 delegate/100 members;
More than 25,000 members; 1 delegate/200 members.

This was amended in 1964; each region and independent service now sends 1 delegate per every 100–250 workers. See art. 9, ZMWU Constitution.

35. Both the 1947 and 1963 Trade Unions Acts prohibit political activity on the part of the union; this has not been interpreted to prevent union leaders from becoming active supporters of a party or running for office themselves, as long as they do not use union funds.

36. Prior to 1958, the General Assembly merely elected a Management Council; this group then elected a president, vice-president and an executive counicl of five.

37. Several hundred copies are kept under lock and key in the president's office for no apparent reason.

38. These latter two assessments caused several thousand workers to strike at Kozlu; they would not return until the union gave them their money back.

39. The author interviewed the president and vice-president of the KDMU in prison shortly after they were arrested. Both were violently opposed to the current leadership of the ZMWU. However, when they were interviewed a year later, they did not seem to hold the same view, even though the leadership had not changed.

40. Zonguldak Mine Workers' Union, *Maden Işçileri Sendikasi 16 nci Dönem Kongresi Raporu* (Mine Workers' Union Activity Report to the 16th Congress), Inkilap Matbaasi, Zonguldak, 1963, p. 3.

41. *Ibid.*, p. 13.

42. This union had, at one time, over 5,000 members. Under the leadership of Ipekçi, perhaps practising what he advocated, the union has gradually disbanded, until today there are fewer than 500 members.

43. ZMWU, 16th Congress Report, *op. cit.*, pp. 5–6.

44. In the election held in September, 1964, after the defeat of Mehmet Alpdündar, over 80 per cent voted. In the election held in May 1966, workers from the villages, for the first time in the union's history, travelled to Zonguldak to vote.

45. This had been held just one month prior to the interviews being conducted.

46. This answer was rather unusual, in that interviewers located miles from one another got essentially the same response from workers using exactly the same phrase; it seemed as though it had been learned somewhere, but the workers had no recollection of where they had heard this said and no explanation of why they held this opinion.

47. There are essentially two kinds of union structures, beyond the local and general unions, that are possible—the national and the federation. The national utilises a system of vertical integration establishing branches in various areas; if one of its affiliates is closed, then all of the others are closed too. This actually happened during the Menderes regime (1950–60). As the ZMWU did not want this to happen, it adopted the federal system. Under this, the affiliates maintain their legal identity and cannot be closed if one of the other affiliates, or the federation itself, is.

48. Characteristically, they have always been short of funds and could never get many unions to affiliate with them.

The Economics of Exporting Labour to the EEC: A Turkish Perspective

Tansu Ciller

The effects of labour emigration on the labour-importing economies of the EEC (mainly Germany, France, Belgium, and Holland) have interested economists to a wide extent in recent years. This paper, however, attempts to analyse the impact of labour emigration on a developing labour-exporting country, namely, Turkey. Since labour exportation is now playing more than one role in the developing economies of many other Mediterranean and Near Eastern countries, case studies such as this one may prove to be beneficial in underlining common experiences in the search for externalities of labour exportation.

The movement of foreign labour to Western European countries is not a new phenomenon. It can be easily dated back to the second half of the nineteenth century. For many labour-exporting countries, however, it is a new concept. In the mid-1950s, Italy was probably the only important source of emigration to the EEC. In January, 1959, the Community established its first regulations, making provisions under which social security benefits were provided to non-nationals. These regulations have helped the Community meet its labour shortages, by permitting over 700,000 Italian workers to find jobs in other countries, and, more recently, by opening the way for increasingly large numbers of non-community workers. Until 1961, the bulk of foreign labour came from Italy, Spain, and Algeria, with smaller contingents from Portugal and Greece.[1] By 1962 and 1963, a change began to take place. As Italy and Spain became more developed, the number of workers sent abroad each year levelled off, and, in the case of Italy, even fell.[2] The demand for labour by the recipient countries had remained high, and therefore labour emigration *to* the EEC countries from both EEC members and non-members increased steadily.[3]

Turkish workers in Europe, like Yugoslav workers in the EEC, are a relatively new development.[4] Turkey, as an associate member of the European Economic Community, along with other members, has agreed to take inspiration from Articles 48, 49, and 50 of the Treaty of Rome, in an effort gradually to develop free movement of labour among the member countries. Although, according to Article 12 of the Ankara Treaty, complete free movement would not be accomplished until the transitionary stage, there has been some effort to negotiate this subject during the preparatory stage as well. The one-way movement of workers between Turkey and the labour-importing nations in Europe has taken place under bilateral arragements, as it has among other European countries as well.[5]

TABLE 1

Some Economic Aspects of Turkish Workers in the EEC.

Years	Annual Total Workers Abroad (Thousands of Persons)	Cumulative Total Workers Abroad (Thousands of Persons)	Annual Total Remittances Sent Home (Million $)	Cumulative Total Remittances Sent Home (Million $)	Transfer of Foreign Exchange P of Workers (In $)
1963	43	43	3·5	3·5	8·4
1964	66	109	9	12·5	82·5
1965	52	161	70	82·5	431
1966	34	195	115	192·5	590
1967	9	204	93	290·5	456
1968	43	247	107	397·5	433
1969	113	360	141	588·5	392
1970	135	495	273	811·5	551
1971	105	600	490	1301·5	817
1972	62	665	+40[a]	2041·5[a]	

Note: [a] Based on unpublished SPO realised data. Estimates for 1973 reached some $950 million.
Source: Data are gathered from Statistics of the Turkish Ministry of Work, *Yurt Disindaki Iscilerimizin, Temel Sorunlari* (Problems of Workers Abroad), pp. 1–22.

LABOUR EXPORTATION AND ITS EFFECTS ON THE TURKISH ECONOMY

During the First Five-Year Plan preparation in 1960–61, there were only a few thousand Turkish workers abroad, and no significant increase in their numbers was expected. The direct remittances that they sent home did not even appear in the 1961 balance-of-payment statistics. Since 1963, the presence of Turkish workers in Western Europe has expanded sharply, as is shown in Table 1.[6]

The Unfavourable Results of Labour Exportation for Turkey

The free migration of labour up to now has been mostly to the advantage of Turkey. There are, however, some unfavourable or costly aspects of it that need to be mentioned:

1. While the educational level of Turkish workers is low by European standards, still it represents an investment in education on the part of Turkey.[7]

The majority of the departing workers has reported five years of schooling or more. One survey of 494 such workers[8] gives the percentage breakdowns on their educational levels, as shown in Table 2. It can be roughly estimated that the education of Turkish workers in the EEC cost the Turkish government over TL 50 million by 1972.

TABLE 2

Educational Breakdown of Turkish Workers Abroad (percentages)

No schooling	2·8
Literate	14·8
Finished primary school	49·0
Vocational school graduate	15·4
Middle school graduate	12·8
Lycée graduate	4·3
University	0·8
Unknown	0·2

Source: Nermin Abadan, *Batl Almanyadaki Isciler ve Sorunlari*, p. 165.

2. No doubt the greatest impact of the increased number of workers abroad on Turkey's development has been through their remittances. This can be seen in columns 3, 4 and 5 of Table 1. One unfortunate result of the increased remittances on the Turkish economy in the short run, however, is that it increased inflationary pressures, mainly due to ineffective fiscal and monetary policy. The workers' remittances practically covered the trade deficit in 1971 and exceeded the trade deficit in 1972.[9] Not being combined with sterilisation policies, this has led to an increased demand for consumption goods; the worker abroad sends money to the family back home, which is converted to Turkish lira and spent on consumption goods. The State Planning organisation reports that, during

the first few months of 1973, the rate of increase of demand for semi-durables and luxury consumption goods has exceeded the rate of increase during the first four months of 1972.[10] Domestic production of these goods is not keeping up with demand. The price increases in consumer goods, therefore, have been above 15 per cent per year on the average during 1971 and 1972. Achieving price stability through importation of consumer goods when necessary has become a feasible policy, due to increased foreign exchange reserves, mainly because of increased workers' remittances. The developing economy's investment requirements, however, necessitate holding on to such increases in the effort to channel them to investment goods in accordance with a higher long-term growth strategy. According to the agreement between the EEC and Turkey, Turkey will eliminate all kinds of restrictions on 45 per cent of imports by 1980. Liberalisation will cover 60 per cent of Turkish imports by 1984, and all imports by 1994. Thus, import liberalisation policy will tend to decrease shortages and inflationary pressures in the consumptions goods sector in the long run. The cost, however, would be in the form of a relative decline in imported investment goods. The dropping out of various young Turkish consumer goods industries is also a probable outcome.

3. The sociologist has yet to study the impact of the Turkish workers abroad on family life as well as on Turkish society. It is not unusual to hear stories of broken homes due to the husband in Germany neglecting all responsibilities toward the family that he left back in the village.

Turkey's long-term interests lie in drawing the migrants back home eventually to profit from the skills acquired abroad.[11] Yet, a survey conducted by the German government states that already 13 per cent of the foreign workers have decided not to return to their homelands, while more than 60 per cent of foreign workers have plans to stay more than one year,[12] and around 40 per cent of the Turkish workers in West Germany stay from four to seven years. Their children usually also end up forgetting the native tongue completely, attending the schools of the EEC countries in which they are being raised. This may imply a decline in workers' remittances in the future, since remittances are usually a function of familial and cultural ties in the society, and they tend to be a reflection of the time interval during which the migrants have been away.

BENEFITS OF LABOUR EXPORTATION

Workers in EEC on the whole, however, have been vital for underdeveloped economies, mainly for the following reasons.[13]

1. Workers' remittances contribute to both foreign exchange earnings and capital formation. Moreover, they are superior to ordinary exports in these respects. This is true, first, because there are no previous payments to factors that can spill over into imports. The remittance multiplier is lower than the export multiplier in part because of this difference in first-round spending. 'A good case can be made for assuming that

spending is probably smaller at the second round as well as because of the high marginal propensity to save out of remittances. The part that is consumed likewise goes to subsistence of low-income groups with limited tastes for foreign articles of consumption.'[14] It is this low marginal propensity to import, combined with the relatively high marginal propensity to save, that causes the remittances to raise savings and consequently to stimulate capital formation. The remittances can sustain high levels of investment with favourable balance of payments effects.[15]

Previous to 1964, Turkish remittances from official channels were negligible. The 25–30 per cent discount at which the lira could be obtained on the free market stopped all transfer at the official rates of exchange. Instead, the Turkish workers who returned home brought cars, tape recorders, and similar consumer items. Consequently, some measures were taken, and by the end of 1964 a total of $9 million was remitted and the amount increased continually thereafter.[16]

2. The importance of emigrant remittances to the Turkish Balance of Payments can be made clearer through the following comparisons. The $70 million sent home in 1965 was equal to 15·2 per cent of the nation's export proceeds; further, this source of foreign exchange then ranked second only to tobacco ($88·5 million), but it was well ahead of hazelnuts, which occupied the third position ($61·6 million). In 1966, remittances sent home ranked first, ahead even of tobacco. In 1970, it again was the top contributor. In that year, due to the devaluation which reduced the value of the Turkish lira from $1 = TL 9 to $1 = TL 15, the remittances from abroad increased to 273 million. This constituted about 26 per cent of the total export proceeds.[17]

Table 4 shows the projections and realisations of workers' remittances as percentages of total export proceeds and value of imports during the second plan.

The realised value of workers' remittances as percentages of export proceeds or import expenditures has exceeded the record plan targets, in spite of the fact that the annual growth target for exports has been

TABLE 4

Remittances as Percentage of Exports Proceeds and Import Expenditures

Year	% of Exports Second Plan Target	% of Exports Second Plan Realised	% of Imports Second Plan Target	% of Imports Second Plan Realised
1968	25·9	21·6	16·7	14·0
1969	26·1	26·0	16·7	17·4
1970	26·0	46·4	16·2	28·8
1971	24·8	76·0	15·9	44·8
1972	23·6	80·0	15·2	42·3

Source: Based on data supplied by the Turkish Ministry of Work.

actualised during the plan interval.[18] The actual remittances transferred in 1972 reached some $740 million, while the trade deficit was only $678 million.[19] The workers' remittances have also an increasing share of total foreign exchange earnings, much needed for developing economies.

3. Another immediate advantage of labour migration lies in its easing unemployment pressures. Turkey has a dual problem of population explosion (2·73 per cent per year greater than the 2·6 per cent for India, for example) and an increasing unemployment rate. The figures in Table 7 will give a better idea about the importance of labour exportation in dealing with domestic unemployment. By 1972, labour supply had reached 16 million people and the domestic economy could absorb only around 13·7 million. The remaining 2·3 million are either employed in the EEC or are unemployed.

4. The workers abroad, upon their return to Turkey, seem to be supplying the needed skilled labour to domestic establishments. A survey on business having employed personnel with European experience revealed that domestic employers find them more 'orderly, productive, industrious, and more willing and able to assume responsibility', even if the workers with European experience seem to be less willing to work overtime.[20] Establishments having employed personnel with European experience thus seem to prefer the 'European experience' over 'domestic experience only'.

TABLE 5

Preferences of Establishments having Employed Personnel with European Experience

	Number	Per cent
European experience preferred	24	58·54
Domestic experience only preferred	8	19·51
No preference	9	21·95
Total	41	100·00

5. Increased remittances are increased savings and can be channelled to investment. There are already some 88 workers' companies in West Germany.[21] Only around 30,000 of the 600,000 Turkish workers there (some 5 per cent of the total) are stockholders. Twenty-three out of 88 companies have projects which started construction and 13 that started production. The distribution of these projects concentrates on construction, food, housing and metal,[22] which has a ready domestic market, a high labour-to-capital ratio,[23] and relatively simple technology. Fourteen of these 36 projects had regional preferences, since workers prefer to invest in their home towns.[24] Some well-established companies, which have taken their place in the economy, could also attract and channel these savings to new investment projects.[25]

TABLE 6

Share of Remittances in Total Foreign Exchange Earnings

	First Plan 1963–67		*Second Plan 1968–72*		*Third Plan 1973–77*	
	In Million $	% Total Foreign Exchange Earnings	In Million $	% Total Foreign Exchange Earnings	In Million $	% Total Foreign Exchange Earnings
Imports	3200		4903		7000	
Exports	2256	88·7	2951	65·1	4500	56·3
Remittances	300	11·3	1561	34·9	3250	40·6
Tourism	−65	—	20	—	250	3·1

Source: Based on Data presented by Turkish Ministry of Labour.

TABLE 7

Year	*Labour Supply (Millions of Persons)*	*Domestic Employment*	*Employment Abroad*	*Unemployed**
1965	13·0	12·65	·16	·19
1966	13·3	12·9	·2	·2
1967	13·7	13·1	·2	·4
1968	14·0	13·3	·25	·45
1969	14·5	13·4	·36	·74
1970	15·0	13·6	·5	·9
1971	15·6	13·7	·6	1·2
1972	16·0	13·7	·7	1·6

Source: Based on the unpublished chart presented by Turkish Ministry of Labour, Summer 1973.
Note: *The figures for the unemployed altogether exclude disguised unemployment.

There is yet much to be done in channelling migrant workers' savings to investment. The Turkish worker is frugal compared to other migrant workers, and saves around 38 per cent of his income. On the average, they send 18 per cent of their income (half of these savings) to families back at home, which is spent there, and keep the other half of their savings in the banks of the employing countries, which annually totals about $15 billion. This could be attributed to Turkey's lack of investment projects,[26] insufficient know-how, and lack of bank credits. A survey by Turk-is among the Turkish workers indicates that workers expect and want government enterpreneurship to participate as stock holders in projects initiated by the government.[27] In these companies, the migrant workers would be offered a guaranteed job upon return to their homeland.[28] Government initiative, therefore, could also be helpful in accumulating large sums of capital required by the investment and goods industries.[29]

SUMMARY

The Turkish labour exportation experience suggests that, on the unfavourable side, it has resulted in a costly loss of investment in education, since the relatively well-educated Turkish worker (according to domestic standards) is now employed in the EEC countries. Remittances not accompanied by sterilisation policies have increased the inflationary pressures in the consumption goods sectors in the short run. New evidence about the plans of a substantial portion of workers not to return back home, among other things, implies a decline in workers' remittances in the long run.

The most favourable impact of the migrant workers abroad, aside from easing domestic unemployment problems, is through their remittances. Workers' remittances contribute both to foreign exchange earnings and to capital formation, and tend to have a smaller multiplier compared to export earnings because there are no previous payments to factors that can spill over into imports.[30] The Turkish experience suggests that remittances can be very effective in capital formation, even if much remains to be done in this field.

Workers in the EEC do not constitute a transitional phenomenon; it is there to stay. In Belgium and France, one out of every 20, and in West Germany one out of every 10 workers is a migrant.

'The German industry would not exist without them', says Wolfgang Baumann of the Federation of German Industries. The Patronat—France's employers' association—and government recruitment expert William Weidenborner, estimate larger manpower deficits in West European industries in the next decade.[31] It is likely, therefore, that the European demand for foreign workers will continue through the 1980s and that other less-developed Mediterranean countries, aside from Turkey, will start exporting labour. There is much to be gained, therefore, in further studying the impact of migrant workers on their relatively less-developed domestic countries, in the attempt to examine externalities of labour exportation.[32]

NOTES

1. Estimates of emigrant remittances from labour-importing to labour-exporting countries were, for example, as follows in 1963.

Received Remittances from European Emigrants		*Paid to European Emigrants*	
Italy	300	Switzerland	335
Spain	200	Germany	250
Portugal	70	France	225
Greece	56		
Turkey	0		

Source: G. P. Kindleberger, 'Emigration and Economic Growth', *Banco Nazionale Del Lavoro Quarterly Review*, no. 74, September, 1965, p. 7.

2. The following statistics show the trend of emigration to Europe from the four leading suppliers.

(Thousands of persons)

	1958	*1959*	*1960*	*1961*	*1962*	*1963*
Italy	157·8	102·8	309·9	329·6	315·8	235·1
Spain	n.a.	24·1	40·8	108·8	150·8	n.a.
Greece	6·6	6·7	26·9	39·6	60·8	74·2
Portugal	4·8	3·7	6·0	7·5	9·2	17·1

Source: R. H. Eldridge, 'Workers Abroad and Turkish Balance of Payments', *Middle East Journal* Summer 1966, p. 297.

3. A comparison of labour emigration *to* EEC from members and non-members, was as follows for the years 1963–64. It should be noted that around two-thirds of the foreign labour force used in the EEC countries came from non-member countries.

	From Members		*From Non-members*		*Thousand of Persons total*	
	1963	*1964*	*1963*	*1964*	*1963*	*1964*
Belgium	5·7	7·1	20·7	26·1	26·4	33·2
Germany	175·0	189·4	202·5	178·5	377·5	467·9
France	15·8	14·4	99·8	139·3	115·5	153·7
Italy	2·0	1·8	2·3	1·7	4·3	3·0
Luxembourg	7·0	7·2	1·8	3·4	8·8	10·6
Holland	4·8	6·7	12·3	24·1	17·1	30·8
Total	210·3	226·6	339·4	473·1	549·6	699·7

Source: Iktisadi Kalkinma Tesisi *Aurupa Ekonomi Toplulugun ve Turkiye* (*EEC and Turkey*) p.25.

4. In West Germany, where close to 90 per cent of migrant Turkish workers are employed, the share of Turkish workers among other foreign workers increased from

13·8 per cent in 1968, to around 22·4 per cent in 1972. 'Distaki Isciler' ('Workers Abroad'), Turkish Ministry of Labour, 22 July, 1973, p. 7.

5. Turkey signed agreements on 30 October, 1961, with Germany; on 15 May, 1964, with Austria; on 19 August, 1964, with Holland; on 16 July, 1964, with Belgium; and on 8 April, 1965, with France. There has also been a separate set of bilateral agreements signed regarding the social problems and security of the Turkish workers beginning in April 1964 with Germany; April 1966 with Holland, and July 1965 with Belgium. Source: Iktisadi Kalkinma Tesisi, *Aurupa Ekonomi Toplulugu ve Turkiye* (EEC and Turkey), Monograph 2, Istanbul 1967, p. 210.

6. These figures only refer to workers going through the Turkish Employment Service, and they do not take account of those who returned home permanently or those who did not go through a government agency. The rough estimates are that 10,000 have returned and 20,000 have gone abroad unofficially. It is also interesting to note the share of Turkish women workers going abroad swelled to 20 per cent in 1965, whereas it had been 7 per cent shortly before that.

7. In an international comparison on the educational level of foreign workers in the EEC, the Yugoslavian workers rank first, and the Portuguese last.

8. The same study revealed the following results. Nearly 95 per cent of the migrants were men in their twenties, mostly married (56 per cent), but without their families (83 per cent). They lived very frugally, sharing rooms. Some 67 per cent of the workers earned about \$75–150 per month, with the average annual net wage amounting to \$1,536, and they saved around 50 per cent of this. (The Turkish industrial wage is \$55 per month.) Some of the workers had previously migrated to large cities in Turkey in search of a job, and not having found one, they emigrated to Germany. The same survey reported the last employment of the emigrants before they left Turkey as follows:

Employment of Turkish Workers Before They Left Turkey (percentages)

Industrial Labour	25·3
Small Craftsmen	20·8
Transport and Communication	9·5
Agriculture	8·8
Administrative Personnel	7·0
Professions (doctor, etc.)	5·2
Sales	4·8
Services	4·2
Mining	2·6
Unclassified	11·8

Source: Nermin Abadan, *Bati Almanyadaki Isciler*, p. 165.

Although Turkey thus seems to be losing industrial workers, these might actually be unskilled workers who migrated to cities and had little experience. In Germany, the Turkish workers were employed in large factories, (55 per cent) in construction (22 per cent), handicraft (14 per cent), and in mining (9 per cent). Even if the workers employed in the large factories actually hold unskilled industrial jobs, this might still be of help in adjusting them to more productive roles upon their return to Turkey.

9. See Table 6.

10. SPO (State Planning Organisation), 'Luks Tuketim Yukseliyor' ('Luxury consumption is increasing'), *Milliyet*, 20 June, 1973, p. 9.

11. Even if there is no doubt of the immediate advantages of drawing migrants back, the readjustment problems of returning workers might be complex indeed. Only 10,000 workers returned permanently as of end 1965. As the number of workers abroad expands, the number returning per year will probably be 50,000, per year. Their reintegration to economic and social life of the country will certainly be a source of friction. Their potential can be put to good use or can be wasted, as in the case of

'Italian Americani' (C. P. Kindleberger, 'Emigration and Economic Growth', p. 312). Also, the demands that returning workers may bring with them regarding active unionism and a social security system of broad scope may be more than the productivity of a developing economy such as Turkey can afford at this time.

12. 'Iscilerin Yuzde onucu Yurda Donmek Istemiyor' ('13 per cent of workers will not return to Homeland'), *Milliyet*, 26 July, 1973, p. 7.

13. In the case of Turkish experience, these results are tied in no direct way to Turkey's entrance to the Common Market. No special concessions have been given to the Turkish workers, and they are in no way treated differently from the Portuguese or Spanish workers in EEC countries. In an economic or industrial crisis, Turkish workers are among the first to be forced out, and there is no direct commitment in the Ankara Treaty to ensure the security of Turkish workers in the EEC. Aside from the indirect stimuli which Turkey's acceptance to EEC provided in this matter, the Ankara Treaty gave no concessions to Turkish workers. During the transitional stage, which Turkey entered in 1970, this problem must receive much attention. Among the Six, Italy will probably oppose Turkey's gaining such concessions, for obvious reasons. But the migration of Turkish labour to the EEC, with the eventual decision to return home, is crucial for Turkish development, indeed, as it already has proved to be. Turkey cannot afford to neglect it.

14. C. P. Kindleberger, 'Emigration and Economic Growth', pp. 7–8. *Banca Nazionale Del Lavoro Quarterly Review*, no. 74, September 1965, pp. 7–8.

15. Ordinarily, the static approach would tend to point out unfavourable impact of increased investment on balance of payments.

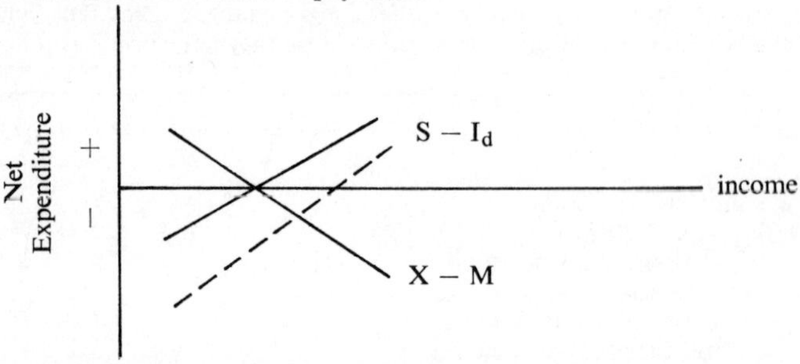

16. It might be well to summarise the measures taken by the government to bring Turkish remittances into official channels and thereby to benefit from their foreign exchange earnings. As the numbers of workers in Europe increased. the government realised that the 25–30 per cent discount on the Turkish Lira in the free market foreclosed any possibility of its benefiting directly from the remittances. In July 1964, Law 499 'Concerning the Savings of Foreign Exchange of Turkish Workers Abroad' was approved and passed by the Senate. It made the exchange rate on transfers 27 per cent above the official rate.

After some further improvements, the worker can now take his foreign exchange earnings to any postal station where he is working, or to any specified commercial or savings bank. The banker PTT notifies one of the designated 19 Turkish banks indicated by the worker, and the Turkish bank issues the equivalent amount of Turkish Lira, plus the 27 per cent bonus (prior to devaluation) to the designated recipient. The banks are reimbursed by Emlak Kredi Bank for the bonus, the latter being reimbursed in turn by the Ministry of Finance from appropriated funds. The actual transfer is simple, inexpensive, and reliable. If the transfer is done through a foreign bank, it takes two weeks; if it is done through a post office, it takes only 2–3 days. The Turkish authorities watch the free rate closely, and they are ready to alter rates to keep workers' transfers competitive.

Other than this, in order to draw the migrants themselves back to Turkey eventually, the workers can also participate in housing and small business loans on the basis of their remittances. The Emlak Kredi Bankasi Housing Credit Fund offers such a programme.

After an emigrant worker has deposited $555 in the fund, he is eligible to borrow up to five times his deposit. But these housing and small business loans have been ineffective in attracting remittances, since only an estimated 1 per cent of all workers have availed themselves of these small business loan facilities.

17. The only discernible seasonal pattern to be found in remittances is the high figures registered in December, since workers return home for the holiday season and bring large amounts of foreign exchange with them.

Seasonal Pattern in Workers' Remittances (in thousands)

	1964	1965
January	65	2,810
February	75	1,919
March	106	2,453
April	241	3,853
May	41	3,696
June	336	4,341
July	377	7,065
August	644	8,176
September	765	7,158
October	896	8,697
November	598	6,364
December	377	15,245

Source: R. H. Eldridge, 'Workers Abroad and the Turkish Balance of Payments', p. 303.

18. SPO, Third Five-Year Plan 1973–77, pp. 57–8.

19. 'Distaki Isci Tessaruflari'. ('Workers Abroad and Their Savings'), *Milliyet*, 22 July, 1973, p. 4.

20. Krahenbuhl, Ronald E. 'Acculturative Effects of International Labour Migration in Turkey'. Paper presented at Middle East Studies Association Annual Meeting, Toronto, 14–15 November, 1969.

21. The source of this and the following information is the unpublished survey conducted by Professor Nevzat Yalcintas.

22. There are also some projects in industries such as chemicals, wood, and tourism.

23. Workers' plans to work in these factories upon their return result in choice of labour-intensive industries.

24. The eastern and most underdeveloped part of Turkey could very well benefit from this.

25. The yet-to-be-approved capital market law foresees the establishment of investment trusts. A corporation, or joint stock company form of partnership would be most appropriate.

26. The Turkish Ministry of Finance reports 20 applications for search of appropriate investment projects. Their total capital amounted to $100 million.

27. 'Distaki Isci Tasarruflari ni Nasil Kullaniriz?' ('What to do with migrant workers' savings?'), *Milliyet*, 29 July, 1973, p. 2.

28. The turnover rate of workers (due to illness, retirement) is around 10–12 per cent of workers employed. Thus, 10 per cent of the work force could be offered to migrants in the form of guaranteed jobs upon their return without creating major over-employment problems.

29. A worker's investment bank type of mechanism could very well be appropriate.

30. C. P. Kindleberger, 'Emigration and Economic Growth', pp. 7–8.

31. 'Europe's imported labour force begins to cost more', *Business Week*, 31 March, 1973, p. 99.

32. See further G. E. Völker, 'Turkish Labour Migration to Germany: Impact on Both Economies', *Middle Eastern Studies*, vol. 12, no. 1—Ed.